Java Precisely

Third Edition

Peter Sestoft

Java Precisely

Third Edition

The MIT Press
Cambridge, Massachusetts
London, England

MIT Press books may be purchased at special quantity discounts for business or sales promotional use.

This book was set in Times by the author using LaTeX and was printed and bound in the United States of America.

Library of Congress Cataloging-in-Publication Data
Names: Sestoft, Peter.
Title: Java precisely / Peter Sestoft.
Description: Third edition. | Cambridge, MA : The MIT Press, [2016] | Includes bibliographical references and index.
Identifiers: LCCN 2015038522 | ISBN 9780262529075 (pbk. : alk. paper)
Subjects: LCSH: Java (Computer program language)
Classification: LCC QA76.73.J38 S435 2015 | DDC 005.13/3–dc23 LC record available at http://lccn.loc.gov/2015038522

10 9 8 7 6 5 4 3 2 1

Contents

vi *Contents*

Preface

This third edition of *Java Precisely* gives a concise description of the Java programming language, version 8.0. It is a quick reference for the reader who has already learned (or is learning) Java from a standard textbook and who wants to know the language in more detail. The book presents the entire Java programming language and essential parts of the class libraries: the collection classes, the input-output classes, the stream library and its facilities for parallel programming, and the functional interfaces used for that.

General rules are shown on left-hand pages mostly, and corresponding examples are shown on right-hand pages only. All examples are fragments of legal Java programs. The complete ready-to-run example programs are available from the book Web site: www.itu.dk/people/sestoft/javaprecisely.

This third edition adds material about new methods for functional parallel processing of arrays (section 8.4); default and static methods on interfaces (section 13.3); the memory visibility effects of `volatile` and `final` (section 20.5); new comparator methods (section 22.10); functional interfaces (chapter 23) and the related lambda expressions (section 11.13) and method reference expressions (section 11.14); stream processing, including parallel programming and collectors (chapter 24); and the Optional class (chapter 25). In general the book has been updated for the changes from Java 5.0 to Java 8.0. The final chapter 29 summarizes and illustrates the new features of Java 8.0 and compares them to the C# programming language.

The book does not cover garbage collection, non-blocking input-output, the executor framework, finalization and weak references, details of IEEE754 floating-point numbers, or Javadoc.

Acknowledgments Thanks to Rasmus Lund, Niels Hallenberg, Hans Henrik Løvengreen, Christian Gram, Jan Clausen, Anders Peter Ravn, Bruce Conrad, Brendan Humphreys, Hans Rischel, Ken Friis Larsen, Dan Becker, Mads Jeppe Tarp-Johansen, Kasper Østerbye, Kasper Bilsted Graversen, Søren Eduard Jacobsen, Paul van Bemmelen, Axel Tobias Schreiner, David Hemmendinger, Baris Aktemur, Jakob Bendsen, Jan Schoubo, and all the anonymous reviewers and copy editors for their useful comments, suggestions, and corrections. Special thanks to Rasmus Lund for letting me adapt his collections diagram for this book, and to Kasper Østerbye for campaigning for a reflection chapter and providing a first draft of it.

It was a pleasure to work with Robert Prior, Valerie Geary, Deborah Cantor-Adams, Krista Magnuson, Marc Lowenthal, Marie Lufkin Lee, Virginia Crossman, and Kathleen Hensley at The MIT Press. Thanks also to the IT University of Copenhagen, Denmark, for support.

Notational Conventions

Symbol	Meaning
a	Expression or value of array type
b	Boolean or byte array
C	Class
cmp	Comparator or Comparer
cs	Character array (type `char[]`)
cseq	Character sequence (type CharSequence)
E	Exception type
e	Expression
f	Field or function
I	Interface
i	Expression or value of integer type
m	Method
o	Expression or value of object type
p	Package or predicate
s	Expression or value of type String
supp	Expression or value of type Supplier
sig	Signature of method or constructor
t	Type (primitive type or reference type)
T, U, K, V	Type parameter in generic type or method
u	Expression or value of thread type
v	Value of any type
x	Variable or parameter or field or array element
xs	Stream

Java Precisely

1   Running Java: Compilation, Loading, and Execution

Before a Java program can be executed, it must be compiled and loaded. The compiler checks that the Java program is *legal:* that the program conforms to the Java syntax, that operators (such as +) are applied to operands (such as 5 and x) of the correct type, and so on. If so, the compiler generates *class files.* Execution may then be started by loading the class files. Thus running a Java program involves three stages: *compilation* (checks that the program is well-formed), *loading* (loads and initializes classes), and *execution* (runs the code). This holds also for a program run from integrated development environments such as Eclipse or IntelliJ.

2   Names and Reserved Names

A *legal name* (of a variable, method, field, parameter, class, interface or package) starts with a letter or dollar sign ($) or underscore (_), and continues with zero or more letters or dollar signs or underscores or digits (0–9). Avoid dollar signs in class and interface names. Uppercase letters and lowercase letters are considered distinct. A legal name cannot be one of the following *reserved names:*

abstract	char	else	for	interface	protected	switch	try
assert	class	enum	goto	long	public	synchronized	void
boolean	const	extends	if	native	return	this	volatile
break	continue	false	implements	new	short	throw	while
byte	default	final	import	null	static	throws	
case	do	finally	instanceof	package	strictfp	transient	
catch	double	float	int	private	super	true	

3   Java Naming Conventions

The following naming conventions are often followed, although not enforced by Java:

- If a name is composed of several words, then each word (except possibly the first one) begins with an uppercase letter. Examples: `setLayout`, `addLayoutComponent`.

- Names of variables, fields, and methods begin with a lowercase letter. Examples: `vehicle`, `myVehicle`.

- Names of classes and interfaces begin with an uppercase letter. Examples: `Cube`, `ColorCube`.

- Named constants (such as `final static` fields and enum values) are written entirely in uppercase, and the parts of composite names are separated by underscores (_). Examples: `CENTER`, `MAX_VALUE`.

- Package names are sequences of dot-separated lowercase names. Example: `java.awt.event`. For uniqueness, they are often prefixed with reverse domain names, as in `com.sun.xml.util`.

4   Comments and Program Layout

Comments have no effect on the execution of the program but may be inserted anywhere to help humans understand the program. There are two forms: one-line comments and delimited comments.

Program layout has no effect on the computer's execution of the program but is used to help humans understand the structure of the program.

Example 1 Comments

```
class Comment {
  // This is a one-line comment; it extends to the end of the line.
  /* This is a delimited comment,
     extending over several lines.
  */
  int /* This delimited comment extends over part of a line */ x = 117;
}
```

Example 2 Recommended Program Layout Style
For reasons of space this layout style is not always followed in this book.

```
class Layout {                           // Class declaration
  int x;

  Layout(int x) {
    this.x = x;                          // One-line body
  }

  int sum(int y) {                       // Multi-line body
    if (x > 0) {                         // If statement
      return x + y;                      // Single statement
    } else if (x < 0) {                  // Nested if-else, block statement
      int res = -x + y;
      return res * 117;
    } else { // x == 0                   // Terminal else, block statement
      int sum = 0;
      for (int i=0; i<10; i++) {         // For loop
        sum += (y - i) * (y - i);
      }
      return sum;
    }
  }

  static boolean checkdate(int mth, int day) {
    int length;
    switch (mth) {                       // Switch statement
    case 2:                              // Single case
      length = 28; break;
    case 4: case 6: case 9: case 11:     // Multiple case
      length = 30; break;
    case 1: case 3: case 5: case 7: case 8: case 10: case 12:
      length = 31; break;
    default:
      return false;
    }
    return (day >= 1) && (day <= length);
  }
}
```

5 Types

A *type* is a set of values and operations on them. A type is either a primitive type or a reference type.

5.1 Primitive Types

A *primitive type* is either `boolean` or one of the *numeric types* `char`, `byte`, `short`, `int`, `long`, `float`, or `double`. The primitive types, example literals (that is, constants), size in bits (where 8 bits equals 1 byte), and value range, are shown in the table opposite. For readability, a number constant may contain underscores (_) anywhere except as the first and last character of the constant.

The integer types are exact within their range. They use signed 2's complement representation (except for `char`), so when the most positive number in a type is *max*, then the most negative number is $-max - 1$. The floating-point types are inexact and follow IEEE754, with the number of significant digits indicated by "sigdig" in the table. For character escape sequences such as `\u0000`, see page 10.

5.2 Reference Types

A *reference type* is a class type defined by a class declaration (section 9.1), or an interface type defined by an interface declaration (section 13.1), or an array type (section 5.3), or an enum type (chapter 14).

A value of reference type is either `null` or a reference to an object or array. The special value `null` denotes "no object." The literal `null`, denoting the `null` value, can have any reference type.

5.3 Array Types

An *array type* has the form `t[]`, where `t` is any type. An array type `t[]` is a reference type. Hence a value of array type `t[]` is either `null` or a reference to an array whose element type is precisely `t` (when `t` is a primitive type), or is a subtype of `t` (when `t` is a reference type).

5.4 Boxing: Wrapping Primitive Types as Reference Types

For every primitive type there is a corresponding wrapper class, which is a reference type. The wrapper classes are listed in the table opposite. An object of a wrapper class contains a single value of the corresponding primitive type.

A wrapper class must be used when a value of primitive type is passed to a method that expects a reference type, or is stored in a variable or field of reference type. For instance, to store an `int` in a collection (chapter 22) one must wrap it as an Integer object.

The conversion from primitive type to wrapper class is called *boxing*, and the opposite conversion is called *unboxing*. Boxing and unboxing are performed automatically when needed. Boxing and unboxing may also be performed explicitly using operations such as `new Integer(i)` to box the integer i, and `o.intValue()` or `(int)o` to unbox the Integer object o. If o is `null`, then unboxing of o will fail at run-time by throwing NullPointerException. Because of automatic unboxing, a Boolean value may be used in conditional statements (`if`, `for`, `while`, and `do-while`) and in logical operators (such as `!`, `&&`, `?:` and so on); and Integer and other integer type wrapper classes may be used in `switch` statements.

A boxed value can be unboxed only to a value of the boxed type, or to a supertype. Thus an Integer object can be unboxed to an `int` or a `long` because `long` is a supertype of `int`, but not to a `char`, `byte`, or `short`.

The wrapper classes Byte, Short, Integer, Long, Float, and Double have the common superclass Number.

Primitive Types

Type	Kind	Example Literals	Size	Range	Wrapper
boolean	logical	false, true	1		Boolean
char	integer	' ', '0', 'A', ...	16	\u0000 ... \uFFFF (unsigned)	Character
byte	integer	0, 1, −1, 117, ...	8	$max = 127$	Byte
short	integer	0, 1, −1, 117, 2_117, ...	16	$max = 32767$	Short
int	integer	0, 1, −1, 117, 2_117, ...	32	$max = 2147483647$	Integer
long	integer	0L, 1L, −1L, 117L, 2_117L, ...	64	$max = 9223372036854775807$	Long
float	floating	−1.0f, 0.49f, 3E8f, ...	32	$\pm 10^{-38} \ldots \pm 10^{38}$, sigdig 6–7	Float
double	floating	−1.0, 0.49, 3E8, ...	64	$\pm 10^{-308} \ldots \pm 10^{308}$, sigdig 15–16	Double

Integer Literals   Integer literals (of type byte, char, short, int, or long) may be written in four bases:

Notation	Base	Distinction	Example Integer Literals
Decimal	10	No leading 0	1_234_567_890, 127, −127
Binary	2	Leading 0b or 0B	0b10, 0b111_1111, −0b111_1111
Octal	8	Leading 0	01234567, 0177, −0177
Hexadecimal	16	Leading 0x or 0X	0xAB_CDEF_0123, 0x7F, −0x7F

Example 3 Automatic Boxing and Unboxing

```
Boolean bb1 = false, bb2 = !bb1;    // Boxing to [false] [true]
Integer bi1 = 117;                  // Boxing to [117]
Double bd1 = 1.2;                   // Boxing to [1.2]
boolean b1 = bb1;                   // Unboxing, result false
if (bb1)                            // Unboxing, result false
  System.out.println("Not true");
int i1 = bi1 + 2;                   // Unboxing, result 119
// short s = bi1;                   // Illegal
long l = bi1;                       // Legal: int is subtype of long
Integer bi2 = bi1 + 2;             // Unboxing, boxing, result [119]
Integer[] biarr = { 2, 3, 5, 7, 11 };
int sum = 0;
for (Integer bi : biarr)
  sum += bi;                        // Unboxing in loop body
for (int i : biarr)                 // Unboxing in loop header
  sum += i;
int i = 1934;
Integer bi4 = i, bi5 = i;
// Prints true true true false; bi4==bi5 is a reference comparison:
System.out.format("%b %b %b %b%n", i==i, bi4==i, i==bi5, bi4==bi5);
Boolean bbn = null;
boolean b = bbn;                    // Compiles OK, fails at run-time
if (bbn)                            // Compiles OK, fails at run-time
  System.out.println("Not true");
Integer bin = null;
Integer bi6 = bin + 2;             // Compiles OK, fails at run-time
```

5.5   Subtypes and Compatibility

A type t1 may be a *subtype* of a type t2, in which case t2 is a *supertype* of t1. Intuitively this means that any value v1 of type t1 can be used where a value of type t2 is expected. When t1 and t2 are reference types, t1 must provide at least the functionality (methods and fields) provided by t2. In particular, any value v1 of type t1 may be bound to a variable or field or parameter x2 of type t2, for instance by the assignment x2 = v1 or by parameter passing. We also say that types t1 and t2 are *compatible*. The following rules determine when a type t1 is a subtype of a type t2:

- Every type is a subtype of itself.
- If t1 is a subtype of t2, and t2 is a subtype of t3, then t1 is a subtype of t3.
- If t1 and t2 are primitive types, and there is a widening (W or L) conversion from t1 to t2 according to the table opposite, then t1 is a subtype of t2.
- If t1 and t2 are classes, then t1 is a subtype of t2 if t1 is a subclass of t2.
- If t1 and t2 are interfaces, then t1 is a subtype of t2 if t1 is a subinterface of t2.
- If t1 is a class and t2 is an interface, then t1 is a subtype of t2 provided that t1 (is a subclass of a class that) implements t2 or implements a subinterface of t2.
- Array type t1[] is a subtype of array type t2[] if reference type t1 is a subtype of reference type t2.
- Any reference type t, including any array type, is also a subtype of predefined class Object.

No primitive type is a subtype of a reference type and no reference type is a subtype of a primitive type. But there are automatic boxing and unboxing conversions between a primitive type and its wrapper class; see section 5.4.

5.6   Signatures and Subsumption

A *signature* has form m(t$_1$, ..., t$_n$), where m is a method or constructor name, and (t$_1$, ..., t$_n$) is a list of non-generic types; see example 36.

We say that a signature sig_1 = m(t$_1$, ..., t$_n$) *subsumes* signature sig_2 = m(u$_1$, ..., u$_n$) if each u$_i$ is a subtype of t$_i$. We also say that sig_2 is *more specific* than sig_1. Note that the method name m and the number *n* of types must be the same in the two signatures. Since every type t$_i$ is a subtype of itself, every signature subsumes itself. In a collection of signatures there may be one that is subsumed by all others; such a signature is called the *most specific* signature.

5.7   Type Conversion

A *type conversion* converts a value from one type to another. A *widening* conversion converts from a type to a supertype (or the type itself). A *narrowing* conversion converts from a type to another type. A narrowing conversion requires an explicit *type cast* (section 11.11), except in an assignment x = e or initialization where e is a compile-time integer constant (section 11.5).

The legal type conversions between primitive types are shown in the table opposite. The primitive type boolean cannot be converted to any other primitive type. A type cast between primitive types never fails at run-time.

Conversion between Primitive Types

The letter C marks a narrowing conversion that requires a type cast `(t)e`, see section 11.11; W marks a widening conversion that preserves the value; and L marks a widening conversion that may cause a loss of precision. A narrowing integer conversion discards those (most significant) bits that cannot be represented in the smaller integer type. Conversion from an integer type to a floating-point type (`float` or `double`) produces a floating-point approximation of the integer value. Conversion from a floating-point type to an integer type discards the fractional part of the number; that is, it rounds toward zero. When converting a too-large floating-point number to a `long` or `int`, the result is the best approximation (that is, the type's largest positive or the largest negative representable number); conversion to `byte`, `short`, or `char` is done by converting to `int` and then to the requested type.

From Type	To Type						
	char	byte	short	int	long	float	double
char	W	C	C	W	W	W	W
byte	C	W	W	W	W	W	W
short	C	C	W	W	W	W	W
int	C	C	C	W	W	L	W
long	C	C	C	C	W	L	L
float	C	C	C	C	C	W	W
double	C	C	C	C	C	C	W

Example 4 Conversion between Primitive Types
This example shows lossy (L) and lossless (W) widening conversions to `float` and `double` as well as narrowing conversions (C) from `int` and `double`. Example 51 shows primitive conversions in assignments.

```
private static void floatdouble(float f, double d)
{ System.out.println(f + " " + d); }
private static void bytecharshort(byte b, char c, short s)
{ System.out.println(b + " " + (int)c + " " + s); }
private static void intint(int i1, int i2)
{ System.out.println(i1 + " " + i2); }
...
int i1 = 1000111222, i2 = 40000, i3 = -1;
floatdouble(i1, i1);                      // L W: 1.00011123E9 1.000111222E9
bytecharshort((byte)i2, (char)i2, (short)i2);  // C C C: 64 40000 -25536
bytecharshort((byte)i3, (char)i3, (short)i3);  // C C C: -1 65535 -1
intint((int)1.9, (int)-1.9);              // C C: 1 -1
intint((int)1.5, (int)-1.5);              // C C: 1 -1
intint((int)2.5, (int)-2.5);              // C C: 2 -2
```

Example 5 Method Signature Subsumption

- `m(double,double)` subsumes itself and `m(double,int)` and `m(int,double)` and `m(int,int)`.
- `m(double,int)` subsumes itself and `m(int,int)`.
- `m(int,double)` subsumes itself and `m(int,int)`.
- `m(double,int)` does not subsume `m(int,double)`, nor the other way around.
- The collection `m(double,int)`, `m(int,int)` has the most specific signature `m(int,int)`.
- The collection `m(double,int)`, `m(int,double)` has no most specific signature.

6   Variables, Parameters, Fields, and Scope

A *variable* is declared inside a method, constructor, initializer block, or block statement (section 12.2). The variable can be used only in that block statement (or method or constructor or initializer block), and only after its declaration.

A *parameter* is a special kind of variable: it is declared in the parameter list of a method or constructor, and is given a value when the method or constructor is called. The parameter can be used only in that method or constructor.

A *field* is declared inside a class, but not inside a method or constructor or initializer block of the class. It can be used anywhere in the class, also textually before its declaration.

6.1   Values Bound to Variables, Parameters, or Fields

A variable, parameter, or field of primitive type holds a *value* of that type, such as the boolean `false`, the integer `117`, or the floating-point number `1.7`. A variable, parameter, or field of reference type `t` either has the special value `null` or holds a reference to an object or array. If it is an object, then the run-time class of that object must be `t` or a subclass of `t`.

6.2   Variable Declarations

The purpose of a variable is to hold a value during the execution of a block statement (or method or constructor or initializer block). A *variable-declaration* has one of the forms

> *variable-modifier type varname1, varname2, ... ;*
> *variable-modifier type varname1 = initializer1, ... ;*

A *variable-modifier* may be `final` or absent. If a variable is declared `final`, then it must be initialized or assigned at most once at run-time (exactly once if it is ever used): it is a *named constant*. However, if the variable has reference type, then the object or array pointed to by the variable may still be modified. A *variable initializer* may be an expression or an array initializer (section 8.2).

Execution of the variable declaration will reserve space for the variable, then evaluate the initializer, if any, and store the resulting value in the variable. Unlike a field, a variable is not given a default value when declared, but the compiler checks that it has been given a value before it is used.

6.3   Scope of Variables, Parameters, and Fields

The *scope* of a name is that part of the program in which the name is visible. The scope of a variable extends from just after its declaration to the end of the innermost enclosing block statement. The scope of a method or constructor parameter is the entire method or constructor body. For a control variable x declared in a `for` statement

> `for (int x = ...; ...; ...)` *body*

the scope is the entire `for` statement, including the header and the body.

Within the scope of a variable or parameter x, one cannot redeclare x. However, one may declare a variable x within the scope of a field x, thus *shadowing* the field. Hence the scope of a field x is the entire class, except where shadowed by a variable or parameter of the same name, and except for initializers preceding the field's declaration (section 9.1).

Example 6 Variable Declarations

```
public static void main(String[] args) {
  int a, b, c;
  int x = 1, y = 2, z = 3;
  int ratio = z/x;
  final double PI = 3.141592653589;
  boolean found = false;
  final int maxyz;
  if (z > y) maxyz = z; else maxyz = y;
}
```

Example 7 Scope of Fields, Parameters, and Variables
This program declares five variables or fields, all called x, and shows where each one is in scope (visible). The variables and fields are labeled #1, ..., #5 for reference.

```
class Scope {
  ...                    //
  void m1(int x) {       // Declaration of parameter x (#1)
    ...                  // x #1 in scope
  }                      //
  ...                    //
  void m2(int v2) {      //
    ...                  // x #5 in scope
  }                      //
  ...                    //
  void m3(int v3) {      //
    ...                  // x #5 in scope
    int x;               // Declaration of variable x (#2)
    ...                  // x #2 in scope
  }                      //
  ...                    //
  void m4(int v4) {      //
    ...                  // x #5 in scope
    {                    //
      int x;             // Declaration of variable x (#3)
      ...                // x #3 in scope
    }                    //
    ...                  // x #5 in scope
    {                    //
      int x;             // Declaration of variable x (#4)
      ...                // x #4 in scope
    }                    //
    ...                  // x #5 in scope
  }                      //
  ...                    //
  int x;                 // Declaration of field x (#5)
  ...                    // x #5 in scope
}
```

7   Strings

A *string* is an object of the predefined class String. It is immutable: once created it cannot be changed. A string literal is a sequence of characters within double quotes: "New York", "A38", "", and so on. Internally, a character is stored as a number using the Unicode [1] character encoding, whose character codes 0–127 coincide with the old ASCII encoding. String literals and character literals may use character *escape sequences*:

Escape Code	Meaning
\b	backspace
\t	horizontal tab
\n	newline
\f	form feed (page break)
\r	carriage return
\"	the double quote character
\'	the single quote character
\\	the backslash character
ddd	the character whose character code is the three-digit octal number *ddd*
\u*dddd*	the character whose character code is the four-digit hexadecimal number *dddd*

A character escape sequence represents a single character. Since the letter A has code 65 (decimal), which is written 101 in octal and 0041 in hexadecimal, the string literal "A\101\u0041" is the same as "AAA". If s1 and s2 are expressions of type String and v is an expression of any type, then

- s1.length() of type int is the length of s1, that is, the number of characters in s1.

- s1.equals(s2) of type boolean is true if s1 and s2 contain the same sequence of characters, and false otherwise; equalsIgnoreCase is similar but does not distinguish lowercase and uppercase.

- s1.charAt(i) of type char is the character at position i in s1, counting from 0. If the index i is less than 0, or greater than or equal to s1.length(), then StringIndexOutOfBoundsException is thrown.

- s1.toString() of type String is the same object as s1.

- String.valueOf(v) returns the string representation of v, which can have any primitive type (section 5.1) or reference type. When v has reference type and is not null, then it is converted using v.toString(); if it is null, then it is converted to the string "null". Any class C inherits from Object a default toString method that produces strings of the form C@2a5734, where 2a5734 is some memory address, but toString may be overridden to produce more useful strings.

- s1 + s2 has the same meaning as s1.concat(s2): it constructs the concatenation of s1 and s2, a new String consisting of the characters of s1 followed by the characters of s2. Both s1 + v and v + s1 are evaluated by converting v to a string with String.valueOf(v), thus using v.toString() when v has reference type, and then concatenating the resulting strings.

- s1.compareTo(s2) returns a negative integer, zero, or a positive integer, according as s1 precedes, equals, or follows s2 in the usual lexicographical ordering based on the Unicode [1] character encoding. If s1 or s2 is null, then the exception NullPointerException is thrown. Method compareToIgnoreCase is similar but does not distinguish lowercase and uppercase.

- s1.substring(int i, int j) returns a new String of the characters from s1 with indexes i..(j-1). Throws IndexOutOfBoundsException if i<0 or i>j or j>s1.length.

- s1.subSequence(int i, int j) is like substring but returns a CharSequence (section 26.7).

- More String methods are described in the Java class library documentation [2].

Example 8 Equality of Strings and the Subtlety of the (+) Operator

```
String s1 = "abc";
String s2 = s1 + "";       // New object, but contains same text as s1
String s3 = s1;            // Same object as s1
String s4 = s1.toString(); // Same object as s1
// The following statements print false, true, true, true, true:
System.out.println("s1 and s2 identical objects: " + (s1 == s2));
System.out.println("s1 and s3 identical objects: " + (s1 == s3));
System.out.println("s1 and s4 identical objects: " + (s1 == s4));
System.out.println("s1 and s2 contain same text: " + (s1.equals(s2)));
System.out.println("s1 and s3 contain same text: " + (s1.equals(s3)));
// These two statements print 35A and A1025 because (+) is left-associative:
System.out.println(10 + 25 + "A");  // Same as (10 + 25) + "A"
System.out.println("A" + 10 + 25);  // Same as ("A" + 10) + 25
```

Example 9 Concatenating All Command Line Arguments
When concatenating many strings, use a string builder instead (chapter 19 and example 104).

```
public static void main(String[] args) {
  String res = "";
  for (int i=0; i<args.length; i++)
    res += args[i];
  System.out.println(res);
}
```

Example 10 Counting the Number of e's in a String

```
static int ecount(String s) {
  int ecount = 0;
  for (int i=0; i<s.length(); i++)
    if (s.charAt(i) == 'e')
      ecount++;
  return ecount;
}
```

Example 11 Determining Whether Strings Occur in Lexicographically Increasing Order

```
static boolean sorted(String[] a) {
  for (int i=1; i<a.length; i++)
    if (a[i-1].compareTo(a[i]) > 0)
      return false;
  return true;
}
```

Example 12 Using a Class That Declares a toString Method
The class Point (example 27) declares a toString method that returns a string of the point coordinates. The operator (+) calls the toString method implicitly to format the Point objects.

```
Point p1 = new Point(10, 20), Point p2 = new Point(30, 40);
System.out.println("p1 is " + p1);      // Prints: p1 is (10, 20)
System.out.println("p2 is " + p2);      // Prints: p2 is (30, 40)
p2.move(7, 7);
System.out.println("p2 is " + p2);      // Prints: p2 is (37, 47)
```

7.1   String Formatting

Formatting of numbers, characters, dates, times, and other data may be done using a formatting string fmt containing *formatting specifiers*, using one of these methods:

- String.format(fmt, v1, ..., vn) returns a String produced from fmt by replacing formatting specifiers with the strings resulting from formatting the values v1, ..., vn.

- strm.format(fmt, v1, ..., vn), where strm is a PrintWriter or PrintStream (section 26.6), constructs a string as above, outputs it to strm, and returns strm.

- strm.printf(fmt, v1, ..., vn) behaves exactly as strm.format(fmt, v1, ..., vn).

These methods exist also in a version that take a Locale object as first argument; see examples 16 and 17. Formatting specifiers are described in sections 7.1.1 and 7.1.2 below. If a value vi is of the wrong type for a given formatting specifier, or if the formatting specifier is ill-formed, then a call to the above methods will throw an exception of class IllegalFormatException or one of its subclasses.

7.1.1   Formatting of Numeric, Character, and General Types

A formatting specifier for numeric, character, and general types has this form:

%[*index*$] [*flags*] [*width*] [.*precision*]*conversion*

The *index* is an integer $1, 2, \ldots$ indicating the value v_{index} to format; the *conversion* indicates what operation is used to format the value; the *width* indicates the minimum number of characters used to format the value; the *flags* indicate how that width should be used (where "–" means left-justification, or padding on the right, and "0" means padding with zero); and *precision* limits the output, such as the number of fractional digits. Each of the four parts in brackets [ ] is optional; the only mandatory parts are the percent sign (%) and the *conversion*.

The documentation for Java API class java.util.Formatter gives the full details of number formatting. The table below shows the legal *conversions* on numbers (I = integers, F = floating-point numbers, IF = both), characters (C), and general types (G). An uppercase conversion such as X produces uppercase output.

Format	conversion	flags	precision	Type
Decimal	d	-+ 0, (		I
Octal	o	-#0		I
Hexadecimal	x or X	-#0		I
Hexadecimal significand and exponent	a or A	-#+ 0		F
General: scientific or fractional	g or G	-#+ 0, (	Max. significant digits	IF
Fixed-point number	f	-#+ 0, (	Fractional digits	IF
Scientific notation	e or E	-#+ 0, (	Fractional digits	IF
Unicode character [1]	c or C	–		C
Boolean: "true" or "false"	b or B	–		Boolean
Hexadecimal hashcode of value, or "null"	h or H	–		G
Determined by value's formatTo method	s or S	–		G
A percent symbol (%)	%	(none)		
Platform-specific newline	n	(none)		

Example 13 Aligning Strings Using the `String.format` Method
The code `%` begins each of the three formatting specifiers, `1$` refers to the first value (`"Oslo"`), conversion `s` means string formatting, width 7 means seven characters minimum width, and "–" means left-justification. The result `res` is `|Oslo|␣␣␣Oslo|Oslo␣␣␣|`, where the symbol ␣ denotes a blank (space).

```
String res = String.format("|%1$s|%1$7s|%1$-7s|", "Oslo");
```

Example 14 Aligning Numbers in Columns Using the `out.format` Method
Three lines each with five numbers in the range 0–999 are printed, with the numbers right-justified in a field four characters wide so that they form five columns. The formatting specifier `%4d` uses implicit indexing; one might equivalently use explicit indexing `#1$4d` for the same effect. Note the use of `%n` to denote a newline.

```
Random rnd = new Random();                              // Random number generator
for (int i=0; i<3; i++) {
  for (int j=0; j<5; j++)
    System.out.format("%4d", rnd.nextInt(1000));        // Random integer 0..999
  System.out.format("%n");                              // Newline
}
```

Some Integer Formatting Specifiers and Their Effect

Number	Formatting Specifier						
	`%d<`	`%+d<`	`%8d<`	`%-8d<`	`%08d`	`%,d`	`%(d`
0	0<	+0<	0<	0 <	00000000	0	0
255	255<	+255<	255<	255 <	00000255	255	255
-255	-255<	-255<	-255<	-255 <	-0000255	-255	(255)
1250662	1250662<	+1250662<	1250662<	1250662 <	01250662	1,250,662	1250662

Number	Formatting Specifier					
	`%+-,11d<`	`%x`	`%#x`	`%X`	`%o`	`%#o`
0	+0 <	0	0x0	0	0	00
255	+255 <	ff	0xff	FF	377	0377
-255	-255 <	ffffff01	0xffffff01	FFFFFF01	37777777401	037777777401
1250662	+1,250,662 <	131566	0x131566	131566	4612546	04612546

Some Floating-Point Number Formatting Specifiers and Their Effect

Number	Formatting Specifier						
	`%f`	`%.2f`	`%7.2f`	`%07.2f`	`%7.0f`	`%.4g`	`%.4e`
0.0	0.000000	0.00	0.00	0000.00	0.	0.0000	0.0000e+00
0.1	0.100000	0.10	0.10	0000.10	0.	0.1000	1.0000e-01
1.0	1.000000	1.00	1.00	0001.00	1	1.0000	1.0000e+00
1.5	1.500000	1.50	1.50	0001.50	2.	1.5000	1.5000e+00
-1.5	-1.500000	-1.50	-1.50	-001.50	-2.	-1.5000	-1.5000e+00
330.8	330.800000	330.80	330.80	0330.80	331.	330.8000	3.3080e+02
1234.516	1234.516000	1234.52	1234.52	1234.52	1235.	1234.5160	1.2345e+03

7.1.2   Formatting of Dates and Times

A formatting specifier for dates and times has this form:

%[*index*$] [*flag*] [*width*] *conversion*

The *index* and *width* are as in section 7.1.1. The only possible *flag* is "–" which causes left-justification (padding on the right) in connection with a *width* specification. The legal *conversions* are shown below.

Format	*conversion*	Example Result
Hour of the day, 24-hour clock, two digits	tH	21
Hour of the day, 12-hour clock, two digits	tI	09
Hour of the day, 24-hour clock, one or two digits	tk	21
Hour of the day, 12-hour clock, one or two digits	tl	9
Minute within the hour, two digits	tM	06
Seconds within the minute, two digits	tS	07
Milliseconds within the second, three digits	tL	870
Nanosecond within the second, nine digits	tN	870000000
Locale-specific morning/afternoon, lowercase	tp	pm
Locale-specific morning/afternoon, uppercase	tP	PM
Numeric time zone offset from UTC (plus is East)	tz	+0100
Alphabetic time zone abbreviation	tZ	CET
Seconds since the epoch (1970-01-01 00:00:00 UTC)	ts	1078517167
Milliseconds since the epoch	tQ	1078517167870
Locale-specific full month name	tB	March
Locale-specific short month name	tb	Mar
Locale-specific full weekday name	tA	Friday
Locale-specific short weekday name	ta	Fri
Century (year divided by 100)	tC	20
Year, four digits	tY	2004
Year, last two digits	ty	04
Day of year, three digits	tj	065
Month number, two digits	tm	03
Day of month, two digits	td	05
Day of month, one or two digits	te	5
Time of day (hour and minute)	tR	21:06
Time of day (hour, minute, seconds)	tT	21:06:07
Time of day (12-hour clock, minute, seconds)	tr	09:06:07 PM
US-style date (month/day/year)	tD	03/05/04
ISO8601 date (year-month-day)	tF	2004-03-05
Date, time, and timezone; similar to POSIX asctime	tc	Fri Mar 05 21:06:07 CET 2004

Example 15 Formatting Dates and Times as Strings

This example prints `2004-09-14 12:09`; months are numbered from 0 in Java's GregorianCalendar class.

```
GregorianCalendar date = new GregorianCalendar(2004, 8, 14, 12, 9, 28);
System.out.format("%1$tF %1$tR%n", date);
```

Example 16 Locale-Specific Formatting of Dates and Times

The formatting of date and time often depends on the locale: language and nationality. For instance, this is the case for the formatting specifier `%tc`. The Locale class is in package `java.util`.

```
Date now = new Date();
System.out.format("%tc%n", now);                      // default locale
System.out.format(Locale.US, "%tc%n", now);           // en_US locale
System.out.format(Locale.GERMANY, "%tc%n", now);      // de_DE locale
```

Example 17 Locale-Specific Formatting of Numbers

Number formatting is locale sensitive: different languages use different decimal separators (point or comma). For instance, this example outputs `1,234,567.90` and `1.234.567,90` and `1 234 567,90` where the spaces in the latter number are special non-breaking spaces (ISO Latin1 character `'\240'`).

```
double d = 1234567.9;
System.out.format(Locale.US,      "%,.2f%n", d);      // en_US locale
System.out.format(Locale.GERMANY, "%,.2f%n", d);      // de_DE locale
System.out.format(Locale.FRANCE,  "%,.2f%n", d);      // fr_FR locale
```

Some Date and Time Formatting Specifiers and Their Effect

Different languages and countries have very different conventions for writing dates, requiring different formatting specifiers for use with `String.format`. In general, the locale mechanism is not sufficient to write locale-specific dates, except when using the `%tc` formatting specifier. To avoid misunderstandings, do give all four digits of the year, and avoid formats such as `03/05/04` that may have different US and UK interpretations.

Formatting Specifier	Result	Locale	Usage
`%tc`	`Fri Mar 05 21:06:07 CET 2004`	en_US	US
`%tc`	`Fr Mrz 05 21:06:07 CET 2004`	de_DE	Germany
`%tc`	`ven. mars 05 21:06:07 CET 2004`	fr_FR	France
`%1$tD`	`03/05/04`	en_US	US
`%1$tm/%1$td/%1$ty`	`03/05/04`	en_US	US
`%1$tm/%1$td/%1$ty %1$tI:%1$tM %1$tP`	`03/05/04 09:06 PM`	en_US	US
`%1$td.%1$tm.%1$tY %1$tH:%1$tM`	`05.03.2004 21:06`	en_US	Germany
`%1$td/%1$tm/%1$tY`	`05/03/2004`	en_US	UK
`%1$td-%1$tb-%1$ty`	`05-Mar-04`	en_US	US/UK
`%1$tB %1$te, %1$tY`	`March 5, 2004`	en_US	US
`%1$tA %1$tB %1$te, %1$tY`	`Friday March 5, 2004`	en_US	US
`%1$tA, %1$te %1$tB %1$tY`	`Friday, 5 March 2004`	en_US	UK
`%1$te. %1$tB %1$tY`	`5. März 2004`	de_DE	Germany
`%1$tA %1$te. %1$tB %1$tY`	`Freitag 5. März 2004`	de_DE	Germany
`%1$tFT%1$tT`	`2004-03-05T21:06:07`	en_US	RFC3339

8   Arrays

An *array* is an indexed collection of variables, called *elements*. An array has a given *length* $\ell \geq 0$ and a given *element type* t. The elements are indexed by the integers $0, 1, \ldots, \ell - 1$. The value of an expression of array type u[] is either null or a reference to an array whose element type t is a subtype of u. If u is a primitive type, then t must equal u.

8.1   Array Creation and Access

A new array of length ℓ with element type t is created (allocated) using an *array creation expression*:

```
new t[ℓ]
```

where ℓ is an expression of type int. If type t is a primitive type, all elements of the new array are initialized to 0 (when t is byte, char, short, int, or long) or 0.0 (when t is float or double) or false (when t is boolean). If t is a reference type, all elements are initialized to null.

If ℓ is negative, then the exception NegativeArraySizeException is thrown.

Let a be a reference of array type u[], to an array with length ℓ and element type t. Then

- a.length of type int is the length ℓ of a, that is, the number of elements in a.

- The *array access* expression a[i] denotes element number i of a, counting from 0; this expression has type u. The integer expression i is called the *array index*. If the value of i is less than 0 or greater than or equal to a.length, then exception ArrayIndexOutOfBoundsException is thrown.

- When t is a reference type, every array element assignment a[i] = e checks that the value of e is null or a reference to an object whose class C is a subtype of the element type t. If this is not the case, then the exception ArrayStoreException is thrown. This check is made before every array element assignment at run-time, but only for reference types.

8.2   Array Initializers

A variable or field of array type may be initialized at declaration, using an existing array or an *array initializer* for the initial value. An array initializer is a comma-separated list of zero or more expressions enclosed in braces { ... }:

```
t[] x = { expression, ..., expression }
```

The type of each *expression* must be a subtype of t. Evaluation of the initializer causes a distinct new array, whose length equals the number of expressions, to be allocated. Then the expressions are evaluated from left to right, their values are stored in the array, and finally the array is bound to x. Hence x cannot occur in the *expressions:* it has not yet been initialized when they are evaluated.

Array initializers may also be used in connection with array creation expressions:

```
new t[] { expression, ..., expression }
```

Multidimensional arrays can have nested initializers (example 22). Note that there are no array constants: a new distinct array is created every time an array initializer is evaluated.

Example 18 Creating and Using One-Dimensional Arrays
The first half of this example rolls a die 1,000 times, then prints the frequencies of the outcomes. The second half creates and initializes an array of String objects.

```
int[] freq = new int[6];                    // All initialized to 0
for (int i=0; i<1000; i++) {                // Roll dice, count frequencies
  int die = (int)(1 + 6 * Math.random());
  freq[die-1] += 1;
}
for (int c=1; c<=6; c++)
  System.out.println(c + " came up " + freq[c-1] + " times");

String[] number = new String[20];           // Create array of null elements
for (int i=0; i<number.length; i++)         // Fill with strings "A0", ..., "A19"
  number[i] = "A" + i;
for (int i=0; i<number.length; i++)         // Print strings
  System.out.println(number[i]);
```

Example 19 Array Element Assignment Type Check at Run-Time
This program compiles, but at run-time a[2]=d throws ArrayStoreException, since the class of the object bound to d (that is, Double) is not a subtype of a's element type (that is, Integer).

```
Number[] a = new Integer[10];        // Length 10, element type Integer
Double d = new Double(3.14);         // Type Double,  class Double
Integer i = new Integer(117);        // Type Integer, class Integer
Number n = i;                        // Type Number,  class Integer
a[0] = i;                            // OK, Integer is subtype of Integer
a[1] = n;                            // OK, Integer is subtype of Integer
a[2] = d;                            // No, Double not subtype of Integer
```

Example 20 Using an Initialized Array
Method checkdate here behaves the same as checkdate in example 2. The array should be declared outside the method, as shown, otherwise a distinct new array is created for every call to the method.

```
static int[] days = { 31, 28, 31, 30, 31, 30, 31, 31, 30, 31, 30, 31 };
static boolean checkdate(int mth, int day)
{ return (mth >= 1) && (mth <= 12) && (day >= 1) && (day <= days[mth-1]); }
```

Example 21 Creating a String from a Character Array
When replacing character c1 by character c2 in a string, the result can be built in a character array because its length is known. This is 50 percent faster than example 105, which uses a string builder.

```
static String replaceCharChar(String s, char c1, char c2) {
  char[] res = new char[s.length()];
  for (int i=0; i<s.length(); i++)
    if (s.charAt(i) == c1)
      res[i] = c2;
    else
      res[i] = s.charAt(i);
  return new String(res);            // A string containing the characters of res
}
```

8.3   Multidimensional Arrays

The types of multidimensional arrays are written $t[][]$, $t[][][]$, and so on. A rectangular n-dimensional array of size $\ell_1 \times \ell_2 \times \cdots \times \ell_n$ is created (allocated) using the array creation expression

    new t[ℓ_1][ℓ_2]...[ℓ_n]

A multidimensional array a of type $t[][]$ is in fact a one-dimensional array of arrays; its component arrays have type $t[]$. Hence a multidimensional array need not be rectangular, and one need not create all the dimensions at once. To create only the first k dimensions of size $\ell_1 \times \ell_2 \times \cdots \times \ell_k$ of an n-dimensional array, leave the $(n-k)$ last brackets empty:

    new t[ℓ_1][ℓ_2]...[ℓ_k][]...[]

To access an element of an n-dimensional array a, use n index expressions: $a[i_1][i_2]...[i_n]$.

8.4   The Utility Class Arrays

Class Arrays from package `java.util` provides static utility methods to compare, fill, sort, and search arrays, and to create a collection (chapter 22) or stream (chapter 24) from an array. The `binarySearch`, `equals`, `fill`, `parallelSort`, and `sort` methods are overloaded also on arrays with element type `byte`, `char`, `short`, `int`, `long`, `float`, `double`, `Object`, and generic type parameter T; and the `equals` and `fill` methods also on type `boolean`. The Object versions of `binarySearch` and `sort` use the `compareTo` method of the array elements, unless an explicit Comparator object (section 22.9) is given.

- `static List<T> asList(T... a)` returns a List<T> view (section 22.2) of the elements of parameter array a, in index order. The resulting list implements interface RandomAccess.
- `static int binarySearch(byte[] a, byte k)` returns an index i>=0 for which a[i]==k, if any; otherwise returns i<0 such that (-i-1) would be the proper position for k. The array a must be sorted, as by sort(a), or else the result is undefined.
- `static int binarySearch(Object[] a, Object k)` works like the preceding method but compares array elements using their `compareTo` method (section 22.9 and example 134).
- `static int binarySearch(Object[] a, Object k, Comparator cmp)` works like the preceding method but compares array elements using the method cmp.compare (section 22.9).
- `static boolean equals(byte[] a1, byte[] a2)` returns true if a1 and a2 have the same length and contain the same elements, in the same order.
- `static boolean equals(Object[] a1, Object[] a2)` works like the preceding method but compares array elements using their `equals` method (section 22.9).
- `static void fill(byte[] a, byte v)` sets all elements of a to v.
- `static void fill(byte[] a, int from, int to, byte v)` sets a[from..(to-1)] to v.

Example 22 Creating Multidimensional Arrays

Consider this rectangular 3-by-2 array and this two-dimensional "jagged" (lower triangular) array:

0.0	0.0		0.0		
0.0	0.0		0.0	0.0	
0.0	0.0		0.0	0.0	0.0

The following program shows two ways (r1, r2) to create the rectangular array, and three ways (t1, t2, t3) to create the "jagged" array:

```
double[][] r1 = new double[3][2];
double[][] r2 = new double[3][];
for (int i=0; i<3; i++)
  r2[i] = new double[2];

double[][] t1 = new double[3][];
for (int i=0; i<3; i++)
  t1[i] = new double[i+1];
double[][] t2 = { { 0.0 }, { 0.0, 0.0 }, { 0.0, 0.0, 0.0 } };
double[][] t3 = new double[][] { { 0.0 }, { 0.0, 0.0 }, { 0.0, 0.0, 0.0 } };
```

Example 23 Using Multidimensional Arrays

The genetic material of living organisms is held in DNA, conceptually a string AGCTTTTCA of nucleotides A, C, G, and T. A triple of nucleotides, such as AGC, is called a codon; a codon may code for an amino acid. This program counts the frequencies of the $4 \cdot 4 \cdot 4 = 64$ possible codons, using a three-dimensional array freq. The auxiliary array fromNuc translates from the nucleotide letters (A,C,G,T) to the indexes (0,1,2,3) used in freq. The array toNuc translates from indexes to nucleotide letters when printing the frequencies.

```
static void codonfreq(String s) {
  int[] fromNuc = new int[128];
  for (int i=0; i<fromNuc.length; i++)
    fromNuc[i] = -1;
  fromNuc['a'] = fromNuc['A'] = 0; fromNuc['c'] = fromNuc['C'] = 1;
  fromNuc['g'] = fromNuc['G'] = 2; fromNuc['t'] = fromNuc['T'] = 3;
  int[][][] freq = new int[4][4][4];
  for (int i=0; i+2<s.length(); i+=3) {
    int nuc1 = fromNuc[s.charAt(i)];
    int nuc2 = fromNuc[s.charAt(i+1)];
    int nuc3 = fromNuc[s.charAt(i+2)];
    freq[nuc1][nuc2][nuc3] += 1;
  }
  final char[] toNuc = { 'A', 'C', 'G', 'T' };
  for (int i=0; i<4; i++)
    for (int j=0; j<4; j++) {
      for (int k=0; k<4; k++)
        System.out.print(" "+toNuc[i]+toNuc[j]+toNuc[k]+": " + freq[i][j][k]);
      System.out.println();
    }
}
```

Methods on utility class Arrays continued:

- `static <T> void parallelPrefix(T[] a, BinaryOperator<T> op)` performs a parallel prefix operation on array `a` using operator `op`, by computing new values `anew[i]` and subsequently assigning the new values to `a`'s elements. The new value `anew[0]` is just `a[0]`. For `i>0` the new value `anew[i]` is the result of `op.apply(anew[i-1],a[i])` computed in some order, and possibly in parallel. The operation makes sense only if `op` is associative and side-effect free; see section 23.1.

- `static <T> void parallelPrefix(T[] array, int from, int to, BinaryOperator<T> op)` performs a parallel prefix operation as above, but on the subarray `a[from..(to-1)]` using `op`.

  Both of the above methods are overloaded also on `double[]`, `int[]` and `long[]`, taking an `op` argument of type {Double,Int,Long}BinaryOperator.

- `static <T> void parallelSetAll(T[] a, IntFunction<T> f)` initializes all elements of the specified array, in parallel, computing element `a[i]` as `f.apply(i)`.

  Overloaded also on `double[]`, `int[]` and `long[]`, taking an `f` argument of type IntToDoubleFunction, IntUnaryOperator, and IntToLongFunction.

- `static void parallelSort(byte[] a)` sorts array `a` into numerical order, using parallel sort.

- `static void parallelSort(byte[] a, int from, int to)` sorts subarray `a[from..(to-1)]` into ascending numerical order.

- `static <T extends Comparable<T>> void parallelSort(T[] a)` sorts array `a` into ascending order, according to the natural ordering of its elements.

- `static <T> void parallelSort(T[] a, Comparator<T> cmp)` sorts array `a` by `cmp`.

- `static <T extends Comparable<T>> void parallelSort(T[] a, int from, int to)` sorts subarray `a[from..(to-1)]` into ascending order, according to the natural ordering of its elements.

- `static <T> void parallelSort(T[] a, int from, int to, Comparator<T> cmp)` sorts subarray `a[from..(to-1)]` in the order specified by `cmp`.

- `static void sort(byte[] a)` sorts the array `a` using quicksort, which is not stable.

- `static void sort(Object[] a)` sorts the array `a` using mergesort, which is stable. Elements are compared using their `compareTo` method (section 22.9).

- `static void sort(T[] a, Comparator<? extends T> cmp)` works like the preceding method, but elements are compared using the method `cmp.compare` (section 22.9). Is stable.

- `static void sort(byte[] a, int from, int to)` sorts `a[from..(to-1)]`.

- `static <T> Stream<T> stream(T[] a)` returns a sequential stream containing the elements of `a`.

- `static <T> Stream<T> stream(T[] array, int from, int to)` returns a sequential stream containing the elements of subarray `a[from..(to-1)]`.

  The last two methods are overloaded also on `double[]`, `int[]`, and `long[]`, producing streams of type {Double,Int,Long}Stream.

Example 24 Sort and Parallel Sort on Arrays

An array of n = 50 million floating-point numbers can be sorted sequentially or in parallel using methods on class Arrays. On a 4-core Intel i7 processor, the parallel sort is four times faster than the sequential sort. In this example the array elements are van der Corput numbers (example 183) in the range $[0, 1]$. After sorting them, one can compute the difference between any two neighbor array elements and find that the maximal difference is 2.98023×10^{-8} or roughly 1 in 33 million, which shows that the 50 million numbers are indeed dense in $[0, 1]$.

```
double[] vdc = vanDerCorput().limit(n).toArray();
Arrays.sort(vdc);
...
double[] vdc = vanDerCorput().limit(n).toArray();
Arrays.parallelSort(vdc);
double min = vdc[0], max = vdc[n-1], maxDiff = 0.0;
for (int i=1; i<n; i++)
  maxDiff = Math.max(maxDiff, vdc[i] - vdc[i-1]);
// min = 1.49012e-08; max = 1.00000; maxDiff = 2.98023e-08
```

Example 25 Prefix Scans on Arrays; Random Motion in One Dimension

A prefix scan on an array a of numbers with operation op = (x,y) -> x+y will update every array element a[i] to contain the sum of all the preceding array elements a[0..i]. If we fill an array with random numbers in the range $[-1, +1]$ then we can consider each array element a step in a random (Brownian) motion of a particle in one dimension. The prefix scan with op = (x,y) -> x+y will then compute the particle's accumulated position after each time step. We can find how far the particle strayed from the origin (0) by taking the absolute value and computing the maximum, all using just array and stream operations, no loops.

```
double[] a = new Random().doubles(n, -1.0, +1.0).limit(n).toArray();
Arrays.parallelPrefix(a, (x,y) -> x+y);
double maxDist = Arrays.stream(a).map(Math::abs).max().getAsDouble();
```

Example 26 Prefix Scans on Arrays; Random Motion in Two Dimensions

We can change example 25 to investigate random motion in two dimensions by defining a class Vec2D to represent 2D vectors. We can initialize an array of vectors (random particle steps) in parallel, use prefix scan to compute their sum (the particle's position at the end of each step), compute the vector lengths (distances from origin $(0,0)$) and find their maximum, still without explicit loops, and using available parallel cores. Note that randomUniform on Vec2D must be thread-safe because it is called from parallelSetAll. Also, for efficiency it should use java.util.concurrent's ThreadLocalRandom rather than an instance of java.util's Random.

```
Vec2D[] a = new Vec2D[n];
Arrays.parallelSetAll(a, i -> Vec2D.randomUniform());
Arrays.parallelPrefix(a, (p1, p2) -> p1.add(p2));
double maxDist = Arrays.stream(a).mapToDouble(Vec2D::length).max().getAsDouble();
...
private static class Vec2D {
  public final double x, y;
  public double length() { return Math.sqrt(x * x + y * y); }
  public Vec2D add(Vec2D that) { return new Vec2D(this.x + that.x, this.y + that.y); }
  public static Vec2D randomUniform() { ... }
}
```

9   Classes

9.1   Class Declarations and Class Bodies

A *class-declaration* of class C has the form

> *class-modifiers* `class` C *extends-clause implements-clause*
>   *class-body*

A declaration of class C introduces a new reference type C. The *class-body* may contain declarations of fields, constructors, methods, nested classes, nested interfaces, and initializer blocks. A class declaration may take type parameters and be generic; see section 21.4. The declarations in a class may appear in any order:

> {
>
>   *field-declarations*
>   *constructor-declarations*
>   *method-declarations*
>   *class-declarations*
>   *interface-declarations*
>   *enum-type-declaration*
>   *initializer-blocks*
>
> }

A field, method, nested class, nested interface, or nested enum type is called a *member* of the class. A member may be declared `static`. A non-static member is also called an *instance member*.

The scope of a member is the entire class body, except where shadowed by a variable or parameter or by a member of a nested class or interface. The scope of a (static) field does not include (static) initializers preceding its declaration, but the scope of a static field does include all non-static initializers. There can be no two nested classes, interfaces, or enum types with the same name, and no two fields with the same name, but a field, a method, and a class (or interface or enum type) may have the same name.

By *static code* we mean expressions and statements in static field initializers, static initializer blocks, and static methods. By *non-static code* we mean expressions and statements in constructors, non-static field initializers, non-static initializer blocks, and non-static methods. Non-static code is executed inside a *current object*, which can be referred to as `this` (section 11.10). Static code cannot refer to non-static members or to `this`, only to static members.

9.2   Top-Level Classes, Nested Classes, Member Classes, and Local Classes

A *top-level class* is a class declared outside any other class or interface declaration. A *nested class* is a class declared inside another class or interface. There are two kinds of nested classes: a *local class* is declared inside a method, constructor, or initializer block; a *member class* is not. A non-static member class, or a local class in a non-static member, is called an *inner class*, because an object of the inner class will contain a reference to an object of the enclosing class. See also section 9.11.

9.3   Class Modifiers

For a top-level class, the *class-modifiers* may be a list of `public` and at most one of `abstract` or `final`. For a member class, they may be a list of `static`, at most one of `abstract` or `final`, and at most one of `private`, `protected`, or `public`. For a local class, they may be at most one of `abstract` or `final`.

Example 27 Class Declaration
The Point class is declared to have two non-static fields x and y, one constructor, and two non-static methods.
It is used in examples 12 and 52.

```
class Point {
  int x, y;

  Point(int x, int y) { this.x = x; this.y = y; }

  void move(int dx, int dy) { x += dx; y += dy; }

  public String toString() { return "(" + x + ", " + y + ")"; }
}
```

Example 28 Class with Static and Non-static Members
The SPoint class declares a static field allpoints and two non-static fields x and y. Thus each SPoint object
has its own x and y fields, but all objects share the same allpoints field in the SPoint class.

  The constructor inserts the new object (this) into the ArrayList object allpoints (section 22.2). The
non-static method getIndex returns the point's index in the array list. The static method getSize returns the
number of SPoints created so far. The static method getPoint returns the i'th SPoint in the array list. Class
SPoint is used in example 59.

```
class SPoint {
  static ArrayList<SPoint> allpoints = new ArrayList<SPoint>();
  int x, y;

  SPoint(int x, int y) { allpoints.add(this); this.x = x; this.y = y; }
  void move(int dx, int dy) { x += dx; y += dy; }
  public String toString() { return "(" + x + ", " + y + ")"; }
  int getIndex() { return allpoints.indexOf(this); }
  static int getSize() { return allpoints.size(); }
  static SPoint getPoint(int i) { return allpoints.get(i); }
}
```

Example 29 Top-Level, Member, and Local Classes
See also examples 42 and 47.

```
class TLC {                          // Top-level class TLC
  static class SMC { ... }           // Static member class

  class NMC { ... }                  // Non-static member (inner) class

  void nm() {                        // Non-static method in TLC
    class NLC { ... }                // Local (inner) class in method
  }

  static void sm() {                 // Static method in TLC
    class SLC { ... }                // Local class in method
  }
}
```

9.4   The Class Modifiers `public`, `final`, `abstract`

If a top-level class C is declared `public`, then it is accessible also outside its package (chapter 17).

If a class C is declared `final`, one cannot declare subclasses of C and hence cannot override any methods declared in C. This is useful for preventing rogue subclasses from violating data representation invariants.

If a class C is declared `abstract`, then it cannot be instantiated, but non-abstract subclasses of C can be instantiated. An abstract class may declare constructors and have initializers, to be executed when instantiating non-abstract subclasses. An abstract class may declare abstract and non-abstract methods; a non-abstract class cannot declare abstract methods. A class cannot be both `abstract` and `final`, because no objects could be created of that class.

9.5   Subclasses, Superclasses, Class Hierarchy, Inheritance, and Overriding

A class C may be declared a *subclass* of class B by an *extends-clause* of the form

```
class C extends B { ... }
```

Class C is a subclass and hence a subtype (section 5.5) of B and its supertypes. It inherits all methods and fields (even private ones, although they are not accessible in class C), but not the constructors, from B.

Class B is called the *immediate superclass* of C. A class can have at most one immediate superclass. The predefined class Object is a superclass of all other classes and has no superclass, so the classes form a *class hierarchy* in which every class is a descendant of its immediate superclass, except Object, which is at the top.

The very first action of a constructor in C may be an explicit call to a constructor in superclass B, like this:

```
super(actual-list);            or            o.super(actual-list);
```

A superclass constructor call may appear only at the very beginning of a constructor body. The second form `o.super(actual-list)` is used when C's superclass B is an inner class. In that case the new C-object needs an enclosing object (sections 9.11 and 10.3); the value of o is that enclosing object and must not be `null`.

If a constructor C(...) in subclass C does not explicitly call `super(...)` as its first action, then it implicitly calls the argumentless *default constructor* B() in superclass B as its first action, as if by `super()`. In this case, B must have a non-private argumentless constructor B(). Conversely, if there is no argumentless constructor B() in B, then C(...) in C must use `super(...)` to explicitly call some other constructor in B.

The declaration of C may *override* a non-final non-static method m inherited from B by declaring a new non-static method m with the exact same signature. An overridden B-method m can be referred to as `super.m` inside C's constructors, non-static methods, and non-static initializers. The overriding method m in C

- must be at least as accessible (section 9.7) as the overridden method in B;
- must have the same signature (disregarding `final`) as the overridden method in B; and must have a return type that is a subtype of that of the overridden method in B;
- either has no *throws-clause*, or has a *throws-clause* that covers no more checked exception classes than the *throws-clause* (if any) of the overridden method in B.

The declaration of C may *hide* a non-final static method m inherited from B by declaring a new static method m with the exact same signature. It is illegal for a static method to hide a non-static one, and vice versa.

The declaration of C may *hide* a non-static field f inherited from B by declaring an additional non-static field of the same name (see section 9.6 and examples 33, 46, and 56). The hidden instance field f inherited from B can be referred to as `super.f` inside C's constructors, non-static methods, and non-static initializers.

Example 30 Abstract Classes, Subclasses, and Overriding

The abstract class Vessel models the notion of a vessel (for holding liquids): it has a field `contents` representing its actual contents, an abstract method `capacity` for computing its maximal capacity, and a method for filling in more, but only up to its capacity (the excess will be lost). The abstract class has subclasses Tank (a rectangular vessel), Cube (a cubic vessel, subclass of Tank), and Barrel (a cylindrical vessel).

The subclasses implement the `capacity` method, they inherit the `contents` field and the `fill` method from the superclass, and they override the `toString` method (inherited from class Object) to print each vessel object appropriately.

```
abstract class Vessel {
  double contents;
  abstract double capacity();
  void fill(double amount) { contents = Math.min(contents + amount, capacity()); }
}
class Tank extends Vessel {
  double length, width, height;
  Tank(double length, double width, double height)
  { this.length = length; this.width = width; this.height = height; }
  double capacity() { return length * width * height; }
  public String toString()
  { return "tank (" + length + ", " + width + ", " + height + ")"; }
}
class Cube extends Tank {
  Cube(double side) { super(side, side, side); }
  public String toString() { return "cube (" + length + ")"; }
}
class Barrel extends Vessel {
  double radius, height;
  Barrel(double radius, double height) { this.radius = radius; this.height = height; }
  double capacity() { return height * Math.PI * radius * radius; }
  public String toString() { return "barrel (" + radius + ", " + height + ")"; }
}
```

Example 31 Using the Vessel Hierarchy from Example 30

The call `vs[i].capacity()` is legal only because the method `capacity`, although abstract, is declared in class Vessel (example 30):

```
public static void main(String[] args) {
  Vessel v1 = new Barrel(3, 10);
  Vessel v2 = new Tank(10, 20, 12);
  Vessel v3 = new Cube(4);
  Vessel[] vs = { v1, v2, v3 };
  v1.fill(90); v1.fill(10); v2.fill(100); v3.fill(80);
  double sum = 0;
  for (int i=0; i<vs.length; i++)
    sum += vs[i].capacity();
  System.out.println("Total capacity is " + sum);
  for (int i=0; i<vs.length; i++)
    System.out.println("vessel number " + i + ": " + vs[i]);
}
```

9.6   Field Declarations in Classes

The purpose of a *field* is to hold a value inside an object (if non-static) or a class (if static). A field must be declared in a class declaration. A *field-declaration* has one of the forms

> *field-modifiers type fieldname1, fieldname2, ... ;*
> *field-modifiers type fieldname1 = initializer1, ... ;*

The *field-modifiers* may be a list of the modifiers `static`, `final`, `transient` (section 26.12), and `volatile`, and at most one of the access modifiers `private`, `protected`, or `public` (section 9.7).

If a field f in class C is declared `static`, then f is associated with class C and can be referred to independently of any objects of class C. The field can be referred to as `C.f` or `o.f`, where o is an expression of type C, or, in the declaration of C, as f. If a field f in class C is not declared `static`, then f is associated with an *object* (also called *instance*) of class C, and every instance has its own copy of the field. The field can be referred to as `o.f`, where o is an expression of type C, or, in non-static code in the declaration of C, as f.

If a field f in class C is declared `final`, the field cannot be modified after initialization. If f has reference type and points to an object or array, the object's fields or the array's elements may still be modified. The initialization must happen either in the declaration or in an initializer block (section 9.13), or if the field is non-static, precisely once in every constructor in class C.

A *field initializer* may be an expression or an array initializer (section 8.2). A static field initializer can refer only to static members of C and can throw no checked exceptions (chapter 15).

A field is given a *default initial value* depending on its type t. If t is a primitive type, the field is initialized to 0 (when t is `byte`, `char`, `short`, `int`, or `long`) or 0.0 (when t is `float` or `double`) or `false` (when t is `boolean`). If t is a reference type, the field is initialized to `null`.

Static fields are initialized when the class is loaded. First all static fields are given default initial values; then the static initializer blocks (section 9.13) and static field initializers are executed, in order of appearance.

Non-static fields are initialized when a constructor is called, at which time all static fields have been initialized already (section 9.10).

If a class C declares a non-static field f, and C is a subclass of a class B that has a non-static field f, then every object of class C has two fields, both called f: one is the B-field f declared in the superclass B, and one is the C-field f declared in C itself. What field is referred to by a field access `o.f` is determined by the compile-time type of o (section 11.9).

9.7   The Member Access Modifiers `private, protected, public`

A member (field, method, nested class, or interface) is always accessible in the class in which it is declared, except where shadowed by a variable, parameter, or field (of a nested class). The *access modifiers* `private`, `protected`, and `public` determine where else the member is accessible.

If a member is declared `private` in top-level class C or a nested class within C, it is accessible on all object instances, not only `this`, in C and its nested classes, but not in their subclasses outside C nor in other classes. If a member in class C is declared `protected`, it is accessible in all classes in the same package (chapter 17) as C and on the same object instance (`this`) in subclasses of C, but not in non-subclasses in other packages. If a member in class C is not declared `private`, `protected`, or `public`, it has *package access*, or *default access*, and is accessible only in classes within the same package as C, not in classes in other packages. If a member in class C is declared `public`, it is accessible in all classes, including classes in other packages. Thus, in order of increasing accessibility, we have `private` access, package (or default) access, `protected` access, and `public` access.

Example 32 Field Declarations
The SPoint class (example 28) declares a static field `allpoints` and two non-static fields x and y.

Example 41 declares a static field `ps` of array type `double[]`. Its field initializer allocates a six-element array and binds it to `ps`, and then the initializer block (section 9.13) stores some numbers into the array.

The Barrel class in example 100 declares two non-static fields `radius` and `height`. The fields are final and therefore must be initialized (which is done in the constructor).

Example 33 Several Fields with the Same Name
An object of class C here has two non-static fields called vf, one declared in the superclass B and one declared in C itself. Similarly, an object of class D has three non-static fields called vf. Class B and class C each have a static field called sf. Class D does not declare a static field sf, so in class D the name sf refers to the static field sf in the superclass C. Examples 46 and 56 use these classes.

```
class B                          // One non-static field vf, one static sf
{ int vf; static int sf; B(int i) { vf = i; sf = i+1; } }

class C extends B                // Two non-static fields vf, one static sf
{ int vf; static int sf; C(int i) { super(i+20); vf = i; sf = i+2; } }

class D extends C                // Three non-static fields vf
{ int vf; D(int i) { super(i+40); vf = i; sf = i+4; } }
```

Example 34 Member Access Modifiers
The vessel hierarchy in example 30 is unsatisfactory because everybody can read and modify the fields of a vessel object. Example 100 presents an improved version of the hierarchy in which (1) the `contents` field in Vessel is made private to prevent modification, (2) a new public method `getContents` permits reading the field, and (3) the fields of Tank and Barrel are declared protected to permit access from subclasses declared in other packages.

Since the field `contents` in Vessel is private, it is not accessible in the subclasses (Tank, Barrel, . . .), but the subclasses still inherit the field. Thus every Vessel subclass object has room for storing the field but can change and access it only by using the methods `fill` and `getContents` inherited from the abstract superclass.

Example 35 Private Member Accessibility
A private member is accessible everywhere inside the enclosing top-level class (and only there).

```
class Access {
  private static int x;
  static class SI {
    private static int y = x;       // Access private x from enclosing class
  }
  static void m() {
    int z = SI.y;                   // Access private y from nested class
  }
}
```

9.8   Method Declarations

A *method* must be declared inside a class. A *method-declaration* declaring method m has the form

> *method-modifiers   return-type* m (*formal-list*)   *throws-clause*
>   *method-body*

The *formal-list* is a comma-separated list of zero or more *formal parameter declarations*, of one of the forms

> *parameter-modifier   type   parameter-name*
> *parameter-modifier   type*... *parameter-name*

The *parameter-modifier* may be final, meaning that the parameter cannot be modified inside the method, or absent. The *type* is any type. Each *parameter-name* must be a distinct name. A formal parameter is an initialized variable; its scope is the *method-body*. The second form of parameter declaration can appear only last and declares a parameter array; see section 9.9. For generic methods with type parameters, see section 21.8.

The method name m together with the list $t_1, \ldots, t_n$ of declared parameter types in the *formal-list* determine the *method signature* m($t_1, \ldots, t_n$), where any generic types in $t_1, \ldots, t_n$ are replaced by the underlying non-generic raw types (section 21.11). The *return-type* is not part of the method signature.

A class may declare more than one method with the same *method-name*, provided they have different signatures (after replacing generic types by raw types). This is called *overloading* of the *method-name*.

The *method-body* is a *block-statement* (section 12.2) and thus may contain statements as well as declarations of variables and local classes. In particular, the *method-body* may contain return statements. If the *return-type* is void, the method does not return a value, and no return statement in the *method-body* can have an expression argument. If the *return-type* is not void but a type, the method must return a value: it must not be possible for execution to reach the end of *method-body* without executing a return statement. Moreover, every return statement must have an expression argument whose type is a subtype of the *return-type*.

The *method-modifiers* may be abstract or a list of static, final, synchronized (section 20.2), and at most one of the access modifiers private, protected, or public (section 9.7).

If a method m in class C is declared static, then m is associated with class C; it can be referred to without any object. The method may be called as C.m(...) or as o.m(...), where o is an expression whose type is a subtype of C, or, inside methods, constructors, field initializers, and initializer blocks in C, simply as m(...). A static method can refer only to static fields and methods of the class.

If a method m in class C is not declared static, then m is associated with an object (instance) of class C. Outside the class, the method must be called as o.m(...), where o is an object of class C or a subclass, or, inside non-static methods, non-static field initializers, and non-static initializer blocks in C, simply as m(...). A non-static method can refer to all fields and methods of class C, whether they are static or not.

If a method m in class C is declared final, it cannot be overridden (redefined) in subclasses.

If a method m in class C is declared abstract, class C must itself be abstract (and so cannot be instantiated). An abstract method cannot be static, final, or synchronized, and its declaration has no method body:

> abstract *method-modifiers   return-type* m (*formal-list*)   *throws-clause*;

The *throws-clause* of a method or constructor has the form throws E1, ..., En where E1, ..., En are the names of exception types covering all the checked exceptions that the method or constructor may throw. If execution of the method or constructor body may throw some exception e, then e must be either an unchecked exception (chapter 15) or a checked exception whose class is a subtype of one of E1, ..., En. An Ei may be a generic type parameter provided it is constrained (section 21.5) to be a subtype of Throwable.

Example 36 Method Name Overloading and Signatures
This class declares four overloaded methods m with signatures m(int) and m(boolean) and m(int, double) and m(double, double); see section 5.6. Some of the overloaded methods are static, others non-static. The overloaded methods may have different return types, as shown here. Example 61 explains the method calls.

It would be legal to declare an additional method with signature m(double, int), but then the method call m(10, 20) would become ambiguous and illegal. Namely, its call signature would be m(int,int) and there is no way to determine whether to call m(int, double) or m(double, int).

```
double m(int i) { return i; }
boolean m(boolean b) { return !b; }
static double m(int x, double y) { return x + y + 1; }
static double m(double x, double y) { return x + y + 3; }
public static void main(String[] args) {
  System.out.println(m(10, 20));          // Prints: 31.0
  System.out.println(m(10, 20.0));        // Prints: 31.0
  System.out.println(m(10.0, 20));        // Prints: 33.0
  System.out.println(m(10.0, 20.0));      // Prints: 33.0
}
```

Example 37 Method Overloading, Overriding, and Hiding
Class C1 declares overloaded method m1 with signatures m1(double) and m1(int) and method m2 with signature m2(int). Its subclass C2 hides C1's static method m1(double) and overloads m2 by declaring additional overloaded variants. These methods are used in example 62.

```
class C1 {
  static void m1(double d) { System.out.println("11d"); }
  void m1(int i) { System.out.println("11i"); }
  void m2(int i) { System.out.println("12i"); }
}
class C2 extends C1 {
  static void m1(double d) { System.out.println("21d"); }
  void m1(int i) { System.out.println("21i"); }
  void m2(double d) { System.out.println("22d"); }
  void m2(Integer ii) { System.out.println("22ii"); }
  void m3(int i)      { System.out.println("23i"); }
  void m4(Integer ii) { System.out.println("24ii"); }
}
```

Example 38 Method Overloading and a Parameter Array
The first declaration of method max has a parameter array xr of type int[], so the method can be called with any number of arguments greater than one. The first argument gets bound to x and the remaining ones to an array bound to xr. However, a call to max(4, 5) will call the second overload max(int, int), because a method that does not require expansion of a parameter array is preferred over one that does.

```
static int max(int x1, int... xr) {
  int res = x1;
  for (int x : xr)
    res = max(res, x);
  return res;
}
static int max(int x, int y) { return x > y ? x : y; }
```

9.9   Parameter Arrays and Variable-Arity Methods

The last parameter of a method may be declared to be a *parameter array*, using the syntax

```
t... x
```

where `t` is a type, `x` is a parameter name, and the three dots `. . .` are part of the concrete syntax. In the method, parameter `x` will have type `t[]`. In a call to the method, its actual arguments may either be given as zero or more arguments of type `t`, in which case `x` gets bound to a new array holding the values of those arguments; or the value may be given by a single array of type `t[]`, in which case `x` gets bound to that array. The first case is used to declare methods that take a variable number of arguments; see example 38.

In overloading resolution, an explicit overload such as `max(int, int)` is preferred over an expansion of a formal parameter array such as `max(int, int...)`.

9.10   Constructor Declarations

The purpose of a constructor in class `C` is to initialize new objects (instances) of the class. A *constructor-declaration* in class `C` has the form

> *constructor-modifiers* `C`(*formal-list*)   *throws-clause*
>   *constructor-body*

The *constructor-modifiers* may be a list of at most one of `private`, `protected`, and `public` (section 9.7); a constructor cannot be `abstract`, `final`, or `static`. A constructor has no return type.

Constructors may be overloaded in the same way as methods: the *constructor signature* (a list of the parameter types in *formal-list*) is used to distinguish constructors in the same class. A constructor may call another overloaded constructor in the same class using the syntax:

> `this`(*actual-list*)

but a constructor may not call itself, directly or indirectly. A call `this(...)` to another constructor, if present, must be the very first action of a constructor, preceding any declaration or statement.

The *constructor-body* is a *block-statement* (section 12.2) and so may contain statements as well as declarations of variables and local classes. The *constructor-body* may contain `return` statements, but no `return` statement can take an expression argument.

A class that does not explicitly declare a constructor implicitly declares a public, argumentless *default constructor* whose only (implicit) action is to call the superclass constructor (section 9.5):

> `public C() { super(); }`

The *throws-clause* of the constructor specifies the checked exceptions that may be thrown by the constructor, in the same manner as for methods (section 9.8).

When `new` creates a new object in memory (section 11.7), the object's non-static fields are given default initial values according to their type. Then a constructor is called to further initialize the object, and the following happens: first, some superclass constructor is called (explicitly or implicitly, see examples 40 and 63) exactly once; then the non-static field initializers and non-static initializer blocks are executed once in order of appearance in the class declaration; and finally the constructor body (except the explicit superclass constructor call, if any) is executed. The call to a superclass constructor will cause a call to a constructor in its superclass, and so on, until reaching `Object()`.

Example 39 Constructor Overloading; Calling Another Constructor

We add a new constructor to the Point class (example 27), thus overloading its constructors. The old constructor has signature `Point(int, int)` and the new one `Point(Point)`. The new constructor makes a copy of the point p by calling the old constructor using the syntax `this(p.x, p.y)`.

```
class Point {
  int x, y;

  Point(int x, int y)                 // Overloaded constructor
  { this.x = x; this.y = y; }

  Point(Point p)                      // Overloaded constructor
  { this(p.x, p.y); }                 // Calls the first constructor

  void move(int dx, int dy)
  { x += dx; y += dy; }

  public String toString()
  { return "(" + x + ", " + y + ")"; }
}
```

Example 40 Calling a Superclass Constructor

The constructor in the ColoredPoint subclass (example 94) calls its superclass constructor using the syntax `super(x, y)`.

Example 41 Field Initializers and Initializer Blocks

Here the static field initializer allocates an array and binds it to field `ps`. The static initializer block fills the array with an increasing sequence of pseudo-random numbers, then scales them so that the last number is 1.0 (this is useful for generating rolls of a random loaded die). This cannot be done using the field initializer alone.

One could delete the two occurrences of `static` to obtain another example, with a non-static field `ps`, a non-static field initializer, and a non-static initializer block. However, non-static fields are usually initialized by a constructor.

```
class InitializerExample {
  static double[] ps = new double[6];

  static {                            // Static initializer block
    double sum = 0;
    for (int i=0; i<ps.length; i++)   // Fill with increasing random numbers
      ps[i] = sum += Math.random();
    for (int i=0; i<ps.length; i++)   // Scale so last ps element is 1.0
      ps[i] /= sum;
  }
  ...
}
```

9.11   Nested Classes, Member Classes, Local Classes, and Inner Classes

A non-static nested class, that is, a non-static member class NMC or a local class NLC in a non-static member, is called an *inner class*. An object of an inner class always contains a reference to an object of the enclosing class C, called the *enclosing object*. That object can be referred to as C.this in non-static code (example 47), so a non-static member x of the enclosing object can be referred to as C.this.x.

An inner class or local class cannot have static members. More precisely, all static fields must also be final, and methods and nested classes in an inner class or local class must be non-static.

A static nested class, that is, a static member class SMC or a local class in a static member, has no enclosing object and cannot refer to non-static members of the enclosing class C. This is the standard restriction on static members of a class (section 9.1). A static member class may itself have static as well as non-static members.

If a local class refers to variables or formal parameters in the enclosing method, constructor, or initializer, those variables or parameters must be declared final or be *effectively final*: not the target of reassignment or of pre/post increment/decrement operators.

9.12   Anonymous Classes

An *anonymous class* is a special kind of local class; hence it must be declared inside a method, constructor, or initializer. An anonymous class can be declared, and exactly one instance created, using the special expression syntax

```
new C(actual-list)
    class-body
```

where C is a class name. This creates an anonymous subclass of class C, with the given *class-body* (section 9.1). Moreover, it creates an object of that anonymous subclass and calls the appropriate C constructor with the arguments in *actual-list*, as if by super(*actual-list*). An anonymous class cannot declare its own constructors.

When I is an interface name, the similar expression syntax

```
new I()
    class-body
```

creates an anonymous local class, with the given *class-body* (section 9.1), that must implement the interface I, and also creates an object of that anonymous class. Note that the parameter list after I must be empty.

9.13   Initializer Blocks, Field Initializers, and Initializers

In addition to field initializers (section 9.6), a class may contain *initializer-blocks*. Initializer blocks may be used when field initializers or constructors do not suffice. We use the term *initializer* to mean field initializers as well as initializer blocks. A *static initializer block* has the form

```
static block-statement
```

The static initializer blocks and field initializers of static fields are executed, in order of appearance in the class declaration, when the class is loaded. A *non-static initializer block* is simply a free-standing *block-statement*.

An initializer is not allowed to throw a checked exception (chapter 15). If execution of a static initializer throws an (unchecked) exception other than Error or one of its subclasses, that exception is discarded and the exception ExceptionInInitializerError is thrown instead.

Example 42 Member Classes and Local Classes

```
class TLC {                                     // Top-level class
  static int sf;
  int nf;
  static class SMC {                            // Static member class
    static int ssf = sf + TLC.sf;               // can have static members
    int snf = sf + TLC.sf;                      // cannot use non-static TLC members
  }
  class NMC {                                    // Non-static member (inner) class
    int nnf1 = sf + nf;                          // can use non-static TLC members
    int nnf2 = TLC.sf + TLC.this.nf;             // cannot have static members
  }
  void nm() {                                    // Non-static method in TLC
    class NLC {                                  // Local (inner) class in method
      int m(int p) { return sf+nf+p; }           // can use non-static TLC members
} } }
```

Example 43 An Iterator as a Local Class

Method `suffixes` returns an object of the local class SuffixIterator, which implements the Iterator<String> interface (section 22.7) to enumerate the non-empty suffixes of the string `s`:

```
class LocalInnerClassExample {
  public static void main(String[] args) {
    Iterator<String> seq = suffixes(args[0]);
    while (seq.hasNext())
      System.out.println(seq.next());
  }
  static Iterator<String> suffixes(final String s) {
    class SuffixIterator implements Iterator<String> {
      int startindex=0;
      public boolean hasNext() { return startindex < s.length(); }
      public String next() { return s.substring(startindex++); }
      public void remove() { throw new UnsupportedOperationException(); }
    }
    return new SuffixIterator();
} }
```

Example 44 An Iterator as an Anonymous Local Class

Alternatively, we may use an anonymous local class in method `suffixes`:

```
static Iterator<String> suffixes(final String s) {
  return
    new Iterator<String>() {
        int startindex=0;
        public boolean hasNext() { return startindex < s.length(); }
        public String next() { return s.substring(startindex++); }
        public void remove() { throw new UnsupportedOperationException(); }
      };
}
```

10 Classes and Objects in the Computer

10.1 What Is a Class?

Conceptually, a class represents a concept, a template for creating instances (objects). In the computer, a class is a chunk of memory, set aside once, when the class is loaded at run-time. A class has the following parts:

- The name of the class
- Room for all the static members of the class

A class can be drawn as a box. The header `class SPoint` gives the class name, and the box itself contains the static members of the class:

```
class SPoint

allpoints  □
```

10.2 What Is an Object?

Conceptually, an object is an instance of a concept (a class). In the computer, an object is a chunk of memory, set aside by an object creation expression `new C(...)`; see section 11.7. Every evaluation of an object creation expression `new C(...)` creates a distinct object, with its own chunk of computer memory. An object has the following parts:

- A reference to the run-time *class* C of the object; this is the class C used when creating the object
- Room for all the non-static members of the object

An object can be drawn as a box. The header `: SPoint` gives the object's class (underlined), and the remainder of the box contains the non-static members of the object:

```
: SPoint

x    12

y    123
```

10.3 Inner Objects

When NMC is an inner class (a non-static member class, or a local class in non-static code) in a class C, then an object of class NMC is an *inner object*. In addition to the object's class and the non-static fields, an inner object always contains a reference to an *enclosing object*, which is an object of the innermost enclosing class C. The enclosing object reference can be written C.this in non-static code in the inner class.

An object of a static nested class SMC, on the other hand, contains no reference to an enclosing object.

Example 45 Objects and Classes

This is the computer memory at the end of the `main` method in example 59, using the SPoint class from example 28. The variables p and s refer to the same object, variable q is `null`, and variable r refers to the rightmost object.

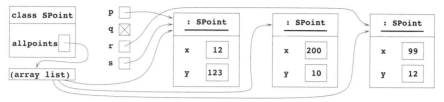

Example 46 Objects with Multiple Fields of the Same Name

This is the computer memory at the end of the `main` method in example 56, using the classes from example 33. The classes B and C each have a single static field `sf`; class D has none. The two objects of class C each have two non-static fields `vf` (called `B/vf` and `C/vf` below), and the class D object has three non-static fields `vf`.

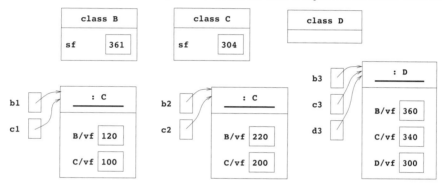

Example 47 Inner Objects

Example 42 declares a class `TLC` with non-static member (inner) class `NMC` and static member class `SMC`. Assume we create a `TLC` object, two `NMC` objects, and an `SMC` object:

```
TLC oo = new TLC();
TLC.NMC io1 = oo.new NMC(), io2 = oo.new NMC();
TLC.SMC sio = new TLC.SMC();
```

Then the computer memory will contain these objects (the classes are not shown):

11   Expressions

An expression is evaluated to obtain a value (such as 117). In addition, evaluation of an expression may change the computer's *state*: the values of variables, fields, and array elements; the contents of files; and so on. More precisely, evaluation of an expression

- terminates normally, producing a value; or
- terminates abruptly by throwing an exception; or
- does not terminate at all (for instance, because it calls a method that does not terminate).

Expressions are built from *literals* (anonymous constants), variables, fields, operators, method calls, array accesses, conditional expressions, the new operator, and so on; see the table of expression forms on the facing page.

One must distinguish the compile-time *type of an expression* from the run-time *class of an object*. An expression has a type (chapter 5) inferred by the compiler. When this is a reference type t, and the value of the expression is an object o, then the class of object o will be a subtype of t but not necessarily equal to t. For instance, the expression (Number)(new Integer(2)) has type Number, but its value is an object whose class is Integer, a subclass of Number.

11.1   Table of Expression Forms

The table of expression forms shows the form, meaning, associativity, argument (operand) types, and result types for expressions. The expressions are grouped according to precedence, as indicated by the horizontal rules, from high precedence to low precedence. Higher-precedence forms are evaluated before lower-precedence forms. Parentheses may be used to emphasize or force a particular order of evaluation.

When an operator (such as +) is left-associative, a sequence e1 + e2 + e3 of operators is evaluated as if parenthesized (e1 + e2) + e3. When an operator (such as =) is right-associative, a sequence e1 = e2 = e3 of operators is evaluated as if parenthesized e1 = (e2 = e3).

In the argument type and result type columns of the table, *integer* stands for any of char, byte, short, int, or long, or their boxed forms Character, Byte, Short, Integer, or Long (section 5.4); and *numeric* stands for integer, float, or double, or their boxed forms Float or Double. The type *boolean* stands for boolean or its boxed form Boolean.

For an operator with one integer or numeric operand, the *promotion type* is double if the operand has type double; it is float if the operand has type float; it is long if the operand has type long; otherwise it is int (that is, if the operand has type byte, char, short, or int).

For an operator with two integer or numeric operands (except the shift operators; section 11.4), the promotion type is double if any operand has type double; otherwise, it is float if any operand has type float; otherwise, it is long if any operand has type long; otherwise, it is int.

Before the operation is performed, the operands are promoted, that is, converted to the promotion type by a widening type conversion (section 5.7).

If the result type is given as numeric also, it equals the promotion type. For example, 10 / 3 has type int, whereas 10 / 3.0 has type double, and c + (byte)1 has type int when c has type char.

Expression	Meaning	Section	Assoc'ty	Argument Types	Result Type
`a[...]`	array access	8.1		`t[]`, integer	`t`
`o.f`	non-static field access	11.9		object `o`	type of `f`
`C.f`	static field access	11.9			type of `f`
`this`	current object reference	9.1, 11.10			this class
`C.this`	enclosing object reference	9.11, 11.10			`C`
`o.m(...)`	instance method call	11.12		object `o`	return type
`C.m(...)`	static method call	11.12			return type
`super.m(...)`	superclass method call	11.12			return type
`C.super.m(...)`	encl. superclass mth. call	11.12			return type
`t.class`	class object for `t`	27.1		type `t`	`Class<t>`
`t::m` or `e::m`	method reference	11.14			
`x++` or `x--`	postincrement/decrement	11.2		numeric	numeric
`++x` or `--x`	preincrement/decrement	11.2		numeric	numeric
`-x`	negation (minus sign)	11.2	right	numeric	numeric
`~e`	bitwise complement	11.4	right	integer	`int/long`
`!e`	logical negation	11.3	right	boolean	boolean
`new t[...]`	array creation	8.1		type `t`	`t[]`
`new C(...)`	object creation	11.7		class `C`	`C`
`(t)e`	type cast	11.11		type, any	`t`
`e1 * e2`	multiplication	11.2	left	numeric	numeric
`e1 / e2`	division	11.2	left	numeric	numeric
`e1 % e2`	remainder	11.2	left	numeric	numeric
`e1 + e2`	addition	11.2	left	numeric	numeric
`e1 + e2`	string concatenation	7	left	String, any	String
`e1 + e2`	string concatenation	7	left	any, String	String
`e1 - e2`	subtraction	11.2	left	numeric	numeric
`e1 << e2`	left shift	11.4	left	integer	`int/long`
`e1 >> e2`	signed right shift	11.4	left	integer	`int/long`
`e1 >>> e2`	unsigned right shift	11.4	left	integer	`int/long`
`e1 < e2`	less than		none	numeric	boolean
`e1 <= e2`	less than or equal to		none	numeric	boolean
`e1 >= e2`	greater than or equal to		none	numeric	boolean
`e1 > e2`	greater than		none	numeric	boolean
`e instanceof t`	instance test	11.8	none	any, reference type	boolean
`e1 == e2`	equal		left	compatible	boolean
`e1 != e2`	not equal		left	compatible	boolean
`e1 & e2`	bitwise and	11.4	left	integer	`int/long`
`e1 & e2`	logical strict and	11.3	left	boolean	boolean
`e1 ^ e2`	bitwise exclusive-or	11.4	left	integer	`int/long`
`e1 ^ e2`	logical strict exclusive-or	11.3	left	boolean	boolean
`e1	e2`	bitwise or	11.4	left	integer	`int/long`
`e1	e2`	logical strict or	11.3	left	boolean	boolean
`e1 && e2`	logical and	11.3	left	boolean	boolean
`e1 || e2`	logical or	11.3	left	boolean	boolean
`e1 ? e2 : e3`	conditional	11.6	right	boolean, any, any	any
`x = e`	assignment	11.5	right	e subtype of `x`	type of `x`
`x += e`	compound assignment	11.5	right	compatible	type of `x`
`x -> ebs`	lambda expression	11.13	right		

11.2 Arithmetic Operators

The value of the postincrement expression x++ is that of x, and its effect is to increment x by 1; and similarly for postdecrement x--, which decrements by 1. The value of the preincrement expression ++x is that of x+1, and its effect is to increment x by 1; and similarly for predecrement --x.

Integer division e1/e2 truncates, that is, rounds toward zero, so 10/3 is 3, and (-10)/3 is −3. The integer remainder x%y equals x-(x/y)*y when y is non-zero; it has the same sign as x. Integer division or remainder by zero throws the exception ArithmeticException. Integer overflow does not throw an exception but wraps around. Thus, in the int type, the expression 2147483647+1 evaluates to −2147483648, and the expression -2147483648-1 evaluates to 2147483647.

The floating point remainder x%y roughly equals x-(((int)(x/y))*y when y is non-zero. Floating-point division by zero and floating-point overflow do not throw exceptions but produce special IEEE754 values (of type float or double) such as Infinity or NaN ("not a number").

11.3 Logical Operators

The operators == and != require the operand types to be compatible: one must be a subtype of the other, possibly after an unboxing operation. Two values of primitive type are equal (by ==) if they represent the same value after conversion to their common supertype. For instance, 10 and 10.0 are equal. Two values of reference type are equal (by ==) if both are null, or both are references to the same object or array, created by the same boxing operation or execution of the new-operator. Hence do not use == or != to compare strings or boxed numbers: two strings s1 and s2 may contain the same sequence of characters and be equal by s1.equals(s2), yet be distinct objects and unequal by s1==s2 (example 8). Similarly for boxed numbers (example 3).

The logical operators && and || perform *shortcut evaluation*: if e1 evaluates to true in e1&&e2, then e2 is evaluated to obtain the value of the expression; otherwise e2 is ignored, and the value of the expression is false. Conversely, if e1 evaluates to false in e1||e2, then e2 is evaluated to obtain the value of the expression; otherwise e2 is ignored, and the value of the expression is true. By contrast, the operators & (logical strict and) and ^ (logical strict exclusive-or) and | (logical strict or) always evaluate both operands, regardless of the value of the left-hand operand. Usually the shortcut operators && and || are preferable.

11.4 Bitwise Operators and Shift Operators

The operators ~ (bitwise complement, or one's complement) and & (bitwise and) and ^ (bitwise exclusive-or) and | (bitwise or) may be used on operands of integer type. The operators work in parallel on all bits of the 2's complement representation of the operands. Thus ~n equals (-n)-1 and also equals (-1)^n.

The shift operators << and >> and >>> shift the bits of the 2's complement representation of the first argument. The two operands are promoted (section 11.1) separately, and the result type is the promotion type (int or long) of the first argument. Thus the shift operation is always performed on a 32-bit (int) or a 64-bit (long) value. In the former case, the length of the shift is between 0 and 31 as determined by the five least significant bits of the second argument; in the latter case, it is between 0 and 63 as determined by the six least significant bits of the second argument.

The left shift n<<s equals n*2*2*...*2 where there are s multiplications. The signed right shift n>>s of a non-negative n equals n/2/2/.../2 where there are s divisions; the signed right shift of a negative n equals ~((~n)>>s). The unsigned right shift n>>>s of a non-negative n equals n>>s; the unsigned right shift of a negative n equals (n>>s)+(2<<~s) if n has type int, and (n>>s)+(2L<<~s) if it has type long, where 2L is the long constant with value 2. See example 91 for a "clever" and intricate use of bitwise operators.

Example 48 Arithmetic Operators

```
public static void main(String[] args) {
  int max = 2147483647;
  int min = -2147483648;
  println(max+1);                              // Prints: -2147483648
  println(min-1);                              // Prints:  2147483647
  println(-min);                               // Prints: -2147483648
  print(   10/3); println(   10/(-3));         // Prints:  3 -3
  print((-10)/3); println((-10)/(-3));         // Prints: -3  3
  print(   10%3); println(   10%(-3));         // Prints:  1  1
  print((-10)%3); println((-10)%(-3));         // Prints: -1 -1
}
static void print(int i)   { System.out.print(i + " "); }
static void println(int i) { System.out.println(i + " "); }
```

Example 49 Logical Operators

Because of shortcut evaluation of `&&`, this expression from example 20 does not evaluate the array access `days[mth-1]` unless $1 \leq$ mth ≤ 12, so the index is never out of bounds:

```
(mth >= 1) && (mth <= 12) && (day >= 1) && (day <= days[mth-1])
```

This returns `true` if `y` is a leap year, namely, if `y` is a multiple of 4 but not of 100, or is a multiple of 400:

```
static boolean leapyear(int y)
{ return y % 4 == 0 && y % 100 != 0 || y % 400 == 0; }
```

Example 50 Bitwise Operators and Shift Operators

```
class Bitwise {
  public static void main(String[] args) throws Exception {
    int a = 0x3;                    // Bit pattern   0011
    int b = 0x5;                    // Bit pattern   0101
    println4(a);                    // Prints:       0011
    println4(b);                    // Prints:       0101
    println4(~a);                   // Prints:       1100
    println4(~b);                   // Prints:       1010
    println4(a & b);                // Prints:       0001
    println4(a ^ b);                // Prints:       0110
    println4(a | b);                // Prints:       0111
  }
  static void println4(int n) {
    for (int i=3; i>=0; i--)
      System.out.print(n >> i & 1);
    System.out.println();
  }
}
```

11.5 Assignment Expressions

In the *assignment expression* x = e, the type of e must be a subtype of the type of x, possibly after boxing or unboxing (section 5.4). The type of the expression is the same as the type of x. The assignment is executed by evaluating expression x and then e, and storing e's value in variable x, after a widening conversion (section 11.11) if necessary. When e is a compile-time constant of type byte, char, short, or int, and x has type byte, char, or short, a narrowing conversion is done automatically, provided the value of e is within the range representable in x (section 5.1). The value of the expression x = e is that of x after the assignment.

The assignment operator is right-associative, so x = y = e means x = (y = e).

When e has reference type (object type or array type), only a reference to the object or array is stored in x. Thus the assignment x = e does not copy the object or array (example 52).

When x and e have the same type, the compound assignment x += e is equivalent to x = x + e; however, x is evaluated only once, so in a[i++] += e the variable i is incremented only once. When the type of x is t, different from the type of e, then x += e is equivalent to x = (t)(x + e), in which the intermediate result (x + e) is converted to type t (section 11.11); again x is evaluated only once. The other compound assignment operators -=, *=, and so on are similar.

Since assignment associates to the right, and the value of sum += e is that of sum after the assignment, one can write ps[i] = sum += e to first increment sum by e and then store the result in ps[i] (example 41).

11.6 Conditional Expressions

The *conditional expression* e1 ? e2 : e3 is legal if e1 has type boolean or Boolean. If the conditional expression appears in the context of assignment, argument, cast, or return, its type may be determined by the context, as for lambda expressions (section 11.13). Otherwise its type is the least common supertype of e2 and e3, possibly after boxing operations. The conditional expression is evaluated by first evaluating e1; if it is true, then e2 is evaluated; otherwise e3 is evaluated—this gives the value of the conditional expression.

11.7 Object Creation Expressions

The *object creation expression*

        new C(*actual-list*)

creates a new object of class C and then calls that constructor in class C whose signature matches the arguments in *actual-list*. The *actual-list* is evaluated from left to right to obtain a list of argument values. These argument values are bound to the constructor's parameters, an object of the class is created in the memory, the non-static fields are given default initial values according to their type, a superclass constructor is called explicitly or implicitly (examples 40 and 63), all non-static field initializers and initializer blocks are executed in order of appearance, and finally the constructor body is executed to initialize the object. The value of the constructor call expression is the newly created object, whose class is C.

When C is an inner class in class D, and o evaluates to an object of class D, then one may create a C-object inside o using the syntax o.new C(*actual-list*); see example 47.

11.8 Instance Test Expressions

The *instance test* e instanceof t is evaluated by evaluating e to a value v. If v is not null and is a reference to an object of class C, where C is a subtype of t, the result is true; otherwise false.

Example 51 Widening, Narrowing, and Truncation in Assignments
The assignment d = 12 performs a widening of 12 from int to double. The assignments b = 123 and b2 = 123+1 perform an implicit narrowing from int to byte, because the right-hand sides are compile-time constants. The assignment b2 = b1+1 would be illegal because b1+1 is not a compile-time constant. The assignment b2 = 123+5 would be illegal because, although 123+5 is a compile-time constant, its value is not representable as a byte (whose range is −128..127).

```
double d;
d = 12;                         // Widening conversion from int to double
byte b1 = 123;                  // Narrowing conversion from int to byte
byte b2;
b2 = 123 + 1;                   // Legal: 123+1 is a compile-time constant
b2 = (byte)(b1 + 1);            // Legal: (byte)(b1 + 1) has type byte
int x = 0;
x += 1.5;                       // Equivalent to: x = (int)(x + 1.5); thus adds 1 to x
```

Example 52 Assignment Does Not Copy Objects
Assignment (and parameter passing) copies the reference, not the object. Class Point is from example 27.

```
Point p1 = new Point(10, 20);
System.out.println("p1 is " + p1);      // Prints: p1 is (10, 20)
Point p2 = p1;                          // p1 and p2 refer to same object
p2.move(8, 8);
System.out.println("p2 is " + p2);      // Prints: p2 is (18, 28)
System.out.println("p1 is " + p1);      // Prints: p1 is (18, 28)
```

Example 53 Compound Assignment Operators
Compute the product of all elements of array xs:

```
static double multiply(double[] xs) {
  double prod = 1.0;
  for (int i=0; i<xs.length; i++)
    prod *= xs[i];                      // Equivalent to: prod = prod * xs[i]
  return prod;
}
```

Example 54 Conditional Expression
The first method returns the absolute value of x. The last two show that the context may determine the type of the conditional expression; the lambda expressions (x -> -x) and (x -> x) do not have a type in isolation.

```
static double absolute(double x) { return (x >= 0 ? x : -x); }
static IntUnaryOperator doInteger(boolean flip) { return flip ? x -> -x : x -> x; }
static DoubleUnaryOperator doDouble(boolean flip) { return flip ? x -> -x : x -> x; }
```

Example 55 Object Creation and Instance Test

```
Number n1 = new Integer(17);
Number n2 = new Double(3.14);
// The following statements print: false, true, false, true.
System.out.println("n1 is a Double:  " + (n1 instanceof Double));
System.out.println("n2 is a Double:  " + (n2 instanceof Double));
System.out.println("null is a Double: " + (null instanceof Double));
System.out.println("n2 is a Number:   " + (n2 instanceof Number));
```

11.9   Field Access Expressions

A *field access* must have one of these three forms:

```
f
C.f
o.f
```

where C is a class and o an expression of reference type.

A class may have several fields of the same name f (section 9.6, example 33, and example 56).

A field access f must refer to a static or non-static field declared in or inherited by a class whose declaration encloses the field access expression (when f has not been shadowed by a field in a nested enclosing class, or by a variable or parameter of the same name). The class declaring the field is the target class TC.

A field access C.f must refer to a static field in class C or a superclass of C. That class is the target class TC.

A field access o.f, where expression o has type C, must refer to a static or non-static field in class C or a superclass of C. That class is the target class TC. To evaluate the field access, the expression o is evaluated to obtain an object. If the field is static, the object is ignored and the value of o.f is the TC-field f. If the field is non-static, the value of o must be non-null and the value of o.f is the value of the TC-field f in object o.

It is informative to contrast a non-static field access and a non-static method call (section 11.12):

- In a non-static field access o.f, the field referred to is determined by the compile-time *type* of the object expression o.

- In a non-static call to a non-private method o.m(...), the method called is determined by the run-time *class* of the target object: the object to which o evaluates.

11.10   The Current Object Reference `this`

The name this may be used in non-static code to refer to the current object (section 9.1). When non-static code in a given object is executed, the object reference this refers to the object as a whole. Hence, when f is a field and m is a method (declared in the innermost enclosing class), then this.f means the same as f (when f has not been shadowed by a variable or parameter of the same name), and this.m(...) means the same as m(...).

When D is an inner class in an enclosing class C, then inside D the notation C.this refers to the C object enclosing the inner D object. See example 42, where TLC.this.nf refers to field nf of the enclosing class TLC.

11.11   Type Cast Expression

A *type cast* of expression e to t is done using this expression, which has type t:

```
(t)e
```

When e is an expression of primitive type and t is a primitive type, the cast is a widening or narrowing conversion (section 5.7). When t is a primitive type and e has the corresponding boxed type, the cast is an unboxing, and when e has primitive type and t is the corresponding boxed type, it is a boxing (section 5.4).

When e is an expression of reference type and t is a reference type, the type cast is evaluated by evaluating e to a value v. If v is null or is a reference to an object or array whose class is a subtype of t, then the type cast succeeds with result v; otherwise the exception ClassCastException is thrown. The type cast is illegal when it cannot possibly succeed at run-time, for instance, when e has type Double and t is Boolean.

Example 56 Field Access

Here we illustrate static and non-static field access in the classes B, C, and D from example 33. Note that the field referred to by an expression of form o.vf or o.sf is determined by the type of expression o, not the class of the object to which o evaluates.

```
public static void main(String[] args) {
  C c1 = new C(100);              // c1 has type C; object has class C
  B b1 = c1;                      // b1 has type B; object has class C
  print(C.sf,  B.sf);             // Prints: 102 121
  print(c1.sf, b1.sf);            // Prints: 102 121
  print(c1.vf, b1.vf);            // Prints: 100 120
  C c2 = new C(200);              // c2 has type C; object has class C
  B b2 = c2;                      // b2 has type B; object has class C
  print(c2.sf, b2.sf);            // Prints: 202 221
  print(c2.vf, b2.vf);            // Prints: 200 220
  print(c1.sf, b1.sf);            // Prints: 202 221
  print(c1.vf, b1.vf);            // Prints: 100 120
  D d3 = new D(300);              // d3 has type D; object has class D
  C c3 = d3;                      // c3 has type C; object has class D
  B b3 = d3;                      // b3 has type B; object has class D
  print(D.sf,  C.sf,  B.sf);      // Prints: 304 304 361
  print(d3.sf, c3.sf, b3.sf);     // Prints: 304 304 361
  print(d3.vf, c3.vf, b3.vf);     // Prints: 300 340 360
}
static void print(int x, int y) { System.out.println(x+" "+y); }
static void print(int x, int y, int z) { System.out.println(x+" "+y+" "+z); }
```

Example 57 Using this When Referring to Shadowed Fields

A common use of this is to refer to fields (this.x and this.y) that have been shadowed by parameters (x and y), especially in constructors, as in the Point class from example 27:

```
class Point {
  int x, y;
  Point(int x, int y) { this.x = x; this.y = y; }
... }
```

Example 58 Using this to Pass the Current Object to a Method

In the SPoint class (example 28), the current object reference this is used in the constructor to add the newly created object to the array list allpoints, and it is used in the method getIndex to look up the current object in the array list:

```
class SPoint {
  static ArrayList<SPoint> allpoints = new ArrayList<SPoint>();
  int x, y;
  SPoint(int x, int y) { allpoints.add(this); this.x = x; this.y = y; }
  int getIndex() { return allpoints.indexOf(this); }
... }
```

11.12 Method Call Expressions

A *method call* expression, or *method invocation*, must have one of these five forms:

    m (*actual-list*)
    super.m (*actual-list*)
    C.m (*actual-list*)
    C.super.m (*actual-list*)
    o.m (*actual-list*)

where m is a method name, C is a class name, and o is an expression of reference type. The *actual-list* is a possibly empty comma-separated list of expressions, called the *arguments* or *actual parameters*. The *call signature* is $csig = m(t_1, \ldots, t_n)$, where $(t_1, \ldots, t_n)$ is the list of types of the n arguments in the *actual-list*. The forms super.m (*actual-list*) and C.super.m (*actual-list*) can be used only in non-static code.

Determining what method is actually called by a method call is complicated because (1) method names may be overloaded, each version having a distinct signature; (2) methods may be overridden, that is, reimplemented in subclasses; (3) methods that are non-static and non-private are called by dynamic dispatch, given a target object; and (4) a method call in a nested class may call a method declared in some enclosing class. Moreover, to make the number and types of actual arguments match the method's signature, it may be necessary to take into account (1a) automatic boxing or unboxing of arguments and (1b) expansion of a parameter array, if any.

Section 11.12.1 describes argument evaluation and parameter passing, when it is clear which method m is being called. Section 11.12.2 describes how to determine which method is being called.

11.12.1 Method Call: Parameter Passing

This section considers the evaluation of a method call m (*actual-list*) when it is clear which method m is called, and focuses on the parameter passing mechanism.

The call is evaluated by evaluating the expressions in the *actual-list* from left to right to obtain the argument values. These argument values are then bound to the corresponding parameters in the method's *formal-list*, in order of appearance. A boxing or unboxing conversion (section 5.4) occurs if necessary, and a widening conversion (section 11.11) occurs if the type of an argument expression is a subtype of the method's corresponding parameter type.

If the last formal parameter x is a parameter array t... (section 9.9), then a new array is created to hold those actual arguments not bound to the preceding parameters, and that array is bound to x.

Java uses *call-by-value* to bind argument values to formal parameters, so the formal parameter holds a copy of the argument value. Thus if the method changes the value of a formal parameter, this change does not affect the argument. For an argument of reference type, the parameter holds a copy of the object reference or array reference, and hence the parameter refers to the same object or array as the actual argument expression. Thus if the method changes that object or array, the changes will be visible after the method returns (example 60).

A non-static method must be called with a target object, for example as o.m (*actual-list*), where the target object is the value of o, or as m (*actual-list*), where the target object is the current object reference this. In either case, during execution of the method body, this will be bound to the target object.

A static method is not called with a target object (and so there is no this reference in a static method).

When the argument values have been bound to the formal parameters, the method body is executed. The value of the method call expression is the value returned by the method if its return type is non-void; otherwise the method call expression has no value. When the method returns, all parameters and local variables in the method are discarded.

Example 59 Calling Non-Overloaded, Non-Overridden Methods

This program uses the SPoint class from example 28. The static methods `getSize` and `getPoint` may be called by prefixing them with the class name SPoint, or by prefixing them with an expression of type SPoint such as q, although the latter is bad style. They may be called before any objects have been created. The non-static method `getIndex` must be called with an object, as in `r.getIndex()`; then the method is executed with the current object reference `this` bound to r.

```
System.out.println("Number of points created: " + SPoint.getSize());
SPoint p = new SPoint(12, 123);
SPoint q = new SPoint(200, 10);
SPoint r = new SPoint(99, 12);
SPoint s = p;
q = null;
System.out.println("Number of points created: " + SPoint.getSize());
System.out.println("Number of points created: " + q.getSize());        // Bad style
System.out.println("r is point number " + r.getIndex());
for (int i=0; i<SPoint.getSize(); i++)
  System.out.println("SPoint number " + i + " is " + SPoint.getPoint(i));
```

Example 60 Parameter Passing Copies References, Not Objects and Arrays

In the method call `m(p, d, a)` shown here, the object reference held in p is copied to parameter pp of m, so p and pp refer to the same object, the integer held in d is copied to dd, and the array reference held in a is copied to aa. At the end of method m, the state of the computer memory is this:

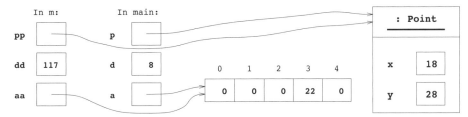

When method m returns, its parameters pp, dd, and aa are discarded. The variables p, d, and a are unmodified, but the object and the array pointed to by p and a have been modified.

```
public static void main(String[] args) {
  Point p = new Point(10, 20);
  int[] a = new int[5];
  int d = 8;
  System.out.println("p is " + p);          // Prints: p is (10, 20)
  System.out.println("a[3] is " + a[3]);     // Prints: a[3] is 0
  m(p, d, a);
  System.out.println("p is " + p);          // Prints: p is (18, 28)
  System.out.println("d is " + d);          // Prints: d is 8
  System.out.println("a[3] is " + a[3]);     // Prints: a[3] is 22
}
static void m(Point pp, int dd, int[] aa) {
  pp.move(dd, dd);
  dd = 117;
  aa[3] = 22;
}
```

11.12.2 Method Call: Determining Which Method Is Called

In general, methods may be overloaded as well as overridden. The overloading is resolved at compile-time by finding the most specific applicable and accessible method signature for the call. Overriding (for non-static methods) is handled at run-time by searching the class hierarchy upwards starting with the run-time class of the object on which the method is called.

At Compile-Time: Determine the Target Type and Signature

Find the target type TC. If the method call has the form m (*actual-list*), the target type TC is the innermost enclosing class containing a method called m that is visible (not shadowed by a method m, regardless of signature, in an intervening class). If the method call has the form super.m (*actual-list*), the target type TC is the superclass of the innermost enclosing class. If the method call has the form C.super.m (*actual-list*), the target type TC is the superclass of the enclosing class C. If the method call has the form C.m (*actual-list*), then TC is C. If the method call has the form o.m (*actual-list*), then TC is the type of the expression o.

Find the target signature tsig. A method in class TC is *applicable* if its signature subsumes the call signature *csig* (section 5.6). Whether a method is *accessible* is determined by its access modifiers (section 9.7). Consider the collection of methods in TC that are both applicable and accessible. The call is illegal (method unknown) if there is no such method. The call is illegal (ambiguous) if there is no method whose signature is most specific, that is, is subsumed by all the others. Thus if the call is legal, there is exactly one most specific signature, the target signature $tsig = m(u_1, \ldots, u_n)$.

Finding the applicable target signatures requires one, two, or three stages. In stage 1, automatic boxing/unboxing and parameter arrays are not taken into account when determining whether a method signature subsumes the call signature. If stage 1 finds no applicable signatures, then stage 2 is performed, now taking automatic boxing/unboxing into account. If stage 2 finds no applicable signatures, then stage 3 is performed, taking both automatic boxing/unboxing and parameter array expansion into account. The net effect is a preference for no boxing/unboxing and no parameter array expansion when possible; see examples 38 and 62.

Determine whether the called method is static. If the method call has the form C.m (*actual-list*), the called method must be static. If the method call has the form m (*actual-list*) or o.m (*actual-list*) or super.m (*actual-list*) or C.super.m (*actual-list*), we use the target type TC and the signature *tsig* to determine whether the called method is static or non-static.

At Run-Time: Determine the Target Object (If Non-static) and Execute the Method

If the method is static, no target object is needed: the method to call is the method with signature *tsig* in class TC. When m is static in a method call o.m (*actual-list*), the expression o is evaluated, but its value is ignored.

If the method is non-static, determine the target object; it will be bound to the object reference this during execution of the method. In the case of m (*actual-list*), the target object is this (if TC is the innermost class enclosing the method call), or TC.this (if TC is an outer class containing the method call). In the case of super.m (*actual-list*), the target object is this. In the case of C.super.m (*actual-list*), the target object is C.this. In the case o.m (*actual-list*), the expression o must evaluate to an object reference. If non-null, that object is the target object; otherwise the exception NullPointerException is thrown. If the method is non-private, the class hierarchy is searched to determine which method to call, starting with the class RTC of the target object. If a method with signature *tsig* is not found in class RTC, then the immediate superclass of RTC is searched, and so on. This search procedure is called *dynamic dispatch*. If the method is private, it must be in the target class TC and no search is needed.

When the method has been determined, arguments are evaluated and bound as described in section 11.12.1.

Example 61 Calling Overloaded Methods

Here we call the overloaded methods m declared in example 36. The call m(10, 20) has call signature m(int, int) and calls the method with signature m(int, double), which is the most specific applicable one. The first two lines call the method m(int, double), and the last two call the method m(double, double).

```
System.out.println(m(10, 20));      // Prints: 31.0
System.out.println(m(10, 20.0));    // Prints: 31.0
System.out.println(m(10.0, 20));    // Prints: 33.0
System.out.println(m(10.0, 20.0));  // Prints: 33.0
```

Example 62 Calling Overridden and Overloaded Methods

Here we use the classes C1 and C2 from example 37. The target type of c1.m1(i) is class C1, which has a non-static method with signature m1(int), so the call is to a non-static method; the target object has class C2, so the called method is m1(int) in C2; and quite similarly for c2.m1(i). The target type for c1.m1(d) is the class C1, which has a static method with signature m1(double), so the call is to a static method, and the object bound to c1 does not matter (and calling a static method through an object is bad style). Similarly for c2.m1(d), whose target type is C2, so it calls m1(double) in C2, which overrides m1(double) in C1.

The calls to c2.m2 with arguments of type int and Integer require no boxing or unboxing because there are overloads c2(int) and c2(Integer). The call to m3 involves unboxing and that to m4 involves boxing.

```
int i = 17;
Integer ii = new Integer(i);
double d = 17.0;
C2 c2 = new C2();                          // Type C2, object class C2
C1 c1 = c2;                                // Type C1, object class C2
c1.m1(i); c2.m1(i); c1.m1(d); c2.m1(d);    // Prints 21i 21i 11d 21d
c1.m2(i);                                  // Prints 12i
c2.m2(i);                                  // Prints 12i,  no boxing/unboxing
c2.m2(ii);                                 // Prints 22ii, no boxing/unboxing
c2.m3(ii);                                 // Prints 23i,  with unboxing
c2.m4(i);                                  // Prints 24ii, with boxing
```

Example 63 Calling Overridden Methods from a Constructor

When d2 is an object of class D2, then d2.m2() calls the method m2 inherited from superclass D1. The call m1() in m2 is equivalent to this.m1(), where this is d2, so the method m1 declared in class D2 is called. Hence d2.m2() prints D1.m2 and D2.m1:7. It prints 7 because field f is initialized to 7 in constructor D2().

Perhaps more surprisingly, the creation d2 = new D2() of an object of class D2 will print D1.m2 and then D2.m1:0. Why does it print 0, not 7? The very first action of constructor D2() is to make an implicit call to the superclass constructor D1(), even *before* executing the assignment f = 7. Hence f will still have its default value 0 when method m1 in D2 is called from method m2 in D1, which in turn is called from constructor D1().

```
class D1 {
  D1() { m2(); }
  void m1() { System.out.println("D1.m1 "); }
  void m2() { System.out.print("D1.m2 "); m1(); }
}
class D2 extends D1 {
  int f;
  D2() { f = 7; }
  void m1() { System.out.println("D2.m1:" + f); }
}
```

11.13   Lambda Expressions (Java 8.0)

A lambda expression evaluates to a function, a value that implements a functional interface (chapter 23). A lambda expression has one of these three forms, each having zero or more parameters and a lambda body:

```
x -> ebs
(x1, ..., xn) -> ebs
(formal-list) -> ebs
```

Here x is a variable, and the lambda body ebs is either an expression or a block statement { ... }. The *formal-list* is the same as for methods in section 9.8. In the two first forms, the parameters are implicitly typed (types are inferred), and in the third form, they are explicitly typed (types are declared). A lambda expression cannot have a mixture of implicitly and explicitly typed parameters.

A lambda expression (like a method reference expression, section 11.14) can appear only on the right-hand side of an assignment, as an argument in a call, in a cast, or in a method return statement. This is because the lambda expression may have many different types and therefore needs a targeted function type such as Function<String,Integer> from section 23.5. The targeted type is provided by the assignment left-hand side, the parameter type, the cast type, or the method return type.

Evaluation of a lambda expression produces an instance fv of a class implementing a functional interface (chapter 23), but does not cause evaluation of the lambda body ebs. To cause evaluation of the lambda body, call the single abstract method of the function interface, as in fv.apply(...); see example 65. If execution of the lambda body throws an exception, then that exception will propagate to the call of the function.

In a lambda body that is a block statement, either no return statement has an associated expression, or else all have the form return e and execution cannot "fall through" by reaching the end of the block statement. A return statement returns from the (innermost) enclosing lambda expression, not from any enclosing method.

A variable captured in a lambda body must be declared final or be effectively final, just as for local classes (section 9.11): it must not be the target of reassignment or of pre/post increment/decrement operators.

An occurrence of this or super in a lambda body ebs means the same as in the lambda expression's context, unlike in an anonymous inner class IC, where this refers to the IC instance and super to methods and fields in the base class of IC.

11.14   Method Reference Expressions (Java 8.0)

A method reference expression has one of these six forms, where t is a type, m a method name, e an expression, and C a class name. Example 67 illustrates all of these:

```
t :: m
e :: m
super :: m
t . super :: m
C :: new
t[]...[] :: new
```

The first five of these can further take optional type arguments <t1...tn> between the :: separator and the method name m; the last form cannot. Such type arguments are used to resolve type parameters of the indicated method m or class C constructor. Also, the number n of type parameters is used to limit the search for applicable methods. Note that one cannot specify the method's actual signature (argument types).

Example 64 Lambda Expressions
This example shows the forms of lambda expressions, where the targeted function type is the variable's type, such as Function<String,Integer>; see page 125 for these types. The fsi1–fsi4 are bound to lambda expressions that parse a string as an integer. The fsis1–fsis3 are bound to lambda expressions that return the three-letter substring of s starting at i. The concat is a function that concatenates its two string arguments. The now is a function that returns the date and time when now.get() is called, not when now is defined. The show1 and show2 are functions with return type void. Example 65 shows how to call these functions. The fsas1–fsas3 are functions that take an array of strings and return their concatenation, with separator ":".

In addition to being bound to variables, lambda expressions are often passed as arguments to methods (in examples 165, 171, 176, and others), or are being returned from methods (in example 173).

```
Function<String,Integer>
  fsi1 = s -> Integer.parseInt(s),
  fsi2 = s -> { return Integer.parseInt(s); },
  fsi3 = (String s) -> Integer.parseInt(s),
  fsi4 = (final String s) -> Integer.parseInt(s);
BiFunction<String,Integer,String>
  fsis1 = (s, i) -> s.substring(i, Math.min(i+3, s.length())),
  fsis2 = (s, i) -> { int to = Math.min(i+3, s.length()); return s.substring(i, to); };
BiFunction<String,String,String>
  concat = (s1, s2) -> s1 + s2;
Supplier<String>
  now = () -> new java.util.Date().toString();
Consumer<String>
  show1 = s -> System.out.println(">>>" + s + "<<<"),
  show2 = s -> { System.out.println(">>>" + s + "<<<"); };
Function<String[],String>
  fsas1 = ss -> String.join(":", ss),
  fsas2 = (String[] ss) -> String.join(":", ss),
  fsas3 = (String... ss) -> String.join(":", ss);
```

Example 65 Calling Lambda-Defined Functions
The function values defined in example 64 can be called as follows, using the method names of the respective functional interfaces, shown on page 125. The type of a function determines how it can be called, so fsas3 above must be called with a single String[] argument, not as a variable-arity function; but see example 163.

```
System.out.println(fsi1.apply("004711"));
System.out.println(fsis1.apply("abcdef", 4));
show1.accept(now.get());
System.out.println(fsas1.apply(new String[] { "abc", "DEF" }));
// fsas3.apply("abc", "DEF");                 // Illegal: Must take one String[] argument
```

Example 66 Higher-Order Lambda Expressions
A lambda expression may be higher-order: return another function as result, or take another function as argument, as illustrated by prefix and twice below. The types look complex but are very descriptive.

```
Function<String,Function<String,String>> prefix = s1 -> s2 -> s1 + s2;
Function<String,String> addDollar = prefix.apply("$");
BiFunction<Function<String,String>,String,String> twice = (f, s) -> f.apply(f.apply(s));
Function<String,String> addTwoDollars = s -> twice.apply(addDollar, s);
prefix.apply("$").apply("100") ... addDollar.apply("100") ... addTwoDollars.apply("100")
```

A method reference expression (like a lambda expression, section 11.13) can appear only on the right-hand side of an assignment, as a method argument, in a cast, or in a method return statement. This is because the method reference expression may have many different types and therefore needs a targeted function type such as Function<String,Integer> from section 23.5. The targeted type is provided by the assignment left-hand side, the parameter type, the cast type, or the method return type.

The compile-time processing of a method reference expression t::m or e::m consists of these steps:

- First, determine which type should be searched for the denoted method. In form t::m, type t must be a reference type, and that is the type to search; in form e::m, expression e must have a reference type, and that is the type to search.

- Second, search that type for applicable methods, based on both the argument count of the targeted function type and the method name m; if there are optional *type arguments* <t1...tn>, the method must have n type parameters. When the targeted function type takes k *normal arguments*, and the method reference expression has form t::m, search both for k-argument static methods and (k-1)-argument instance methods; if the method reference expression has form e::m, search only for k-argument instance methods.

- Third, if there are any applicable methods, then search among them for static as well as instance methods with appropriate receiver and argument types for the targeted function type. If t in t::e is a raw type such as ArrayList, this involves finding appropriate type parameters for t, to obtain for instance ArrayList<String>. If this search produces a unique method M, the search is successful; otherwise the method reference expression is rejected, because it refers to either no methods or to more than one.

A method reference expression of form C::new evaluates to an instance constructor with argument count and parameter types determined by the targeted function type.

A method reference expression of form t[]::new or t[][]::new and so on evaluates to an array allocation function taking a single integer argument, such as i -> new t[i] or i -> new t[i][] and so on; the argument determines the length of the array's first dimension only. As with normal array instance creation, the element type t must not be a generic type instance such as ArrayList<Integer> or a type parameter.

At run-time, a method reference expression must evaluate to a functional value fv, through these steps:

- First, in an expression of the form e::m, evaluate e to a reference rec, and if it is null, throw an exception.

- Second, the functional value fv is produced. This must be an instance of an internally generated class FC that implements the targeted functional interface and therefore must have a method such as apply; see chapter 23. The value fv is produced either by creating a new class instance or by finding and returning an appropriate existing instance. The apply method of class FC may perform boxing or unboxing of arguments and result to implement the functional interface's single abstract method and to pass appropriate arguments to the method M previously found during the compile-time method reference search; this is needed for charat in example 67. Also, if a reference rec was obtained in the first run-time step, then rec will be stored in the FC instance and used as the receiver argument of instance method M.

The run-time evaluation of a method reference expression to function value fv does not involve calling the method M found by the compile-time search. Only when fv is called, as in fv.apply(...), will M be called.

The Java Language Specification [3] gives many more details, especially on the compile-time search.

In addition to the examples opposite, further uses of method reference expressions are illustrated by examples 155, 161, 179, and 180.

Example 67 Method Reference Expressions

The method reference expression bound to `charat` below is a t::m reference to an instance method; `parseint` is a t::m to a static method; `hex1` is an c::m reference giving an explicit receiver e (the string) to method `charAt` on class String. The `makeConverter` method shows that the expression part e of an e::m reference can be complex. Variable `makeC` is bound to the C(int) constructor of class C shown further below.

Variable `make1DArray` refers to a method equivalent to i -> new Double[i]. In `mkDoubleList`, the type parameter list <Double> is for the generic class ArrayList; in `sorter`, the type parameter list <Double> is for the (static) generic method `sort` on non-generic class Arrays. Class C shows how `this` and `super` can be used to resolve a method reference e::getVal to either class C's or superclass B's `getVal` method.

```
BiFunction<String,Integer,Character> charat = String::charAt;          // t::m
Function<String,Integer> parseint = Integer::parseInt;                 // t::m
Function<Integer,Character> hex1 = "0123456789ABCDEF"::charAt;         // e::m
Function<Integer,C> makeC = C::new;                                    // C::new
Function<Integer,Double[]> make1DArray = Double[]::new;                // t[]::new
Consumer<String> print = System.out::println;                          // e::m
Function<Integer,ArrayList<Double>> mkDoubleList = ArrayList<Double>::new;  // t::new
BiConsumer<Double[],Comparator<Double>> sorter = Arrays::<Double>sort;  // t::<t1>m
private static Function<Integer,Character> makeConverter(boolean uppercase)
{ return (uppercase ? "0123456789ABCDEF" : "0123456789abcdef") :: charAt; }  // e::m
class B {
  protected int val;
  public int getVal() { return val; }
}
class C extends B {
  public C(int val) { this.val = val; }
  public Supplier<Integer> getBVal() { return super::getVal; }          // super::m
  public Supplier<Integer> getCVal() { return this::getVal; }           // this::m
  public int getVal() { return 117 * val; }
}
```

Example 68 A Lambda Expression or Method Reference Expression Needs a Targeted Function Type

A lambda expression or method reference expression has no type in itself and so must appear in a context where it has a targeted function type; four such contexts are shown below. In particular, a method reference expression cannot appear directly as the receiver of a method call as in `Double::toHexString.andThen(...)`:

```
// int len0 = Double::toHexString.andThen(String::length).apply(123.5); // Illegal
Function<Double,String> hexFun;
hexFun = Double::toHexString;                          // Legal: Assignment right-hand side
int len1 = hexFun.andThen(String::length).apply(123.5);
int len2 = applyAndMeasure(Double::toHexString, 123.5);  // Legal: Argument position
// Legal: In cast context:
int len3 = ((Function<Double,String>)Double::toHexString).andThen(String::length).apply(123.5);
int len4 = makeToHex().andThen(String::length).apply(123.5);
static int applyAndMeasure(Function<Double,String> hexFun, double d) {
  return hexFun.andThen(String::length).apply(d);
}
static Function<Double,String> makeToHex() {
  return Double::toHexString;                          // Legal: In return context
}
```

12   Statements

A *statement* may change the computer's *state*: the value of variables, fields, and array elements; the contents of files; and so on. More precisely, execution of a statement

- terminates normally (meaning execution will continue with the next statement, if any); or
- terminates abruptly by throwing an exception; or
- exits by executing a `return` statement (if inside a method or constructor); or
- exits a switch or loop by executing a `break` statement (if inside a switch or loop); or
- exits the current iteration of a loop and starts a new iteration by executing a `continue` statement (if inside a loop); or
- does not terminate at all, for instance, by executing `while (true) {}`.

12.1   Expression Statements

An *expression statement* is an *expression* followed by a semicolon:

    expression ;

It is executed by evaluating the *expression* and ignoring its value. The only forms of *expression* that may be legally used in this way are assignment expressions (section 11.5), increment and decrement expressions (section 11.2), method call expressions (section 11.12), and object creation expressions (section 11.7).

For example, an assignment statement `x=e;` is an assignment expression `x=e` followed by a semicolon.

Similarly, a method call statement is a method call expression followed by a semicolon. The value returned by the method, if any, is discarded; the method is executed only for its side effect.

12.2   Block Statements

A *block-statement* is a sequence of zero or more *statements*, *variable-declarations*, or *class-declarations*, in any order, enclosed in braces. Within a block, a variable or class can be used only after its declaration.

    {
      variable-declarations
      class-declarations
      statements
    }

12.3   The Empty Statement

An *empty statement* consists of a semicolon only. It is equivalent to the block statement { } that contains no statements or declarations, and it has no effect at all:

    ;

Example 69 Block Statements
The body of this `main` method, like all method bodies and constructor bodies, is a block statement. It contains a variable declaration, a class declaration, and two further block statements. The two `p1` variables have nothing to do with each other: each block statement introduces its own scope; see section 6.3.

```
public static void main(String[] args) {
  int offset = 10;
  class Pair {
    public final int fst, snd;
    public Pair(int fst, int snd) { this.fst = fst; this.snd = snd; }
    public String toString() { return String.format("(%d,%d)", fst, snd); }
  }
  {
    Pair p1 = new Pair(10, 10+offset);
    System.out.println(p1);
  }
  {
    Pair p1 = new Pair(200, 300);
    System.out.println(p1);
  }
}
```

Example 70 Empty Statement and Infinite Loop Because of Misplaced Semicolon
Here a misplaced semicolon (;) causes the loop body to be an empty statement; the increment `i++` is not part of the loop body. Hence the `while` loop will not terminate but go on forever.

```
int i=0;
while (i<10);
  i++;
```

Example 71 Single `if-else` Statement
This method behaves the same as `absolute` in example 54.

```
static double absolute(double x) {
  if (x >= 0)
    return x;
  else
    return -x;
}
```

Example 72 Sequence of `if-else` Statements
We cannot use a switch here, because a switch can work only on integer and enum types. But see example 75.

```
static int wdayno1(String wday) {
  if      (wday.equals("Monday"))    return 1;
  else if (wday.equals("Tuesday"))   return 2;
  else if (wday.equals("Wednesday")) return 3;
  else if (wday.equals("Thursday"))  return 4;
  else if (wday.equals("Friday"))    return 5;
  else if (wday.equals("Saturday"))  return 6;
  else if (wday.equals("Sunday"))    return 7;
  else return -1;                             // Here used to mean 'not found'
}
```

12.4   Choice Statements

12.4.1   The `if` Statement

An `if` statement has the form

> if (*condition*)
>   *truebranch*

The *condition* must have type `boolean` or Boolean, and *truebranch* is a statement. If *condition* evaluates to `true`, then *truebranch* is executed, otherwise not.

12.4.2   The `if-else` Statement

An `if-else` statement has the form:

> if (*condition*)
>   *truebranch*
> else
>   *falsebranch*

The *condition* must have type `boolean` or Boolean, and *truebranch* and *falsebranch* are statements. If *condition* evaluates to `true`, then *truebranch* is executed; otherwise *falsebranch* is executed.

The `if-else` statement is illustrated by examples 71 and 72 on the preceding page.

12.4.3   The `switch` Statement

A `switch` statement has the form

> switch (*expression*) {
> case *constant1*: *branch1*
> case *constant2*: *branch2*
> . . .
> default: *branchn*
> }

The type of *expression* must be `int`, `short`, `char`, `byte`, or a boxed version of these, or an enum type (chapter 14) or String. Each *constant* must be a *compile-time constant* expression, consisting only of literals, `final` variables, `final` fields declared with explicit field initializers, and operators; or it must be an unqualified enum value. All *constants* must be distinct. Each *constant* must have a subtype of the type of *expression*.

Each *branch* is preceded by one or more `case` clauses and is a possibly empty sequence of statements, usually terminated by `break` or `return` (if inside a method or constructor) or `continue` (inside a loop). There can be at most one `default` clause, placed anywhere inside the `switch` statement, not necessarily last.

The `switch` statement is executed as follows: the *expression* is evaluated to obtain a value v. If v equals one of the *constants*, then the corresponding *branch* is executed. If v does not equal any of the *constants*, then the *branch* following `default` is executed; if there is no `default` clause, nothing is executed. If a *branch* is not exited by `break`, `return`, or `continue`, then execution continues with the next *branch* in the switch regardless of the `case` clauses, until a *branch* exits or the switch ends.

Example 73 A `switch` Statement
Here we could have used a sequence of `if-else` statements, but a `switch` is both faster and clearer.

```
static String findCountry(int prefix) {
  switch (prefix) {
  case 1:   return "North America";
  case 44:  return "Great Britain";
  case 45:  return "Denmark";
  case 299: return "Greenland";
  case 46:  return "Sweden";
  case 7:   return "Russia";
  case 972: return "Israel";
  default:  return "Unknown";
  }
}
```

Example 74 A `switch` Statement on an Enum Type
One can switch on a value m of enum type, here type Month from example 97. Enum members such as Apr and Jun appear unqualified in the `case` expressions.

```
switch (m) {
case Apr: case Jun: case Sep: case Nov:
  return 30;
case Feb:
  return leapYear(y) ? 29 : 28;
default:
  return 31;
}
```

Example 75 The `switch` Statement and Strings
As shown below, it is straightforward to switch on values of String type, such as the name of a weekday entered at run-time.

   Before Java version 7 this was not possible. Instead one might use a sequence of `if` statements as in example 72, or if the number of choices is large, use a hashmap (section 22.5) to map each string to an Integer, and then switch on the Integer. A serious drawback of that approach was that the programmer had to maintain consistency between the hashmap and the case labels (numbers), typically appearing in different parts of the code.

```
double hours = Double.parseDouble(args[1]);
switch (args[0]) {
case "Monday":
  System.out.format("Monday: pay is %.2f%n", 10+7.42*hours);
  break;
case "Tuesday": case "Wednesday": case "Thursday": case "Friday":
  System.out.format("Workday: pay is %.2f%n", 7.42*hours);
  break;
case "Saturday": case "Sunday":
  System.out.format("Weekend: pay is %.2f%n", 20+1.25*7.42*hours);
  break;
default:
  System.out.format("Unknown weekday: %s%n", args[0]);
}
```

12.5   Loop Statements

12.5.1   The `for` Statement

A `for` statement has the form

```
for (initialization; condition; step)
    body
```

where *initialization* is a *variable-declaration* (section 6.2) or an *expression*, *condition* is an *expression* of type `boolean` or Boolean, *step* is an *expression*, and *body* is a *statement*. More generally, the *initialization* and *step* may also be comma-separated lists of *expressions*; the expressions in such a list are evaluated from left to right. The *initialization*, *condition*, and *step* may be empty. An empty *condition* is equivalent to `true`. Thus `for` (;;) *body* means "forever execute *body*." The `for` statement is executed as follows:

1. The *initialization* is executed.
2. The *condition* is evaluated. If it is `false`, the loop terminates.
3. If it is `true`, then (a) the *body* is executed; (b) the *step* is executed; and (c) execution continues at (2).

Hence the `for` statement above is equivalent to this statement using `while` (section 12.5.3):

```
initialization
while (condition) {
    body
    step
}
```

12.5.2   Using the `for` Statement on Iterables

A variant of the `for` statement can be used to iterate over the values of an iterator:

```
for (tx x : expression)
    body
```

The *expression* must have type Iterable<t> (section 22.7) where t is a subtype of type `tx`, a boxed version of `tx`, or an array whose element type is a subtype of `tx` or is a boxed version of `tx`. Thus iterators obtained from *expression* will produce elements that can be assigned to x, possibly after an unboxing operation. The *body* must be a statement.

First the *expression* is evaluated to obtain an iterable, and its `iterator()` method is called to obtain an iterator. Then the *body* is executed for each element produced by the iterator, with variable x bound to that element, possibly after an unboxing operation.

Unlike in C#, variable x is not read-only (final) in the *body*, but it is considered distinct on every iteration, so if *body* does not update it, x is effectively final. Hence x may safely be captured in lambda expressions and inner classes; see example 78. This is not the case for loop variables in classic `for`-loops (section 12.5.1).

It is safe to modify the elements of an array while iterating over the array, but in general, modification to an object being iterated over can produce unpredictable effects.

This variant of the `for` statement is sometimes called the foreach statement, but "foreach" is not a keyword, and the statement must be written as shown above.

Example 76 Nested `for` Loops
This program prints a four-line triangle of asterisks (*):

```
for (int i=1; i<=4; i++) {
  for (int j=1; j<=i; j++)
    System.out.print("*");
  System.out.println();
}
```

Example 77 Using the Enhanced `for` Statement on an Array

```
int[] iarr = { 2, 3, 5, 7, 11 };
int sum = 0;
for (int i : iarr)
  sum += i;
System.out.println(sum);
```

Example 78 Using the Enhanced `for` Statement on an Iterable
The first `for` statement iterates over the elements of an Iterable<Integer>, that is, a generator of Integer sequences. Method `fromTo`, which creates the iterable, is defined in example 143. Examples 79 and 82 show other ways to iterate over the integer sequence.

  The second `for` statement populates an array list `functions` of functions from `int` to `int`, and shows that the iteration variable i is effectively final and may be used in the lambda expression (j -> j * i).

  The third `for` statement iterates over the array list and calls each function with the argument 10.

```
public static void main(String[] args) {
  for (int i : fromTo(13, 17))
    System.out.println(i);
  List<IntUnaryOperator> functions = new ArrayList<>();
  for (int i : fromTo(13, 17))
    functions.add(j -> j * i);
  for (IntUnaryOperator f : functions)
    System.out.println(f.applyAsInt(10));
}
public static Iterable<Integer> fromTo(final int m, final int n) { ... }
```

Example 79 Explicitly Going through an Iterable Using `for`
The enhanced `for` statement in example 78 is equivalent to this `for` loop: obtain an iterable by calling `fromTo(13, 17)`, obtain an iterator from the iterable, and then go through the iterator's elements using the iterator's `hasNext` and `next` methods. Note that the `for` loop's *step* is empty; the call to `next()` in the loop body ensures progress. See also example 82.

```
Iterable<Integer> ible = fromTo(13, 17);
for (Iterator<Integer> iter = ible.iterator(); iter.hasNext(); /* none */) {
  int i = iter.next();
  System.out.println(i);
}
```

12.5.3   The `while` Statement

A `while` statement has the form

> `while` (*condition*)
>   *body*

where *condition* is an expression of type `boolean` or Boolean, and *body* is a statement. It is executed as follows:

1. The *condition* is evaluated. If it is `false`, the loop terminates.
2. If it is `true`, then
    a. The *body* is executed.
    b. Execution continues at (1).

Just after the `while` loop, the negation of *condition* must hold (unless the loop is exited by `break`). This fact provides useful information about the program's state after the loop; see example 80.

   When a *loop invariant*—a property that always holds at the beginning and end of the loop body—is known as well, then one can combine it with the negation of the *condition* to get precise information about the program's state after the `while` loop. This often helps in understanding short but subtle loops; see example 81.

12.5.4   The `do-while` Statement

A `do-while` statement has the form

> `do`
>   *body*
> `while` (*condition*);

where *condition* is an expression of type `boolean` or Boolean, and *body* is a statement. The *body* is executed at least once, because the `do-while` statement is executed as follows:

1. The *body* is executed.
2. The *condition* is evaluated. If it is `false`, the loop terminates.
3. If it is `true`, then execution continues at (1).

Hence the `do-while` statement above is equivalent to the following statement using `while`:

> *body*
> `while` (*condition*)
>   *body*

So a `do-while` statement does not test the loop *condition* before the first execution of the loop *body*. Mistakenly using a `do-while` statement where a `while` statement should have been used leads to program errors. Such errors are discovered only when some day the program encounters an empty input file, a zero-element result set from a database, or a similar borderline situation.

   Therefore you should usually prefer `while` over `do-while`. But there are cases where `do-while` is more natural; see example 83.

Example 80 Linear Array Search Using a `while` Loop
This method behaves as `wdayno1` in example 72. The negation of the loop condition holds just after the loop; note that together with (`i < wdays.length`), it implies that `wday` equals `wdays[i]`.

```
static int wdayno2(String wday) {
  int i=0;
  while (i < wdays.length && ! wday.equals(wdays[i]))
    i++;
  // Now i >= wdays.length or wday equals wdays[i]
  if (i < wdays.length)
    return i+1;
  else
    return -1;                              // Here used to mean 'not found'
}
static final String[] wdays =
{ "Monday", "Tuesday", "Wednesday", "Thursday", "Friday", "Saturday", "Sunday" };
```

Example 81 Binary Search of a Sorted Array Using a `while` Loop
Assume `arr` is sorted and imagine that `arr[-1]` is minus infinity and `arr[arr.length]` is plus infinity; then `arr[a-1]<x<arr[b+1]` is a loop invariant. If the loop terminates (without `return`), then it holds just after the loop that `arr[b]<x<arr[a]`, and so inserting x at `arr[a]` would keep the array sorted. If x is found, return i, which is non-negative; if x is not found, return the one's complement ~a, which is negative (because a>=0).

```
public static int binarySearch(double[] arr, double x) {
  int a=0, b=arr.length-1;
  while (a<=b) { // Loop invariant: arr[a-1] < x < arr[b+1]
    int i = (a+b)/2;
    if (arr[i] < x)      a = i+1;
    else if (arr[i] > x) b = i-1;
    else                 return i;    // because arr[i] == x
  }
  // Now a>b, in fact a==b+1 and b==a-1, and so arr[b] < x < arr[a]
  return ~a;
}
```

Example 82 Explicitly Going through an Iterable Using `while`
This `while` loop is very similar in structure to the `for` loop in example 79.

```
Iterable<Integer> ible = fromTo(13, 17);
Iterator<Integer> iter = ible.iterator();
while (iter.hasNext()) {
  int i = iter.next();
  System.out.println(i);
}
```

Example 83 Using `do-while` to Roll a Die and Compute Sum Until 5 or 6 Comes Up

```
int sum = 0, eyes;
do {
  eyes = (int)(1 + 6 * Math.random());
  sum += eyes;
} while (eyes < 5);
```

12.6   Returns, Labeled Statements, Exits, and Exceptions

12.6.1   The `return` Statement

The simplest form of a `return` statement, without an expression argument, is

```
return;
```

That form of `return` statement must occur in a method whose return type is `void`, or in a constructor. Execution of the `return` statement exits the method or constructor and continues execution at the place from which the method or constructor was called. Alternatively, a `return` statement may have an expression argument:

```
return expression;
```

That form of `return` statement must occur inside the body of a method (not constructor) whose return type is a supertype or boxed or unboxed version of the type of the *expression*. The `return` statement is executed as follows: First the *expression* is evaluated to some value `v`. Then it exits the method and continues execution at the method call expression that called the method; the value of that expression will be `v`, possibly after the application of a widening, boxing, or unboxing conversion.

12.6.2   Labeled Statements

A labeled statement has the form

label : *statement*

where *label* is a name. The scope of *label* is *statement*, where it can be used in `break` (section 12.6.3) and `continue` (section 12.6.4). The *label* cannot be reused inside *statement*, except inside a local class.

12.6.3   The **break** Statement

A `break` statement is legal only inside a switch or loop and has one of the forms

```
break;
break label;
```

Executing `break` exits the innermost enclosing switch or loop and continues execution after that switch or loop. Executing `break` *label* exits the enclosing statement that has label *label*, and continues execution after that statement. Such a statement must exist in the innermost enclosing method, constructor, or initializer block.

12.6.4   The **continue** Statement

A `continue` statement is legal only inside a loop and has one of the forms

```
continue;
continue label;
```

Executing `continue` terminates the current iteration of the innermost enclosing loop and continues the execution at the *step* in `for` loops (section 12.5.1) or the *condition* in `while` and `do-while` loops (sections 12.5.3 and 12.5.4). Executing `continue` *label* terminates the current iteration of the enclosing loop that has label *label*, and continues the execution at the *step* or the *condition*. There must be such a loop in the innermost enclosing method, constructor, or initializer block.

Example 84 Using `return` to Terminate a Loop Early
This method behaves the same as `wdayno2` in example 80:

```
static int wdayno3(String wday) {
  for (int i=0; i < wdays.length; i++)
    if (wday.equals(wdays[i]))
      return i+1;
  return -1;                                 // Here used to mean 'not found'
}
```

Example 85 Using `break` to Terminate a Loop Early

```
double prod = 1.0;
for (int i=0; i<xs.length; i++) {
  prod *= xs[i];
  if (prod == 0.0)
    break;
}
```

Example 86 Using `continue` to Start a New Iteration (Not Recommended)
This method decides whether `query` is a substring of `target`. When a mismatch between the strings is found, `continue` starts the next iteration of the outer `for` loop, thus incrementing `j`:

```
static boolean substring1(String query, String target) {
  nextposition:
    for (int j=0; j<=target.length()-query.length(); j++) {
      for (int k=0; k<query.length(); k++)
        if (target.charAt(j+k) != query.charAt(k))
          continue nextposition;
      return true;
    }
  return false;
}
```

Example 87 Using `break` to Exit a Labeled Statement Block (Not Recommended)
This method behaves as `substring1` from example 86. It uses `break` to exit the entire statement block labeled `thisposition`, thus skipping the first `return` statement and starting a new iteration of the outer `for` loop:

```
static boolean substring2(String query, String target) {
  for (int j=0; j<=target.length()-query.length(); j++)
    thisposition: {
      for (int k=0; k<query.length(); k++)
        if (target.charAt(j+k) != query.charAt(k))
          break thisposition;
      return true;
    }
  return false;
}
```

12.6.5   The **throw** Statement

A throw statement has the form

> throw *expression*;

where the type of the *expression* must be a subtype of class Throwable (chapter 15). The throw statement is executed as follows: The *expression* is evaluated to obtain an exception object v. If it is null, then a NullPointerException is thrown; otherwise the exception object v is thrown. Thus a thrown exception is never null. In any case, the enclosing block statement terminates abruptly (chapter 15). The thrown exception may be caught by a dynamically enclosing try-catch statement (section 12.6.6). If the exception is not caught, then the entire program execution will be aborted, and information from the exception will be printed on the console (for example, at the command prompt, or in the Java Console inside a Web browser).

12.6.6   The **try-catch-finally** Statement

A try-catch statement is used to catch (particular) exceptions thrown by a code block; it has this form:

```
try
    body
catch (E1 x1) catchbody₁
catch (E21 | E22 | ... | E2k x2) catchbody₂
...
finally finallybody
```

where E1, E21, E22, ... are exception types; x1, x2, ... are variable names; and *body*, *catchbody$_i$*, and *finallybody* are *block-statements* (section 12.2). There can be zero or more catch clauses, and the finally clause may be absent, but a try-catch-finally statement must have least one catch or finally clause. By contrast, a try-with-resources statement (section 12.7) is not required to have catch or finally clauses.

A single-catch clause of the form catch (Ei x1) matches any exception type E1 that is a subtype of (or possibly equal to) Ei. A multi-catch clause of the form catch (Ei1 | ... | Eik xi) must have k>=1 and matches any exception type that is a subtype of (or possibly equal to) one of the Eij.

The try-catch-finally statement is executed by executing the *body*. If the execution of the *body* terminates normally, or exits by return, break, or continue (when inside a method, constructor, switch, or loop), then the catch clauses are ignored. If the *body* terminates abruptly by throwing exception e of class E, then the first matching catch clause (if any) is located, say the i'th one; variable xi is bound to e; and the corresponding *catchbody$_i$* is executed. The *catchbody$_i$* may terminate normally; loop infinitely; exit by executing return, break, or continue; or throw an exception (possibly xi). If there is no finally clause, this determines how the entire try-catch statement terminates. A thrown exception e is never null (section 12.6.5), so xi is guaranteed not to be null either. If there is no matching catch clause, then the entire try-catch statement terminates abruptly with exception e.

If there is a finally clause, then *finallybody* will be executed regardless of whether the execution of *body* terminated normally; regardless of whether *body* exited by executing return, break, or continue; regardless of whether any exception thrown by *body* was caught by a catch clause; and regardless of whether the catch clause exited by executing return, break, or continue, or by throwing an exception. If execution of *finallybody* terminates normally, then the entire try-catch-finally terminates as determined by *body* (or *catchbody$_i$*, if one was executed and terminated abruptly or exited). If execution of *finallybody* terminates abruptly, then that determines how the entire try-catch-finally terminates (example 99).

Example 88 Throwing an Exception to Indicate Failure

Instead of returning the bogus error value `-1` as in method `wdayno3` (example 84), throw a WeekdayException (example 98). Note the `throws` clause (section 9.8) in the method header.

```
static int wdayno4(String wday) throws WeekdayException {
  for (int i=0; i < wdays.length; i++)
    if (wday.equals(wdays[i]))
      return i+1;
  throw new WeekdayException(wday);
}
```

Example 89 A `try-catch` Statement

This example calls the method `wdayno4` (example 88) inside a `try-catch` statement that catches exceptions of class WeekdayException (example 98) and its superclass Exception. The second `catch` clause will be executed (for example) if the array access `args[0]` fails because there is no command line argument (since ArrayIndexOutOfBoundsException is a subclass of Exception). If an exception is caught, it is bound to the variable `x` and printed by an implicit call (chapter 7) to the exception's `toString` method.

```
public static void main(String[] args) {
  try {
    System.out.println(args[0] + " is weekday number " + wdayno4(args[0]));
  } catch (WeekdayException x) {
    System.out.println("Weekday problem: " + x);
  } catch (Exception x) {
    System.out.println("Other problem: " + x);
  }
}
```

Example 90 A `try-finally` Statement or a Try-with-Resources Statement

Assume we want to read three lines from a text file (section 26.4), each containing a single floating-point number. To make sure to close the text file regardless of whether anything goes wrong during reading (premature end-of-file, ill-formed number), we can use a `try-finally` statement (section 12.6.6) or more elegantly, a try-with-resources statement (section 12.7). The example code is assumed to be inside a method, and `res` is an already allocated array of `double`:

```
BufferedReader breader = new BufferedReader(new FileReader(filename));
try {
  res[0] = Double.parseDouble(breader.readLine());
  res[1] = Double.parseDouble(breader.readLine());
  res[2] = Double.parseDouble(breader.readLine());
  return res;
} finally {
  breader.close();
}
...
try (BufferedReader breader = new BufferedReader(new FileReader(filename))) {
  res[0] = Double.parseDouble(breader.readLine());
  res[1] = Double.parseDouble(breader.readLine());
  res[2] = Double.parseDouble(breader.readLine());
  return res;
}
```

12.7   The Try-with-Resources Statement

A try-with-resources statement consists of a number of semicolon separated initialized *variable-declarations* (section 6.2) followed by a statement block *body* possibly followed by `catch` clauses and/or a `finally` clause as in section 12.6.6:

```
try (initialized-variable-declarations)
    body
optional catch-finally-clauses
```

A variable declared in the *variable-declarations* is called a resource and is implicitly final. Its type must implement interface AutoCloseable from package `java.lang` with method `void close()`. All stream interfaces (chapter 24) and input-output classes (chapter 26) implement AutoCloseable. The try-with-resources statement is executed by evaluating the *variable-declarations* from left to right to initialize the resources, then executing the *body*, then calling `close()` on the non-`null` resources in reverse order of initialization, regardless of whether the *body* terminates normally, by `return`, or by throwing an exception. The optional *catch-finally-clauses* are considered after the `close()` calls, and so may handle exceptions thrown during closing.

12.8   The `assert` Statement

The `assert` statement has one of the following forms:

```
assert boolean-expression ;
assert boolean-expression : expression ;
```

The *boolean-expression* must have type `boolean` or Boolean. The type of *expression* must be `boolean`, `char`, `double`, `float`, `int`, `long`; a boxed version of these; or Object.

Under ordinary execution of a program, an `assert` statement has no effect at all. However, assertions may be enabled at run-time by specifying the option `-ea` or `-enableassertions` when executing a program `C` (chapter 16) as in the `java -enableassertions C` command line.

When assertions are enabled at run-time, every execution of the `assert` statement will evaluate the *boolean-expression*. If the result is `true`, program execution continues normally. If the result is `false`, the assertion fails, and an AssertionError will be thrown; moreover, in the second form of the `assert` statement, the *expression* will be evaluated, and its value will be passed to the appropriate AssertionError constructor. Thus the value of the *expression* will be reported along with the exception in case of assertion failure. This simplifies troubleshooting in a malfunctioning program.

An AssertionError signals the failure of a fundamental assumption in the program and should not be caught by a `try-catch` statement in the program; it should be allowed to propagate to the top level.

An `assert` statement can serve two purposes: to document the programmer's assumption about the state at a certain point in the program, and to check (at run-time) that the assumption holds (provided the program is executed using the `enableassertions` option).

One may put an `assert` statement after a particularly complicated piece of code, to check that it has achieved what it was supposed to (example 91).

In a class that has a data representation invariant, one may assert the invariant at the end of every method that could modify the state of the current object (example 92).

One should not use `assert` statements to check the validity of user input or the arguments of public methods or constructors, because the check will be performed only if assertions are enabled at run-time. Instead, use ordinary `if` statements and throw an exception in case of error.

Example 91 Using `assert` to Specify and Check the Result of an Algorithm

The integer square root of $x \geq 0$ is an integer y such that $y^2 \leq x$ and $(y+1)^2 > x$. The precondition $x \geq 0$ is always checked, using an `if` statement. The postcondition on y is specified by an `assert` statement, and checked if assertions are enabled at run-time. This is reassuring, given that the correctness of this algorithm is none too obvious. The assertion uses casts to `long` to avoid arithmetic overflow in the `assert` statement.

```
static int sqrt(int x) {  // Algorithm by Borgerding, Hsieh, Ulery
  if (x < 0)
    throw new IllegalArgumentException("sqrt: negative argument");
  int temp, y = 0, b = 0x8000, bshft = 15, v = x;;
  do {
    if (v >= (temp = (y<<1)+b << bshft--)) {
      y += b; v -= temp;
    }
  } while ((b >>= 1) > 0);
  assert (long)y * y <= x && (long)(y+1)*(y+1) > x;
  return y;
}
```

Example 92 Using `assert` to Specify and Check Invariants

A word list is a sequence of words to be formatted as a line of text. Its `length` is the minimum number of characters needed to format the words and the interword spaces, that is, the lengths of the words plus the number of words minus 1. Those methods that change the word list use `assert` statements to specify the invariant on `length`, and to check it if assertions are enabled at run-time.

```
class WordList {
  private LinkedList<String> strings = new LinkedList<String>();
  private int length = -1;          // Invariant: equals word lengths plus inter-word spaces
  public int length() { return length; }

  public void addLast(String s) {
    strings.addLast(s);
    length += 1 + s.length();
    assert length == computeLength() + strings.size() - 1;
  }

  public String removeFirst() {
    String res = strings.removeFirst();
    length -= 1 + res.length();
    assert length == computeLength() + strings.size() - 1;
    return res;
  }

  private int computeLength() { ... } // For checking the invariant only
}
```

An algorithm for formatting a sequence of words into a text with a straight right-hand margin should produce lines res of a specified length `lineWidth`, unless there is only one word on the line or the line is the last one. This requirement can be expressed and checked using an `assert` statement. The complete example file, available online (see the book's preface), gives the details of the formatting algorithm itself.

```
assert res.length()==lineWidth || wordCount==1 || !wordIter.hasNext();
```

13   Interfaces

13.1   Interface Declarations

An *interface* describes fields and methods but does not implement them. An *interface-declaration* may contain field descriptions, method descriptions, class declarations, and interface declarations, in any order.

```
interface-modifiers interface I extends-clause {
    field-descriptions
    method-descriptions
    method-declarations
    class-declarations
    interface-declarations
}
```

An interface may be declared at top level or inside a class or interface but not inside a method, constructor, or initializer. At top level, the *interface-modifiers* may be `public` or absent. A public interface is accessible also outside its package. Inside a class or interface, the *interface-modifiers* may be `static` (always implicitly understood) and at most one of `public`, `protected`, or `private`. An interface declaration may take type parameters and be generic; see section 21.7.

The *extends-clause* may be absent or have the form `extends I1, I2, ...` where `I1, I2, ...` is a non-empty list of interface names. If the *extends-clause* is present, then interface `I` describes all those members described by `I1, I2, ...`, and interface `I` is a *subinterface* (and hence subtype) of `I1, I2, ...`. Interface `I` can describe additional fields and methods but cannot override inherited members.

A *field-description* in an interface declares a named constant and must have the form

```
field-desc-modifiers type f = initializer;
```

where *field-desc-modifiers* is a list of `static`, `final`, and `public`, none of which needs to be given explicitly, as all are implicitly understood. The field initializer must be an expression involving only literals, operators, and static members of classes and interfaces.

A *method-description* for method `m` must have the form

```
method-desc-modifiers return-type m(formal-list) throws-clause;
```

where *method-desc-modifiers* is a list of `abstract` and `public`, none of which needs to be given explicitly.

A *method-declaration* (section 9.8) must have modifier `default` or `static`; see section 13.3.

A *class-declaration* inside an interface is always implicitly `static` and `public`.

13.2   Classes Implementing Interfaces

A class `C` may be declared to implement one or more interfaces by an *implements-clause*:

```
class C implements I1, I2, ...
    class-body
```

In this case, `C` is a subtype (section 5.5) of `I1, I2`, and so on, and `C` must declare all the methods described by `I1, I2, ...` with exactly the prescribed signatures and return types. A class may implement any number of interfaces. Fields, classes, and interfaces declared in `I1, I2, ...` can be used in class `C`.

Example 93 Three Interface Declarations
The Colored interface describes method getColor, interface Drawable describes method draw, and Colored-Drawable describes both. The methods are implicitly public.

```
import java.awt.*;
interface Colored { Color getColor(); }
interface Drawable { void draw(Graphics g); }
interface ColoredDrawable extends Colored, Drawable {}
```

Example 94 Classes Implementing Interfaces
The methods getColor and draw must be public as in the interface declarations (example 93).

```
class ColoredPoint extends Point implements Colored {
  Color c;
  ColoredPoint(int x, int y, Color c) { super(x, y); this.c = c; }
  public Color getColor() { return c; }
}

class ColoredDrawablePoint extends ColoredPoint implements ColoredDrawable {
  ColoredDrawablePoint(int x, int y, Color c) { super(x, y, c); }
  public void draw(Graphics g) { g.fillRect(x, y, 1, 1); }
}

class ColoredRectangle implements ColoredDrawable {
  int x1, x2, y1, y2;    // (x1, y1) upper left, (x2, y2) lower right corner
  Color c;

  ColoredRectangle(int x1, int y1, int x2, int y2, Color c)
  { this.x1 = x1; this.y1 = y1; this.x2 = x2; this.y2 = y2; this.c = c; }
  public Color getColor() { return c; }
  public void draw(Graphics g) { g.drawRect(x1, y1, x2-x1, y2-y1); }
}
```

Example 95 Using Interfaces as Types
A Colored value has a getColor method; a ColoredDrawable value has a getColor method and a draw method:

```
static void printcolors(Colored[] cs) {
  for (int i=0; i<cs.length; i++)
    System.out.println(cs[i].getColor().toString());
}

static void draw(Graphics g, ColoredDrawable[] cs) {
  for (int i=0; i<cs.length; i++) {
    g.setColor(cs[i].getColor());
    cs[i].draw(g);
  }
}
```

13.3   Default and Static Methods on Interfaces (Java 8.0)

An interface can declare *default methods*, which must have a body in the form of a block statement. The method body can refer only to the interface's (abstract, default, or static) methods and (final static) fields, as well as other static methods. A default method is inherited by any class that implements the interface or any of its subinterfaces. Many predefined functional interfaces have default methods; see chapter 23 and example 214.

An interface can declare *static methods*, which have a body in the form of a block statement. The method body can refer only to other static methods and (final static) fields of the interface. A static method m declared on interface I can be called directly on the interface type as I.m(...) and must be called like this also in implementing classes and in subinterfaces; it is not "inherited" by them.

13.4   Annotation Type Declarations

An annotation type @Anno is a special kind of interface; its declaration has this form:

> *interface-modifiers* @interface Anno { *annotation-members* }

Each *annotation-member* has one of these forms, where an *annotation-member-expression* is a constant:

> *type* f();
> *type* f() default *annotation-member-expression*;
> final *type* f = *constant*;

Several meta-annotations may be used when declaring an annotation type. The @Target({...}) meta-annotation specifies the legal targets for an annotation type; the default is any target:

@Target Value	Legal Targets
ANNOTATION_TYPE	Annotation type declarations
CONSTRUCTOR	Constructor declarations
FIELD	Field declarations or enum value declarations
LOCAL_VARIABLE	Local variable declarations
METHOD	Method declarations
PACKAGE	Package declarations
PARAMETER	Parameter declarations in method or constructor
TYPE	Class, interface, or enum type declarations
TYPE_PARAMETER	Type parameter of generic class, interface, method or constructor

The @Retention(...) meta-annotation specifies the retention policy for an annotation type:

Value	Meaning
SOURCE	The annotation is discarded by the compiler and will not be stored in the class file
CLASS	The annotation is stored in the class-file (default) but unavailable at run-time
RUNTIME	The annotation is available for reflective inspection at run-time

Annotations with retention policy RUNTIME can be accessed using reflection (chapter 27) at run-time. Methods getAnnotations and getDeclaredAnnotations on classes Class, Field, Method, and Constructor return the annotations of the given target in an array of type Annotation[ ].

If an annotation that has meta-annotation @Inherited is used on a class declaration, then the subclasses of this class will inherit the annotation. Chapter 28 describes other standard annotations and their use.

Example 96 Declaring and Using a Custom Annotation Type

An Author annotation is a custom annotation that holds an author name, a month (of enum type Month from example 97), a diet, and a weekly workload. Its legal targets are classes and methods. Author annotations are retained until run-time, so they can be inspected using reflection. We use static import (chapter 17) to avoid prefixing TYPE and METHOD with their declaring enum type java.lang.annotation.ElementType. An Authors annotation holds an array of Author annotations; the meta-annotation @Repeatable(Authors.class) on Author says that repeated use is shorthand for an Authors annotation.

```java
import java.lang.annotation.*;                         // Annotation
import static java.lang.annotation.ElementType.*;      // @Target arguments
import static java.lang.annotation.RetentionPolicy.*;  // @Retention arguments
import java.lang.reflect.*;                            // Method

@Target({TYPE, METHOD})     // Attribute can be used on types and methods only
@Retention(RUNTIME)         // Attribute values are kept until run-time
@Repeatable(Authors.class)  // Attribute may be repeated as a shorthand for @Authors(...)
@interface Author {
  public final int oneHour = 60 * 60 * 1000;
  public String name();
  public Month month();
  public String[] diet() default { "Coffee", "Cola", "Mars bars" };
  public int weeklyWork() default 56 * oneHour;
}

@Target({TYPE, METHOD})     // Attribute can be used on types and methods only
@Retention(RUNTIME)         // Attribute values are kept until run-time
@interface Authors { public Author[] value(); }

class TestAnnotations {
  @Author(name="Peter", month=Month.NOV, diet={ "Dr. Pepper" })
  public void myMethod1() { }

  @Author(name="Jens", month=Month.JUL)
  public void myMethod2() { }

  @Author(name="Ulrik", month=Month.JUL)
  @Author(name="Andrzej", month=Month.AUG, diet = { "Tea" })
  // Alternative, with the same meaning:
  // @Authors({@Author(name="Ulrik", month=Month.JUL),
  //           @Author(name="Andrzej", month=Month.AUG, diet = { "Tea" })})
  public void myMethod3() { }

  ...
  Class ty = TestAnnotations.class;
  for (Method mif : ty.getMethods()) {
    if (mif.getName().startsWith("myMethod")) {
      System.out.println("\nGetting the annotations of " + mif.getName());
      Annotation[] annos = mif.getDeclaredAnnotations();    // Find RUNTIME annotations
      System.out.println("The annotations are:");
      for (Annotation anno : annos)
        System.out.println(anno);
} } }
```

14   Enum Types

An enum type is used to declare distinct enum values; an enum type is a reference type. An *enum-type-declaration* is a specialized form of class declaration that begins with a list of enum value declarations:

> *enum-modifiers* `enum` `t` *implements-clause* {
>   *enum-value-list* ;
>   *field-declarations*
>   *constructor-declarations*
>   *method-declarations*
>   *class declarations*
>   *interface-declarations*
>   *initializer-blocks*
> }

The declarations of fields, methods, nested types, and initializer blocks are as for ordinary classes (section 9.1); these declarations may appear in any order. In fact, the enum type `t` is implemented as a class and is a reference type, and there is exactly one instance (object) of that implementation class for each declared enum value.

The *enum-modifiers* control the accessibility of the enum type and follow the same rules as class access modifiers (section 9.3). The modifiers `abstract` and `final` cannot be used. An enum type may be declared to implement any number of interfaces but cannot be declared to have a superclass; it implicitly has the superclass java.lang.Enum<t>. An enum type is implicitly final and cannot be used as a superclass. A nested enum type is implicitly static (the `static` modifier is allowed but is implicitly understood and not required) and cannot refer to instance fields of an enclosing type.

An enum declaration can declare private constructors only, and an enum value cannot be explicitly created using `new` `t`(*actual-list*). Instead enum values are created by the *enum-value-list*, which is a (possibly empty) comma-separated list of enum value declarations. An enum value declaration has the form *enum-value* or *enum-value*(*actual-list*). The first one corresponds to a call to the enum type's argumentless constructor and the second one to a call to the constructor overload appropriate for the enum value's *actual-list*.

A declared enum value has the type `t` of the enclosing enum type and is similar to a public static final field. Unlike most reference type values, enum values can be used in `switch` statements (example 74). The *ordinal value* of an enum value is given by its position in the *enum-value-list*; the first one is zero. There are no predefined conversions between enum values and integers, and no numeric operations such as (+), nor comparisons such as (<), on enum values. A value of an enum type always equals a declared *enum-value*.

Outside its declaration, an enum value must be written in fully qualified form (`Month.JAN`) if not using static import (chapter 17), except inside `switch` statements, where it must be written in unqualified form (`JAN`).

Let `v1` and `v2` be enum values of the same type; then the following operations are defined:

- `v1.ordinal()` of type `int` is the ordinal value of the enum value, such as 3.

- `v1.toString()` of type String is the declared name of the enum value, such as `"Thu"`.

- `v1.compareTo(v2)` returns an integer that is negative, zero, or positive, according as `v1` precedes, equals, or follows `v2` in the declaring enum value list, as if comparing `v1.ordinal()` to `v2.ordinal()`.

- `v1==v2` is true if `v1` and `v2` evaluate to the same enum value; otherwise false.

- The static method `values()` returns a new array of type `t[]` holding references to all enum values in the enum type. A new array is created at every call to this method, so an application should call it at most once and cache the result if possible, as shown by example 97.

Example 97 Representing Weekdays and Months Using Enum Types
When specifying a date, it is desirable to use numbers for years (2004), dates (11), and ISO week numbers (28), but symbolic values for weekdays (SUN) and months (JUL). In calendrical calculations it is useful to assign numbers 0–6 to the weekdays (MON–SUN) and numbers 1–12 to the months (JAN–DEC). This is done in the enum types Day and Month below by declaring methods to convert integers to enum values and back.

The Month enum type declares a field `days` to hold the number of days in the month (in a non-leap year), and a constructor to initialize the field. It also declares a method `succ()` that computes the next month. Note the use of reference comparison of enum values in method `days(int)`.

```
enum Day {
  MON, TUE, WED, THU, FRI, SAT, SUN;
  private final static Day[] day = values();        // Cache the array
  public static Day toDay(int n) { return day[n]; }
  public int toInt() { return ordinal(); }
}
enum Month {
  JAN(31), FEB(28), MAR(31), APR(30), MAY(31), JUN(30),
  JUL(31), AUG(31), SEP(30), OCT(31), NOV(30), DEC(31);
  private final int days;
  private Month(int days) { this.days = days; }
  private final static Month[] month = values();     // Cache the array
  public int days(int year) {
    return this == FEB && MyDate.leapYear(year) ? 29 : days;
  }
  public static Month toMonth(int n) { return month[n-1]; }
  public int toInt() { return ordinal()+1; }
  public Month succ() { return toMonth(toInt()+1); }
}

class MyDate {
  final int yy /* 0-9999 */, dd /* 1-31 */;
  final Month mm;
  public MyDate(int yy, Month mm, int dd) throws Exception { ... }
  ...
  public static MyDate fromDaynumber(int n) {
    ...
    Month m = Month.JAN;
    int mdays;
    while ((mdays = m.days(y)) < d) {
      d -= mdays;
      m = m.succ();
    }
    return new MyDate(y, m, d);
    ...
  }
  public static Day weekday(int y, Month m, int d) {
    return Day.toDay((toDaynumber(y, m, d)+6) % 7);
  }
  public String toString() { // ISO format such as 2015-07-26
    return String.format("%4d-%02d-%02d", yy, mm.toInt(), dd);
  }
}
```

15   Exceptions, Checked and Unchecked

An *exception* is an object of an exception type: a non-generic subclass of Throwable. It is used to signal and describe an abnormal situation during program execution. The evaluation of an expression or the execution of a statement may throw an exception, either by executing a `throw` statement (section 12.6.5) or by executing a primitive operation, such as array element assignment, that may throw an exception.

A thrown exception may be caught in a dynamically enclosing `try-catch` statement (section 12.6.6). If the exception is not caught, then the entire program execution will be aborted, and information from the exception will be printed on the console. What is printed is determined by the exception's `toString` method.

There are two kinds of exception types: *checked* (those that must be declared in the *throws-clause* of a method or constructor; see section 9.8) and *unchecked* (those that need not be). If the execution of a method or constructor body can throw a checked exception of class E, then class E or a supertype of E must be declared in the *throws-clause* of the method or constructor. The following table shows part of the exception class hierarchy.

Class	Status	Package
Throwable	checked	java.lang
Error	unchecked	java.lang
AssertionError	unchecked	java.lang
ExceptionInInitializerError	unchecked	java.lang
OutOfMemoryError	unchecked	java.lang
StackOverflowError	unchecked	java.lang
Exception	checked	java.lang
ClassNotFoundException	checked	java.lang
InterruptedException	checked	java.lang
IOException	checked	java.io
CharConversionException	checked	java.io
EOFException	checked	java.io
FileNotFoundException	checked	java.io
InterruptedIOException	checked	java.io
ObjectStreamException	checked	java.io
InvalidClassException	checked	java.io
NotSerializableException	checked	java.io
SyncFailedException	checked	java.io
UnsupportedEncodingException	checked	java.io
UTFDataFormatException	checked	java.io
RuntimeException	unchecked	java.lang
ArithmeticException	unchecked	java.lang
ArrayStoreException	unchecked	java.lang
ClassCastException	unchecked	java.lang
ConcurrentModificationException	unchecked	java.util
IllegalArgumentException	unchecked	java.lang
IllegalFormatException	unchecked	java.util
IllegalMonitorStateException	unchecked	java.lang
IllegalStateException	unchecked	java.lang
IndexOutOfBoundsException	unchecked	java.lang
ArrayIndexOutOfBoundsException	unchecked	java.lang
StringIndexOutOfBoundsException	unchecked	java.lang
NegativeArraySizeException	unchecked	java.util
NoSuchElementException	unchecked	java.util
NullPointerException	unchecked	java.lang
UncheckedIOException	unchecked	java.io
UnsupportedOperationException	unchecked	java.lang

Example 98 Declaring a Checked Exception Class
This is the class of exceptions thrown by method `wdayno4` (example 88). Passing a string to the constructor of the superclass (that is, class Exception) causes method `toString` to append that string to the name of the exception.

```
class WeekdayException extends Exception {
  public WeekdayException(String wday) {
    super("Illegal weekday: " + wday);
  }
}
```

Example 99 All Paths through a `try-catch-finally` Statement
To exercise all 18 paths through the `try-catch-finally` statement (section 12.6.6) in method m in the following program, run it with each of these command line arguments: 101 102 103 201 202 203 301 302 303 411 412 413 421 422 423 431 432 433. The `try` clause terminates normally on arguments 1*yz*, exits by `return` on 2*yz*, and throws an exception on 3*yz* and 4*yz*. However, when *z* is 2 or 3, the `finally` clause determines whether the statement terminates successfully or throws an exception; see below. The `catch` clause ignores exceptions thrown on 3*yz* but catches those thrown on 4*yz*. The `catch` clause terminates normally on 411, exits by `return` on 421, and throws an exception on 431. The `finally` clause terminates normally on *xy*1 (and so lets the `try` or `catch` clause determine how the execution terminates), exits by `return` on *xy*2 (including on 102 and so on), and throws an exception on *xy*3 (including on 103 and so on).

Exits by `break` and `continue` statements are handled similarly to `return`; a more involved example could be constructed to illustrate their interaction.

```
class TryCatchFinally {
  public static void main(String[] args) throws Exception
  { System.out.println(m(Integer.parseInt(args[0]))); }

  static String m(int a) throws Exception {
    try {
      System.out.print("try ... ");
      if (a/100 == 2) return "returned from try";
      if (a/100 == 3) throw new Exception("thrown by try");
      if (a/100 == 4) throw new RuntimeException("thrown by try");
    } catch (RuntimeException x) {
      System.out.print("catch ... ");
      if (a/10%10 == 2) return "returned from catch";
      if (a/10%10 == 3) throw new Exception("thrown by catch");
    } finally {
      System.out.println("finally");
      if (a%10 == 2) return "returned from finally";
      if (a%10 == 3) throw new Exception("thrown by finally");
    }
    return "terminated normally with " + a;
  }
}
```

16   Compilation, Source Files, Class Names, and Class Files

A *Java program* consists of one or more *source files* (with file name suffix .java). A source file may contain one or more class or interface declarations. A source file can contain at most one declaration of a top-level public class or interface, which must then have the same name as the file (minus the file name suffix). A source file myprog.java is compiled to Java class files (with file name suffix .class) by a Java compiler:

```
javac myprog.java
```

This creates one class file for each class or interface declared in the source file myprog.java. A class or interface C declared in a top-level declaration produces a class file called C.class. A nested class or interface D declared inside class C produces a class file called C$D.class. A local class D declared inside a method in class C produces a class file called C1D.class or similar.

A Java class C that declares the method public static void main(String[] args) can be executed using the Java run-time system java by typing a command line of the form

```
java C arg1 arg2 ...
```

This will execute the body of method main with the command line arguments *arg*1, *arg*2, ... bound to the array elements args[0], args[1], ... inside the method main (examples 9 and 104).

17   Packages and Jar Files

Java source files may be organized in *packages*. Every source file in package p must begin with the declaration

```
package p;
```

and must be stored in a subdirectory called p. A class declared in a source file with no package declaration belongs to the anonymous *default package*. A source file not belonging to package p may refer to class C from package p by using the qualified name p.C, in which the class name C is prefixed by the package name. To avoid using the package name prefix, the source file may begin with an import declaration (possibly following a package declaration) of one of three forms:

```
import p.C;
import p.*;
import static p.C.*;
```

The first form allows C to be used unqualified, without the package name, and the second one allows all accessible classes and interfaces in package p to be used unqualified. The third form allows all static members of class C to be used unqualified. The Java class library package java.lang is implicitly imported, so all java.lang classes can be used unqualified in Java source files. Note that java.lang is a composite package name, so class java.lang.String is declared in file java/lang/String.java.

The files in p and its subdirectories can be collected in a *jar file* by executing jar vcf p.jar p on the command line. The packages in the resulting jar file p.jar can be made available to other Java programs by moving the file to the directory /usr/java/jdk1.5.0/jre/lib/ext or similar under Unix, or to the directory c:\jdk1.5\jre\lib\ext or similar under MS Windows. The jar file may contain more than one package; it need only contain class files (not source files); and its name is not significant.

Example 100 The Vessel Hierarchy as a Package

The package vessel here contains part of the vessel hierarchy (example 30). The fields in classes Tank and Barrel are final, so they cannot be modified after object creation. They are protected, so they are accessible in subclasses declared outside the vessel package, as shown in file Usevessels.java, which is in the anonymous default package, not in the vessel package.

The file vessel/Vessel.java

```
package vessel;
public abstract class Vessel {
  private double contents;
  public abstract double capacity();
  public final void fill(double amount)
  { contents = Math.min(contents + amount, capacity()); }
  public final double getContents() { return contents; }
}
```

The file vessel/Tank.java

```
package vessel;
public class Tank extends Vessel {
  protected final double length, width, height;
  public Tank(double l, double w, double h) { length = l; width = w; height = h; }
  public double capacity() { return length * width * height; }
  public String toString()
  { return "tank (l,w,h) = (" + length + ", " + width + ", " + height + ")"; }
}
```

The file vessel/Barrel.java

```
package vessel;
public class Barrel extends Vessel {
  protected final double radius, height;
  public Barrel(double r, double h) { radius = r; height = h; }
  public double capacity() { return height * Math.PI * radius * radius; }
  public String toString() { return "barrel (r, h) = (" + radius + ", " + height + ")"; }
}
```

The file Usevessels.java

Subclass Cube of class Tank may access the field length because that field is declared protected in Tank above. The main method is unmodified from example 31.

```
import vessel.*;
class Cube extends Tank {
  public Cube(double side) { super(side, side, side); }
  public String toString() { return "cube (s) = (" + length + ")"; }
}
class Usevessels {
    public static void main(String[] args) { ... }
}
```

18   Mathematical Functions

Class Math provides static methods to compute standard mathematical functions. Floating-point numbers (double and float) include positive and negative infinities as well as non-numbers (NaN), following the IEEE754 standard [4]. There is also a distinction between positive zero and negative zero, ignored here.

The Math methods return non-numbers (NaN) when applied to illegal arguments, and return infinities in case of overflow; they do not throw exceptions. Also, the methods return NaN when applied to NaN arguments, except where noted, and behave sensibly when applied to positive or negative infinities.

Angles are given and returned in radians, not degrees. Methods that round to the nearest integer will round to the nearest even integer in case of a tie. The methods abs, min, and max are overloaded on float, int, and long arguments also. There are also hyperbolic trigonometric functions cosh, sinh, and tanh.

- static double E is the constant $e \approx 2.71828$, the base of the natural logarithm.
- static double PI is the constant $\pi \approx 3.14159$, the circumference of a circle with diameter 1.
- static double abs(double x) is the absolute value: x if x>=0, and -x if x<0.
- static double acos(double x) is the arc cosine of x, in the range $[0, \pi]$, for -1<=x<=1.
- static double asin(double x) is the arc sine of x, in the range $[-\pi/2, \pi/2]$, for -1<=x<=1.
- static double atan(double x) is the arc tangent of x, in the range $[-\pi/2, \pi/2]$.
- static double atan2(double y, double x) is the arc tangent of y/x in the quadrant of the point (x, y), in the range $]-\pi, \pi]$. When x is 0, the result is $\pi/2$ with the same sign as y.
- static double ceil(double x) is the smallest integral double value >=x.
- static double cbrt(double x) is the cube root x; for negative x, cbrt(x) equals -cbrt(-x).
- static double cos(double x) is the cosine of x, in the range $[-1, 1]$.
- static double exp(double x) is the exponential of x, that is, e to the power x.
- static double floor(double x) is the largest integral double value <=x.
- static double IEEEremainder(double x, double y) is the remainder of x/y, that is, x-y*n, where n is the mathematical integer closest to x/y.
- static double log(double x) is the natural logarithm (to base e) of x, for x>=0.
- static double log10(double x) is the logarithm (to base 10) of x, for x>=0.
- static double max(double x, double y) is the greatest of x and y.
- static double min(double x, double y) is the smallest of x and y.
- static double pow(double x, double y) is x to the power y, that is, x^y. If y is 0, then the result is 1.0. If y is 1, then the result is x. If x<0 and y is not integral, then the result is NaN.
- static double random() returns a uniformly distributed pseudo-random number in $[0, 1[$.
- static double rint(double x) is the integral double value that is closest to x.
- static long round(double x) is the long value that is closest to x.
- static int round(float x) is the int value that is closest to x.
- static double sin(double x) is the sine of x radians.
- static double signum(double x) is -1.0 or 0.0 or $+1.0$ according as x is negative, zero, or positive.
- static double sqrt(double x) is the positive square root of x, for x>=0.
- static double tan(double x) is the tangent of x radians.
- static double toDegrees(double r) is the number of degrees corresponding to r radians.
- static double toRadians(double d) is the number of radians corresponding to d degrees.

Example 101 Floating-Point Factorial
This method computes the factorial function $n! = 1 \cdot 2 \cdot 3 \cdots (n-1) \cdot n$ using logarithms.

```
static double fact(int n) {
  double res = 0.0;
  for (int i=1; i<=n; i++)
    res += Math.log(i);
  return Math.exp(res);
}
```

Example 102 Generating Gaussian Pseudo-Random Numbers
This example uses the Box-Muller transformation to generate N Gaussian, or normally distributed, pseudo-random numbers with mean 0 and standard deviation 1.

```
for (int i=0; i<N; i+=2) {
  double x1 = Math.random(), x2 = Math.random();
  print(Math.sqrt(-2 * Math.log(x1)) * Math.cos(2 * Math.PI * x2));
  print(Math.sqrt(-2 * Math.log(x1)) * Math.sin(2 * Math.PI * x2));
}
```

Example 103 Mathematical Functions: Infinities, NaNs, and Special Cases

```
print("Illegal arguments, NaN results:");
print(Math.sqrt(-1));             // NaN
print(Math.log(-1));              // NaN
print(Math.pow(-1, 2.5));         // NaN
print(Math.acos(1.1));            // NaN
print("Infinite results:");
print(Math.log(0));               // -Infinity
print(Math.pow(0, -1));           // Infinity
print(Math.exp(1000.0));          // Infinity (overflow)
print("Infinite arguments:");
double infinity = Double.POSITIVE_INFINITY;
print(Math.sqrt(infinity));       // Infinity
print(Math.log(infinity));        // Infinity
print(Math.exp(-infinity));       // 0.0
print("NaN arguments and special cases:");
double nan = Math.log(-1);
print(Math.sqrt(nan));            // NaN
print(Math.pow(nan, 0));          // 1.0 (special case)
print(Math.pow(0, 0));            // 1.0 (special case)
print(Math.round(nan));           // 0   (special case)
print(Math.round(1E50));          // 9223372036854775807 (Long.MAX_VALUE)
// For all (x, y) except (0.0, 0.0):
// sign(cos(atan2(y, x))) == sign(x) && sign(sin(atan2(y, x))) == sign(y)
for (double x=-100; x<=100; x+=0.125) {
  for (double y=-100; y<=100; y+=0.125) {
    double r = Math.atan2(y, x);
    if (!(sign(Math.cos(r))==sign(x) && sign(Math.sin(r))==sign(y)))
      print("x = " + x + "; y = " + y);
  }
}
```

19   String Builders and String Buffers

A String object s1, once created, cannot be modified. Using s1 + s2, one can append another string s2 to s1, but that creates a new string object, copying all the characters from s1 and s2; there is no way to extend s1 itself by appending more characters to it. Thus to concatenate n strings each of length k by repeated string concatenation (+), we copy $k + 2k + 3k + \cdots + nk = kn(n+1)/2$ characters, and the time required to do this is proportional to kn^2, which grows rapidly as n grows.

String builders, which are objects of the predefined class java.lang.StringBuilder, provide extensible and modifiable strings. Characters can be appended to a string builder without copying those characters already in the string builder; the string builder is automatically and efficiently extended as needed. To concatenate n strings each of length k using a string builder requires only time proportional to kn, considerably faster than kn^2 for large n. Thus to gradually build a string, use a string builder. This is needed only for repeated concatenation in a loop, as in example 9. The expression s1 + $\cdots$ + sn is efficient; it actually means new StringBuilder().append(s1).$\cdots$.append(sn).toString().

Let sb be a StringBuilder, s a String, and v an expression of any type. Then

- new StringBuilder() creates a new empty string builder.

- sb.append(v) appends the string representation of the value v to the string builder, converting v by String.valueOf(v); see chapter 7. Extends sb as needed. Returns sb.

- sb.charAt(int i) returns character number i (counting from zero) in the string builder. Throws StringIndexOutOfBoundsException if i<0 or i>=sb.length().

- sb.delete(from, to) deletes the characters with index from..(to-1) from the string builder, reducing its length by to-from characters. Throws StringIndexOutOfBoundsException if from<0 or from>to or to>sb.length(). Returns sb.

- sb.insert(from, v) inserts the string representation of v obtained by String.valueOf(v) into the string builder, starting at position from, extending sb as needed. Returns sb. Throws StringIndexOutOfBoundsException if from<0 or from>sb.length().

- sb.length() of type int is the length of sb, that is, the number of characters currently in sb.

- sb.replace(from, to, s) replaces the characters with index from..(to-1) in the string builder by the string s, extending sb if needed. Throws StringIndexOutOfBoundsException if from<0 or from>to or from>sb.length(). Returns sb.

- sb.reverse() reverses the character sequence in the string builder. Returns sb.

- sb.setCharAt(i, c) sets the character at index i to c. Throws StringIndexOutOfBoundsException if i<0 or i>=sb.length().

- sb.toString() of type String is a new string containing the characters currently in sb.

- Method append is fast, but delete, insert, and replace may be slow when they need to move large parts of the string builder—when both from and to are much smaller than length().

A StringBuffer has the same methods as a StringBuilder, but is thread-safe: several concurrent threads (chapter 20) can safely modify the same string buffer. Both classes implement the Appendable and CharSequence interfaces (section 26.7). More StringBuffer methods are described in the Java class library documentation [2].

Example 104 Efficiently Concatenating All Command Line Arguments
When there are many (more than 50) command line arguments, this is much faster than example 9.

```
public static void main(String[] args) {
  StringBuilder res = new StringBuilder();
  for (int i=0; i<args.length; i++)
    res.append(args[i]);
  System.out.println(res.toString());
}
```

Example 105 Replacing Occurrences of a Character by a String
To replace occurrences of character c1 with the string s2 in string s, it is best to use a string builder for the result, since the size of the resulting string is not known in advance. This works well also when replacing a character c1 with another character c2, but in that case the length of the result is known in advance (it equals the length of s), and one can use a character array instead (example 21). Solving this problem by repeated string concatenation (using res += s2) would be very slow.

```
static String replaceCharString(String s, char c1, String s2) {
  StringBuilder res = new StringBuilder();
  for (int i=0; i<s.length(); i++)
    if (s.charAt(i) == c1)
      res.append(s2);
    else
      res.append(s.charAt(i));
  return res.toString();
}
```

Example 106 Inefficiently Replacing Occurrences of a Character by a String
The problem from example 105 can also be solved by destructively modifying a string builder with replace. However, repeatedly using replace is inefficient: for a string of 200,000 random characters, this method is approximately 100 times slower than the one in example 105.

```
static void replaceCharString(StringBuilder sb, char c1, String s2) {
  int i = 0;                              // Inefficient
  while (i < sb.length()) {               // Inefficient
    if (sb.charAt(i) == c1) {             // Inefficient
      sb.replace(i, i+1, s2);             // Inefficient
      i += s2.length();                   // Inefficient
    } else                                // Inefficient
      i += 1;                             // Inefficient
} }                                       // Inefficient
```

Example 107 Padding a String to a Given Width
A string s may be padded with spaces to give it a certain minimum width, to align data into columns when using a fixed-pitch font. But this is supported also by the string formatting facilities; see section 7.1.

```
static String padLeft(String s, int width) {
  StringBuilder res = new StringBuilder();
  for (int i=width-s.length(); i>0; i--)
    res.append(' ');
  return res.append(s).toString();
}
```

20   Threads, Concurrent Execution, and Synchronization

20.1   Threads and Concurrent Execution

The preceding chapters described sequential program execution, in which expressions are evaluated and statements are executed one after the other: they considered only a single thread of execution, where a *thread* is an independent sequential activity. A Java program may execute several threads concurrently, that is, potentially overlapping in time. For instance, one part of a program may continue computing while another part is blocked waiting for input (example 108). For much more on concurrency in Java, see [5].

A thread is created and controlled using an object of the Thread class found in the package `java.lang`. A thread executes the method `public void run()` in an object of a class implementing the Runnable interface, also found in package `java.lang`. To every thread (independent sequential activity) there is a unique controlling Thread object, so the two are often thought of as being identical.

One way to create and run a thread is to declare a class `U` as a subclass of Thread, overwriting its (trivial) `run` method. Then create an object `u` of class `U` and call `u.start()`. This will enable the thread to execute `u.run()` concurrently with other threads (example 108).

Alternatively, declare a class `C` that implements Runnable, create an object `o` of that class, create a thread object `u = new Thread(o)` from `o`, and execute `u.start()`. This will enable the thread to execute `o.run()` concurrently with other threads (example 112).

Threads can communicate with each other via shared state, namely, by using and assigning static fields, non-static fields, array elements, and pipes (section 26.16). By the design of Java, local variables and method parameters cannot be shared between threads and hence are always thread-safe.

States and State Transitions of a Thread

A thread is alive if it has been started and has not died. A thread dies by exiting its `run()` method, either by returning or by throwing an exception. A live thread is in one of the states Enabled (ready to run), Running (actually executing), Sleeping (waiting for a timeout), Joining (waiting for another thread to die), Locking (trying to obtain the lock on object `o`), or Waiting (for notification on object `o`). The thread state transitions are shown in the following table and the figure on the facing page:

From State	To State	Reason for Transition
Enabled	Running	System schedules thread for execution
Running	Enabled	System preempts thread and schedules another one
	Enabled	Thread executes `yield()`
	Waiting	Thread executes `o.wait()`, releasing lock on `o`
	Locking	Thread attempts to execute `synchronized (o) { ... }`
	Sleeping	Thread executes `sleep()`
	Joining	Thread executes `u.join()`
	Dead	Thread exited `run()` by returning or by throwing an exception
Sleeping	Enabled	Sleeping period expired
	Enabled	Thread was interrupted; throws InterruptedException when run
Joining	Enabled	Thread `u` being joined died, or join timed out
	Enabled	Thread was interrupted; throws InterruptedException when run
Waiting	Locking	Another thread executed `o.notify()` or `o.notifyAll()`
	Locking	Wait for lock on `o` timed out
	Locking	Thread was interrupted; throws InterruptedException when run
Locking	Enabled	Lock on `o` became available and was given to this thread

Example 108 Multiple Threads

The main program creates a new thread, binds it to u, and starts it. Now two threads are executing concurrently: one executes main, and another executes run. While the main method is blocked waiting for keyboard input, the new thread keeps incrementing i. The new thread executes yield() to make sure that the other thread is allowed to run (when not blocked). The volatile modifier on i is needed; see section 20.5.1 and example 113.

```
class Incrementer extends Thread {
  public volatile int i;
  public void run() {
    for (;;) {                               // Forever
      i++;                                   //   increment i
      yield();
    }
} }
class ThreadDemo {
  public static void main(String[] args) throws IOException {
    Incrementer u = new Incrementer();
    u.start();
    System.out.println("Repeatedly press Enter to get the current value of i:");
    for (;;) {
      System.in.read();                      // Wait for keyboard input
      System.out.println(u.i);
} } }
```

States and State Transitions of a Thread. A thread's transition from one state to another may be caused by a method call performed by the thread itself (shown in the monospace font), by a method call possibly performed by another thread (shown in the *slanted monospace* font); and by timeouts and other actions.

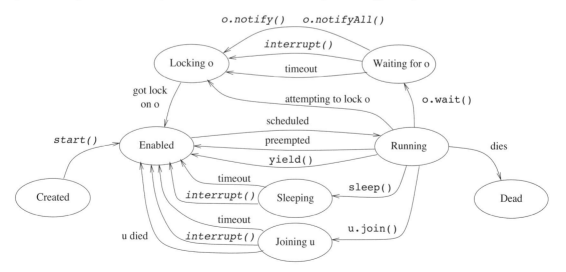

20.2 Locks and the `synchronized` Statement

Concurrent threads are executed independently. Therefore, when multiple concurrent threads access the same fields or array elements, there is considerable risk of creating an inconsistent state (example 110). To avoid this, threads may synchronize the access to shared state, such as objects and arrays. A single *lock* is associated with every object, array, and class. A lock can be held by at most one thread at a time. A thread may explicitly request the lock on an object or array by executing a `synchronized` statement, which has this form:

> synchronized (*expression*)
> *block-statement*

The *expression* must have reference type. The *expression* must evaluate to a non-null reference o; otherwise a NullPointerException is thrown. After the evaluation of the *expression*, the thread becomes Locking on object o; see the figure on the previous page. When the thread obtains the lock on object o (if ever), the thread becomes Enabled and may become Running so that the *block-statement* is executed. When the *block-statement* terminates or is exited by `return`, `break`, or `continue`, or by throwing an exception, then the lock on o is released.

A `synchronized` non-static method declaration (section 9.8) is shorthand for a method whose body has the form

> synchronized (this)
> *method-body*

That is, the thread will execute the method body only when it has obtained the lock on the current object. It will release the lock when it leaves the method body.

A `synchronized` static method declaration (section 9.8) in class C is shorthand for a method whose body has the form

> synchronized (C.class)
> *method-body*

That is, the thread will execute the method body only when it has obtained the lock on the object C.class, which is the unique object of class Class associated with class C; see section 27.1. It will hold the lock until it leaves the method body and release it at that time.

Constructors and initializers cannot be synchronized.

Mutual exclusion is ensured only if *all* threads accessing a shared object lock it before use. For instance, if we add an unsynchronized method roguetransfer to a bank object (example 110), we can no longer be sure that a thread calling the synchronized method transfer has exclusive access to the bank object: any number of threads could be executing roguetransfer at the same time.

A *monitor* is an object whose fields are private and are manipulated only by synchronized methods of the object, so that all field access is subject to synchronization (example 111).

If a thread u needs to wait for some condition to become true, or for a resource to become available, it may temporarily release its lock on object o by calling o.wait(). The thread must hold the lock on object o, otherwise exception IllegalMonitorStateException is thrown. The thread u will be added to the *wait set* of o, that is, the set of threads waiting for notification on object o. This notification must come from another thread that has obtained the lock on o and that executes o.notify() or o.notifyAll(). The notifying thread does not release its lock on o. After being notified, u must obtain the lock on o again before it can proceed. Thus when the call to wait returns, thread u will hold the lock on o just as before the call (example 111).

For detailed rules governing the behavior of unsynchronized Java threads, see chapter 17 of *Java Language Specification* [3].

Example 109 Mutual Exclusion

A Printer thread forever prints a dash (–) followed by a slash (/). If we create and run two concurrent printer threads using `new Printer().start()` and `new Printer().start()`, then only one of the threads can hold the lock on object `mutex` at a time, so no other symbols can be printed between (–) and (/) in one iteration of the `for` loop. Thus the program must print `-/-/-/-/-/-/-/` and so on. However, if the synchronization is removed, it may print `--//--/-/-/--/--//` and so on. The call `Util.pause(200)` pauses the thread for 200 ms, whereas `Util.pause(100,300)` pauses it between 100 and 300 ms. This is done only to make the inherent nondeterminacy of unsynchronized concurrency more easily observable.

```
class Printer extends Thread {
  final static Object mutex = new Object();
  public void run() {
    for (;;) {
      synchronized (mutex) {
        System.out.print("-");
        Util.pause(100,300);
        System.out.print("/");
      }
      Util.pause(200);
} } }
```

Example 110 Synchronized Methods in an Object

The Bank object here has two accounts. Money is repeatedly being transferred from one account to the other by clerks. Clearly the total amount of money should remain constant (at 30 euro). This holds true when the transfer method is declared synchronized, because only one clerk can access the accounts at any one time. If the synchronized declaration is removed, the sum will differ from 30 most of the time, because one clerk is likely to overwrite the other's deposits and withdrawals.

```
class Bank {
  private int account1 = 10, account2 = 20;
  synchronized public void transfer(int amount) {
    int new1 = account1 - amount;
    Util.pause(10);
    account1 = new1; account2 = account2 + amount;
    System.out.println("Sum is " + (account1+account2));
} }

class Clerk extends Thread {
  private Bank bank;
  public Clerk(Bank bank) { this.bank = bank; }
  public void run() {
    for (;;) {                              // Forever
      bank.transfer(Util.random(-10, 10));  //   transfer money
      Util.pause(200, 300);                 //   then take a break
} } }

... Bank bank = new Bank();
... new Clerk(bank).start(); new Clerk(bank).start();
```

20.3   Operations on Threads

The current thread, whose state is Running, may call these methods among others. Further Thread methods are described in the Java class library documentation [2].

- `Thread.yield()` changes the state of the current thread from Running to Enabled, and thereby allows the system to schedule another Enabled thread, if any.

- `Thread.sleep(n)` sleeps for n milliseconds: the current thread becomes Sleeping and after n milliseconds becomes Enabled. May throw InterruptedException if the thread is interrupted while sleeping.

- `Thread.currentThread()` returns the current thread object.

- `Thread.interrupted()` returns and clears the *interrupted status* of the current thread: `true` if there has been no call to `Thread.interrupted()` and no InterruptedException thrown since the last interrupt; otherwise `false`.

Let u be a thread (an object of a subclass of Thread). Then

- `u.start()` changes the state of u to Enabled so that its `run` method will be called when a processor becomes available.

- `u.interrupt()` interrupts the thread u: if u is Running or Enabled or Locking, then its interrupted status is set to `true`. If u is Sleeping or Joining, it will become Enabled, and if it is Waiting, it will become Locking; in these cases u will throw InterruptedException when and if it becomes Running (and the interrupted status is set to `false`).

- `u.isInterrupted()` returns the interrupted status of u (and does not clear it).

- `u.join()` waits for thread u to die; may throw InterruptedException if the current thread is interrupted while waiting.

- `u.join(n)` works as `u.join()` but times out and returns after at most n milliseconds. There is no indication whether the call returned because of a timeout or because u died.

20.4   Operations on Locked Objects

A thread that holds the lock on an object o may call the following methods, inherited by o from class Object.

- `o.wait()` releases the lock on o, changes its own state to Waiting, and adds itself to the set of threads waiting for notification on o. When notified (if ever), the thread must obtain the lock on o, so when the call to `wait` returns, it again holds the lock on o. May throw InterruptedException if the thread is interrupted while waiting.

- `o.wait(n)` works like `o.wait()` except that the thread will change state to Locking after n milliseconds regardless of whether there has been a notification on o. There is no indication whether the state change was caused by a timeout or a notification.

- `o.notify()` chooses an arbitrary thread among the threads waiting for notification on o (if any) and changes its state to Locking. The chosen thread cannot actually obtain the lock on o until the current thread has released it.

- `o.notifyAll()` works like `o.notify()`, except that it changes the state to Locking for *all* threads waiting for notification on o.

Example 111 Producers and Consumers Communicating via a Monitor

A Buffer has room for one integer and has a method `put` for storing into the buffer (if empty) and a method `get` for reading from the buffer (if non-empty); it is a monitor (section 20.2). A thread calling `get` must obtain the lock on the buffer. If it finds that the buffer is empty, it calls `wait` to (release the lock and) wait until something has been put into the buffer. If another thread calls `put` and thus `notifyAll`, then the getting thread will start competing for the buffer lock again, and if it gets it, will continue executing. Here we have used a `synchronized` statement in the method body (instead of making the method `synchronized`) to emphasize that synchronization, `wait`, and `notifyAll` all work on the same buffer object `this`.

```
class Buffer {
  private int contents;
  private boolean empty = true;
  public int get() {
    synchronized (this) {
      while (empty)
        try { this.wait(); } catch (InterruptedException x) {};
      empty = true;
      this.notifyAll();
      return contents;
  } }
  public void put(int v) {
    synchronized (this) {
      while (!empty)
        try { this.wait(); } catch (InterruptedException x) {};
      empty = false;
      contents = v;
      this.notifyAll();
  } }
}
```

Example 112 Graphic Animation Using the Runnable Interface

Class AnimatedCanvas here is a subclass of Canvas and so cannot be a subclass of Thread also. Instead it declares a `run` method and implements the Runnable interface. The constructor creates a Thread object u from the AnimatedCanvas object `this` and then starts the thread. The new thread executes the `run` method, which repeatedly sleeps and repaints, thus creating an animation.

```
class AnimatedCanvas extends Canvas implements Runnable {
  AnimatedCanvas() { Thread u = new Thread(this); u.start(); }

  public void run() {                            // From interface Runnable
    for (;;) { // Forever sleep and repaint
      try { Thread.sleep(100); } catch (InterruptedException e) { }
      ...
      repaint();
    }
  }

  public void paint(Graphics g) { ... }          // From class Canvas
  ...
}
```

20.5   The Java Memory Model and Visibility Across Threads

Concurrent threads in Java communicate via shared mutable memory, for instance, in the form of mutable fields accessible to multiple threads. This raises the question of *visibility of writes across threads*: when will a write x = 42 to shared field x performed by thread A be visible to another thread B that reads x? Due to optimizations performed by the Java JIT compiler and due to the memory caches of modern multicore processors, the surprising answer may be "never" or "later than you would think"; see examples 113 and 114.

However, the Java Memory Model (since Java 5.0) guarantees that writes to a shared field x or shared array element a[i] by thread A are visible to reads performed by thread B in these cases:

- Thread A releases a lock after the write to x or a[i], and then thread B acquires the same lock before the read. Hence leaving and then entering synchronized methods and blocks enforce visibility.

- Field x itself is declared volatile, and the write in A precedes the read in B in real time.

- Thread A writes to some volatile field after the write to x or a[i], and then thread B reads the volatile field before reading x or a[i]. Hence the visibility of x or a[i] may "piggyback" on the visibility effects of writing and then reading any volatile field.

- Thread A starts thread B using method start from section 20.3: a thread can see every write that its creator thread did.

- Thread A terminates, and B awaits the termination of A using join from section 20.3; a thread can see every write performed by a thread it knows has terminated.

- Concurrent collection operations from the java.util.concurrent package and atomic operations from the java.util.concurrent.atomic package also have visibility effects.

20.5.1   The volatile Field Modifier

The volatile field modifier applied to a field x ensures that every write to x by thread A, and every other prior write performed by A, becomes visible to another thread B upon later reading x. The volatile modifier prevents the Java JIT compiler from performing certain optimizations, and it causes extra work at run-time to make one processor core's writes visible to other processor cores. This may slow down the code; see example 115.

Declaring a field a of array type volatile does *not* affect the visibility of writes to the array's elements a[i]. To ensure visibility of array element writes, one must build on the Java Memory Model guarantees listed above: use locking or synchronized; piggyback on writes and subsequent reads of other volatile fields; use atomic operations; and so on.

20.5.2   The final Field Modifier

If an instance field x is declared final, then the value assigned to x by a constructor is visible by any thread that obtains the reference returned by the constructor. Since the final modifier has visibility effect and also ensures that the field cannot be modified (section 9.6), it can be used to implement thread-safe immutable objects. This is useful in connection with functional programming (chapter 23) with parallel streams (chapter 24) and can also be used to avoid locking in some scenarios.

Example 113 Field Writes May Remain Forever Invisible

Without the `volatile` modifier on field `value`, the `mi.set(42)` performed by the main thread may remain forever invisible to the thread executing the `while` loop, which may therefore never terminate.

```
class MutableInteger {
  private /* volatile */ int value = 0;
  public void set(int value) { this.value = value; }
  public int get() { return value; }
}
...
final MutableInteger mi = new MutableInteger();
Thread t = new Thread(new Runnable() { public void run() { while (mi.get() == 0) { } }});
t.start();
mi.set(42);
```

Example 114 Field Writes May Happen in a Surprising Order

Without the `volatile` modifier on the A and B fields, the hardware memory system may delay the writes to fields A and B so that both writes appear to happen after both reads of !B and !A. Thus when executing methods ThreadA and ThreadB concurrently, one may observe bizarre outcomes such as both AWon and BWon becoming 1, which does not correspond to any interleaving of the sequential operations performed by the two methods. On a 4-core Intel i7 processor, this happens frequently; with the `volatile` modifier, it cannot happen.

```
class StoreBufferExample {
  public /* volatile */ boolean A = false, B = false;
  public int AWon = 0, BWon = 0;
  public void ThreadA() {
    A = true;
    if (!B) AWon = 1;
  }
  public void ThreadB() {
    B = true;
    if (!A) BWon = 1;
} }
```

Example 115 The `volatile` Modifier Precludes Some Optimizations

Each iteration of the `for` loop in method `isSorted` seems to read the `array` field three times: once for the array length test, and twice for the array element accesses. Without the `volatile` modifier on `array`, the Java JIT compiler will optimize this code to read the `array` field just once before the loop, and use that reference for the duration of the loop. This enables array bounds check elimination and makes the code run five times faster. When the `volatile` modifier is present, such optimizations would be wrong and are not performed.

```
class IntArray {
  private /* volatile */ int[] array;
  public boolean isSorted() {
    for (int i=1; i<array.length; i++)
      if (array[i-1] > array[i])
        return false;
    return true;
  }
}
```

21   Generic Types and Methods

Generic types and methods provide a way to strengthen type checking at compile-time while at the same time making programs more expressive, reusable and readable. The ability to have generic types and methods is also known as *parametric polymorphism*.

21.1   Generics: Safety, Generality, and Efficiency

The original Java language did not support generic types and methods. Therefore a library for manipulating arbitrary kinds of values would have to cast those values to type Object. For instance, we might use an ArrayList `cool` to hold Person objects, but the `add` and `get` methods of the `cool` array list would have to accept and return values of type Object. This works but has several negative consequences that can be avoided by using generic types; see examples 116 and 117.

21.2   Generic Types, Type Parameters, and Type Instances

A *generic class* declaration `class C<T1,...,Tn> { ... }` has one or more *type parameters* `T1,...,Tn`. The body of the declaration is an ordinary class body (section 9.1) in which the type parameters `Ti` can be used almost as if they were ordinary types; see section 21.6. A generic class is also called a *parametrized class*.

A generic class `C<T1>` is not itself a class. Rather, it is a mechanism or template from which classes such as C<Integer> or C<String> or even C<C<String>>, and so on, can be generated, by replacing the type parameter `T1` by a type expression `t1`, such as Integer, String, or C<String>. The resulting classes are called *type instances*. The type `t1` used to replace the type parameter `T1` can be any reference type expression—a class, an array type, an interface—or it can itself be a type instance. However, it cannot be a primitive type such as `int`, nor the pseudo-type `void` (which can be used only to indicate that a method has no return value).

Generic interfaces (section 21.7) can be declared also, and type instances can be created from them. Again, a generic interface is not an interface, but a type instance of a generic interface is an interface.

Generic methods (section 21.8) can be declared by specifying type parameters on the method declaration in addition to any type parameters specified on the enclosing class or interface type.

Section 21.11 compares the implementation of Java generic types and methods with C++ templates and C# generic types and methods.

21.3   How Can Type Instances Be Used?

A type instance such as C<Integer> can be used almost anywhere an ordinary reference type can be used: as the type of a field, variable, parameter or return type; as the element type in an array type in the same contexts; as a constructor name `new C<T>(...)`; and so on. However, there are the following restrictions:

- One can use a type instance in cast expression such as `(C<Integer>)e` but such a cast is sometimes reported by the compiler to be unchecked (see section 21.6).

- One cannot use a type instance in an instance test expression such as `(e instanceof C<Integer>)`.

- One cannot use a type instance as the element type of an array in an array creation expression such as `new C<Integer>[5]`. But `new ArrayList<C<Integer>>()` is legal; see section 21.11.

Example 116 Using Non-Generic ArrayList: Run-Time Type Checks and Wrapping of Values
The java.util.ArrayList `cool` should hold only Person objects, but without generic types, the compiler cannot check that only Person objects are added to `cool`. Hence at run-time the program must check and cast objects when extracting them from the list. These checks take time and may fail. The Java compiler can only warn that maybe the `add` operations are suspicious:

```
ArrayList cool = new ArrayList();
cool.add(new Person("Kristen"));
cool.add(new Person("Bjarne"));
cool.add(new Exception("Larry"));    // Wrong, but no compile-time check
cool.add(new Person("Anders"));
Person p = (Person)(cool.get(2));    // Compiles OK, but fails at run-time
```

Example 117 Using Generic ArrayList: Compile-Time Type Checks
With generic types, `cool` can be declared to have type java.util.ArrayList<Person>, the compiler can check that only Person objects are passed to the `cool.add` method, and therefore the array list `cool` can contain only Person objects. Thus generic types make the programmer's intention clear in the source code and improve our trust in the program.

However, Java generic types do not improve efficiency: the cast to class Person after `cool.get(2)` is still performed at run-time, but it does not appear explicitly in the source code.

```
ArrayList<Person> cool = new ArrayList<Person>();
cool.add(new Person("Kristen"));
cool.add(new Person("Bjarne"));
cool.add(new Exception("Larry"));    // Wrong, detected at compile-time
cool.add(new Person("Anders"));
Person p = cool.get(2);              // No explicit cast or check needed
```

Example 118 A Generic Class Type for Pairs
A pair of two values of type T and U can be represented by a generic class Pair<T,U>. The generic class has read-only fields for holding the components, and a constructor for creating pairs.

```
class Pair<T,U> {
  public final T fst;
  public final U snd;
  public Pair(T fst, U snd) {
    this.fst = fst;
    this.snd = snd;
  }
}
...
Pair<String,Integer> p1 = new Pair<String,Integer>("Niels", 1947);
Pair<Double,Integer> p2 = new Pair<Double,Integer>(2.718, 1);
Pair<Date,String> p3 = new Pair<Date,String>(new Date(), "now");
```

21.4   Generic Classes

A declaration of a *generic class* C<T1,...,Tn> may have this form:

> *class-modifiers* class C<T1,...,Tn> *class-base-clause*
> *class-body*

The T1,...,Tn are *type parameters*. The *class-modifiers*, *class-body*, and *class-base-clause* are as for a non-generic class declaration (section 9.1).

   In addition, each type parameter Ti may have constraints c_1, c_2, ..., c_n, in which case its entry in the parameter list is written Ti extends c_1 & c_2 & ... & c_n instead of just Ti; see section 21.5.

   The type parameters T1,...,Tn may be used wherever a type is expected in the *class-base-clause* and in non-static members of the *class-body*, and so may the type parameters of any enclosing generic class, if the present class is a non-static member class. See section 21.6 for details.

   A generic class C<T1,...,Tn> in itself is not a class. However, each *type instance* C<t1,...,tn> is a class, just like a class declared by replacing each type parameter Ti with the corresponding type ti in the *class-body*. A type ti that is substituted for a type parameter Ti in a type instance can be any reference type—a class, an array type, an interface, an enum type—or it can itself be a type instance. However, it cannot be a primitive type nor the pseudo-type void; the void pseudo-type can be used only to indicate that a method has no return value.

   All type instances of a generic class C<T1,...,Tn> are represented by the same *raw type* C at run-time. All type instances of a generic class C<T1,...,Tn> share the same static fields (if any) declared in the *class-body*. As a consequence, the type parameters of the class cannot be used in any static members.

   An object instance of a type instance C<t1,...,tn> of a generic class is created using the new operator to invoke a constructor of the type instance, as in new C<t1,...,tn>() for an argument-less constructor. If the type arguments t1,...,tn can be inferred from the context, the argument list may be left empty as a "diamond" <> as in new C<>(). In particular, this works if the object creation expression is the right-hand side of an initialized variable declaration Log<Date> log2 = new Log<>(...) as in example 119, also when the left-hand side is a supertype of the right-hand side, as in List<String> alist2 = new ArrayList<>().

   A type instance C<t1,...,tn> is accessible when all its parts are accessible. Thus if the generic class C<T1,...,Tn> or any of the type arguments t1,...,tn is private, then the type instance is private also.

   A scope can have only one class, generic or not, with the same name C, regardless of its number of type parameters.

   A generic class declaration is illegal if there are types t1,...,tn such that the type instance C<t1,...,tn> would contain two or more method declarations with the same signature.

   The usual conversion rules hold for generic classes and generic interfaces. When generic class C<T1> is declared to be a subclass of generic class B<T1> or is declared to implement interface I<T1>, then the type instance C<t1> is a subtype of the type instances B<t1> and I<t1>: an expression of type C<t1> can be used wherever a value of type B<t1> or I<t1> is expected.

   However, generic classes and interfaces are invariant in their type parameters. Hence even if t11 is a subtype of t12, the type instance C<t11> is not a subtype of the type instance C<t12>. For example, LinkedList<String> is not a subtype of LinkedList<Object>. If it were, one could create a LinkedList<String>, cast it to LinkedList<Object>, store an Object into it, and rather unexpectedly get an Object back out of the original LinkedList<String>. Thus for type system soundness, generic types must in general be invariant in their type parameters. Some of the programming flexibility lost thereby can be regained by using wildcard type arguments in generic types; see section 21.9.

Example 119 A Generic Class for Logging
Generic class Log<T> implements a simple log that stores the last few objects of type T written to it. To create a Log<T> one must provide an array of type T[] to hold the log entries. Method add accepts new log entries of type T and method getLast returns the latest log entry. Method getAll returns an ArrayList<T> of all the available log entries; it cannot create and return an array of type T[]; see section 21.11.

```
class Log<T> {
  private final int size;
  private static int instanceCount = 0;
  private int count = 0;
  private T[] log;
  public Log(T[] log) { this.log = log; this.size = log.length; instanceCount++; }
  public void add(T msg) { log[count++ % size] = msg; }
  public T getLast() { return count==0 ? null : log[(count-1)%size]; }
  public void setLast(T value) { ... }
  public ArrayList<T> getAll() { ... }
}
...
// Log<Date> log2 = new Log<Date>(new Date[5]);          // Shorthand for the above
Log<Date> log2 = new Log<>(new Date[5]);
log2.add(new Date());                                    // now
```

Example 120 A Generic Linked List Class
An object of generic class MyLinkedList<T> is a linked list whose elements have type T; it implements interface MyList<T> (example 124). The generic class declaration has a static nested class Node<U>; two constructors, one of which takes a variable number of arguments of type T; methods that take arguments of type T; an equals method that casts its argument to MyList<T> (by an unchecked cast); and a method that returns an Iterator<T>. See also example 129.

```
class MyLinkedList<T> implements MyList<T> {
  protected int size;                 // Number of elements in the list
  protected Node<T> first, last;      // Invariant: first==null iff last==null
  protected static class Node<U> {  // Static nested generic class
    public Node<U> prev, next;
    public U item;
    ...
  }
  public MyLinkedList() { first = last = null; size = 0; }
  public MyLinkedList(T... arr) { ... }          // Variable-arity constructor
  public void add(T item) { insert(size, item); }
  public void insert(int i, T item) { ... }
  public void removeAt(int i) { ... }
  public boolean equals(Object that) {
    return equals((MyList<T>)that);              // Unchecked cast
  }
  public boolean equals(MyList<T> that) { ... }
  public Iterator<T> iterator() { ... }
  ...
}
```

21.5   Constraints on Type Parameters

A type parameter of a generic class C<T1, ..., Tn> may have type parameter constraints. The constraints on a type parameter are given in-line in the type parameter list by a *constraint-clause* of this form:

Ti extends c_1 & c_2 & ... & c_n

In the constraint clause, Ti is one of the type parameters T1, ..., Tn, each c_j is a *constraint* on Ti, and $n \geq 1$. A *constraint* c must be a type expression: an interface, a non-final class type, or one of the preceding type parameters Tj where $1 \leq j \leq i-1$.

The type expression may be a type instance and may involve any of the type parameters T1, ..., Tn. An array type cannot be used as a constraint.

Only the first constraint c_1 can be a class type or a type parameter Tj; the following constraints must be interfaces. If the first constraint is a type parameter Tj, then that must be the only constraint.

Forward references to type parameters are permitted in a constraint that is a generic type instance such as D<T2>, as in class C<T1 extends D<T2>, T2> { ... }, but they are not permitted when the constraint is a naked type parameter such as T2, as in class C<T1 extends T2, T2> { ... }. This ensures that there can be no constraint cycles.

The types t1, ..., tn used when creating a generic type instance C<t1, ..., tn> must satisfy the *constraints*: if type parameter Ti is replaced by type ti throughout its *constraint-clause*, where the resulting constraint is ti extends c_1 & c_2 & ... & c_n, it must hold that ti is a subtype of c_1 and of c_2 and so on up to c_n.

21.6   How Can Type Parameters Be Used?

Within the body { ... } of a generic class class C<T1, ..., Tn> { ... } or generic interface, a type parameter Ti may be used almost as if it were a public type.

- One can use type parameter Ti as a type argument in the supertype and in the implemented interfaces of the generic class or generic interface (but Ti itself cannot be used as superclass or implemented interface).

- One can use type parameter Ti in the return type, variable types, parameter types, and throws clauses of non-static methods and their local inner classes, as well as in the type and initializer of non-static fields and non-static constructors. In these contexts, Ti can be used in type instances C1<..., Ti, ...> of generic types C1.

- One can use type parameter Ti for the same purposes in non-static member classes, but not in static member classes nor in member interfaces.

- One can use (Ti)e for type casts, but such casts are sometimes reported by the compiler to be unchecked. This is due to Java's implementation of generic types; see section 21.11 and examples 123 and 131.

- One cannot use new Ti[10] to create a new array whose element type is Ti (see example 132); one cannot use (o instanceof Ti) to test whether o is an instance of Ti; one cannot use Ti.class to obtain the canonical object representing the type Ti; one cannot use new Ti() to create an instance of Ti; and one cannot call static methods on a type parameter Ti, as in Ti.m(), or otherwise refer to the static members of a type parameter. Again, this is due to Java's implementation of generic types; see section 21.11.

Example 121 Type Parameter Constraints
Interface Printable describes a method `print` that will print an object on a PrintWriter. The generic PrintableLinkedList<T> can implement Printable provided the list elements (of type T) do.

```
class PrintableMyLinkedList<T extends Printable>
  extends MyLinkedList<> implements Printable
{
  public void print(PrintWriter fs) {
    for (T x : this)
      x.print(fs);
  }
}
interface Printable { void print(PrintWriter fs); }
```

Example 122 Constraints Involving Type Parameters
The elements of a type T are mutually comparable if any T-value x can be compared to any T-value y using `x.compareTo(y)`. This is the case if type T implements Comparable<T>; see section 22.9. The requirement that T implements Comparable<T> is expressible by the constraint `T extends Comparable<T>`.

Type ComparablePair<T,U> is a type of ordered pairs of (T,U)-values. For (T,U)-pairs to support comparison, both T and U must support comparison, so constraints are required on both T and U.

```
class ComparablePair<T extends Comparable<T>, U extends Comparable<U>>
  implements Comparable<ComparablePair<T,U>> {
  public final T fst;
  public final U snd;
  public ComparablePair(T fst, U snd) { this.fst = fst; this.snd = snd; }
  public int compareTo(ComparablePair<T,U> that) {    // Lexicographic ordering
    int firstCmp = this.fst.compareTo(that.fst);
    return firstCmp != 0 ? firstCmp : this.snd.compareTo(that.snd);
  }
}
```

Example 123 Unchecked Cast to Type Parameter
Generic class Hold<T> can hold one element of type T. The `set`-method accepts an Object x and casts it to T before storing it; a saner version would just take an argument of type T. Here the point is that the "unchecked" cast `(T) x` in `set` is actually not performed, so `set` accepts any type of argument and never throws ClassCastException. However, an attempt to obtain a non-T result from `get` will throw ClassCastException. The corresponding type-erased code in example 131 shows why.

```
class Hold<T> {
  private T contents;
  public void set(Object x) { contents = (T)x; }    // Unchecked cast
  public T get() { return contents; }
}
...
Hold<Integer> h = new Hold<Integer>();
h.set("foo");                    // Succeeds at run-time
h.get();                         // Succeeds at run-time
// String s = h.get();           // Illegal, rejected by compiler
Integer i = h.get();             // Legal, but fails at run-time
```

21.7   Generic Interfaces

A declaration of a *generic interface* I<T1, ..., Tn> has this form:

> *interface-modifiers* interface I<T1,...,Tn> *extends-clause*
> *interface-body*

The T1, ..., Tn are type parameters as for generic classes (section 21.4), and the *interface-modifiers*, *extends-clause*, and *interface-body* are as for non-generic interfaces (section 13.1). Each type parameter Ti may have type parameter constraints just as for a generic class; see section 21.5.

A type instance of the generic interface has form I<t1,...,tn> where the t1,...,tn are types. The types t1,...,tn must satisfy the parameter constraints, if any, on the generic interface I<T1,...,Tn> as described in section 21.5.

A generic interface is a subinterface of the interfaces mentioned in its *extends clause*. Like a generic class, a generic interface is not covariant in its type parameters. That is, I<String> is not a subtype of I<Object>, although String is a subtype of Object.

Example 124 A Generic List Interface

The generic interface MyList<T> extends the Iterable<T> interface (section 22.7) with methods to add and remove list elements, methods to get and set the element at a particular position, and a generic method (section 21.8) called <U> map that takes an argument of type Mapper<T,U> (example 125) and builds a list of type MyList<U>. Note that the generic method <U> map has an additional type parameter U.

```
interface MyList<T> extends Iterable<T> {
  int getCount();                    // Number of elements
  T get(int i);                      // Get element at index i
  void set(int i, T item);           // Set element at index i
  void add(T item);                  // Add element at end
  void insert(int i, T item);        // Insert element at index i
  void removeAt(int i);              // Remove element at index i
  <U> MyList<U> map(Mapper<T,U> f);  // Map f over all elements
}
```

Example 125 A Generic Interface Representing a Function

The generic interface Mapper<A,R> describes a single method `call` that takes an argument of type A and returns a result of type R. In other words, Mapper<A,R> is the type of functions from type A to type R, and objects of type Mapper<A,R> can be used where one would use delegates in C# or functions as values in functional languages. Starting with Java 8.0, such single-method *functional interfaces* are part of the class library (chapter 23), and one might use Function<A,R> (section 23.5) instead of Mapper<A,R>. This generic interface is used in examples 124 and 129.

```
interface Mapper<A,R> {
  R call(A x);
}
```

Example 126 Subtype Relations between Generic Classes and Interfaces

A LabelPoint<L> is a point with a label of type L; such a point is Movable. A ColorLabelPoint<L,C> is a LabelPoint<L> that additionally has a "color" of type C. Hence the type instance LabelPoint<String> is a subtype of Movable, and both ColorLabelPoint<String,Integer> and ColorLabelPoint<String,Color> are subtypes of LabelPoint<String> and Movable.

```
interface Movable { void move(int dx, int dy); }
class LabelPoint<L> implements Movable {
  protected int x, y;
  private L lab;
  public LabelPoint(int x, int y, L lab) { this.x = x; this.y = y; this.lab = lab; }
  public void move(int dx, int dy) { x += dx; y += dy; }
}
class ColorLabelPoint<L, C> extends LabelPoint<L> {
  private C c;
  public ColorLabelPoint(int x, int y, L lab, C c) { super(x, y, lab); this.c = c; }
}
```

21.8   Generic Methods

A generic method is a method that takes one or more type parameters. A generic method may be declared inside a generic or non-generic class or interface.

A declaration of a generic method m<T1,...,Tn> has this form:

> *method-modifiers* <T1,...,Tn> *returntype* m(*formal-list*)
> *method-body*

The *method-modifiers*, *returntype*, and *formal-list* are as for non-generic methods (section 9.8). The main syntactic difference is that a generic method has a list of type parameters T1,...,Tn before its *returntype*. Each type parameter Ti may have type parameter constraints just as for a generic class; see section 21.5.

The type parameters T1,...,Tn may be used as types in the *returntype*, *formal-list*, and *method-body*, as may the type parameters of any enclosing generic class if the method is non-static. A type parameter Ti of a generic method may have the same name as a type parameter of an enclosing generic class.

Generic methods of the same name m are not distinguished by their number of generic type parameters, and a generic method is not distinguished from a non-generic method of the same name. For example, these three methods

```
void m() { ... }
<T> void m() { ... }
<T,U> void m() { ... }
```

are not considered distinct, and at most one of them can be declared in a given scope.

If a generic method overrides a generic method declared in a superclass or implements a generic method described in an interface, then it must have the same parameter constraints as those methods. The names of the type parameters are not significant; only their ordinal positions in the type parameter list T1,...,Tn matter.

A call of a generic method can be written without type arguments as in o.m(...), or with explicit generic type arguments as in o.<t1,...,tn>m(...). In the former case, the compiler will attempt to infer the appropriate type arguments t1,...,tn automatically. Type parameter constraints are not taken into account during such inference, but must be satisfied by the resulting type arguments t1,...,tn when inference is successful.

Explicit generic type arguments can be given in four of the syntactic forms of method call (section 11.12):

> o.<t1,...,tn>m(*actual-list*)
> super.<t1,...,tn>m(*actual-list*)
> C.<t1,...,tn>m(*actual-list*)
> C.super.<t1,...,tn>m(*actual-list*)

Note that to give type arguments to a static method m in class C, one must explicitly prefix the method call with the class name, as in C.<t1,...,tn>m(...). Similarly, to give type arguments to an instance method in the current object, one must explicitly prefix the method call with the current object reference, as in this.<t1,...,tn>m(...). In any case, either none or all type arguments must be given.

Example 127 A Generic Quicksort Method Using a Comparator Object

Generic method qsort sorts arr[a..b] where arr has type T[] and T is a type parameter. The Comparator<T> parameter determines the element ordering; see section 22.9. The method (assumed to be in class GenericFun-Quicksort) is called without and with explicit type argument. Class IntegerComparator is from example 144.

```
private static <T> void qsort(T[] arr, Comparator<T> cmp, int a, int b) {
  if (a < b) {
    int i = a, j = b;
    T x = arr[(i+j) / 2];
    do {
      while (cmp.compare(arr[i], x) < 0) i++;
      while (cmp.compare(x, arr[j]) < 0) j--;
      if (i <= j) {
        T tmp = arr[i]; arr[i] = arr[j]; arr[j] = tmp;
        i++; j--;
      }
    } while (i <= j);
    qsort(arr, cmp, a, j);
    qsort(arr, cmp, i, b);
  }
}
...
GenericFunQuicksort.qsort(ia, new IntegerComparator(), 0, ia.length-1);
GenericFunQuicksort.<Integer>qsort(ia, new IntegerComparator(), 0, ia.length-1);
```

Example 128 A Generic Quicksort Method for Comparable Values

This method sorts an array of type T[] whose elements of type T must be comparable to themselves. This is expressed by the method's parameter constraint as in example 122.

```
private static <T extends Comparable<T>> void qsort(T[] arr, int a, int b) {
  ...
  while (arr[i].compareTo(x) < 0) i++;
  while (x.compareTo(arr[j]) < 0) j--;
  ...
}
```

Example 129 A Generic Method in a Generic Class

The generic class MyLinkedList<T> in example 120 can be equipped with a generic method <U> map that takes an additional type parameter U and returns a new list of type MyLinkedList<U>. The generic interface MyList<T> is from example 124, and the generic interface Mapper<T,U> is from example 125.

```
class MyLinkedList<T> implements MyList<T> {
  ...
  public <U> MyList<U> map(Mapper<T,U> f) {       // Map f over all elements
    MyLinkedList<U> res = new MyLinkedList<U>();
    for (T x : this)
      res.add(f.call(x));
    return res;
  }
}
```

21.9   Wildcard Type Arguments

A *wildcard type* is a type expression that denotes some unknown type. A wildcard type can be used only as a type argument in a generic type instance, as in Shop<?> where Shop<T> is a generic type from example 130; a wildcard cannot be used as a type on its own. A wildcard type is useful when one must give a type argument in a generic type or method but does want to specify the exact type. There are three forms of wildcard types:

```
<?>
<? extends tb>
<? super tb>
```

Here the tb is a type expression, possibly involving further occurrences of wildcard type expressions (which then stand for unrelated types). The first form of wildcard represents some unknown type; the second form represents some unknown type that is tb or a subtype of tb; and the third form represents some unknown type that is tb or a supertype of tb.

A wildcard type expression should not be confused with a type parameter constraint in the declaration of a generic type or method (section 21.5); in particular a parameter constraint cannot have the form T super tb.

Consider the Shop<T> example opposite, where a Shop<T> is a shop that deals in objects of type T.

First, a Shop<Car> is a shop to which we can sell objects of type Car (or a subclass); and when we buy from the shop, we know that we get a Car or something that is a subtype of Car.

A Shop<?> is a shop that deals in some unknown type of object. The shop might be a Shop<Vehicle> or a Shop<Sedan> or a Shop<Painting>. Therefore we know only that what we buy from the shop is an Object; and we cannot sell anything to the shop at all, not knowing the type of objects it will accept.

A Shop<? extends Car> is a shop that deals in some unknown subtype of Car. Therefore what we buy from the shop must be a Car; but we cannot sell anything to the shop, not knowing what type Cars it will accept.

A Shop<? super Car> is a shop that deals in some unknown supertype of Car. Obviously, what we buy from the shop must be an Object, and we know that we can sell Cars (or even Sedans) to the shop.

A variable b of type Shop<?> can be given (assigned or passed) a value of type Shop<t> for any type t. A variable b of type Shop<? extends tb> can be assigned a value of type Shop<t> only if type t is a subtype of tb. For instance, a variable of type Shop<? extends Car> can be assigned a Shop<Sedan> or a Shop<Car> but not a Shop<Vehicle>. Conversely, a variable b of type Shop<? super tb> can be assigned a value of type Shop<t> only if type t is a supertype of tb. For instance, a variable of type Shop<? super Car> can be assigned a Shop<Car> or Shop<Vehicle> but not Shop<Sedan>. Thus the subtype relations between Shops are these:

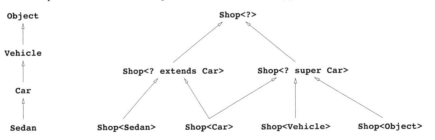

In general, the wildcard type <? extends tb> is useful as type argument when a value of a generic type must be usable as a producer of objects of type tb. Conversely, the wildcard type <? super tb> is useful as a type argument when a value of a generic type must be usable as a consumer of objects of type tb.

Wildcards are used extensively in the parameter types and type constraints in the generic collection library (chapter 22). Examples 150 and 151 explain two of the more intricate cases.

Example 130 Wildcard Types

Assume we have three classes Vehicle, Car, and Sedan, where Vehicle has subclass Car, and Car has subclass Sedan (a closed car). Now consider a generic class Shop<T> that represents a shop or broker from which we can buy and to which we can sell things of type T. A Shop<T> has a method T buyFrom() that allows us to buy a T from the shop, and a method void sellTo(T) that allows us to sell a T to the shop.

```
class Vehicle { }
class Car extends Vehicle { }
class Sedan extends Car { }
class Shop<T> {
  private T thing;
  public T buyFrom() { return thing; }
  public void sellTo(T thing) { this.thing = thing; }
}
```

The table below shows well-typed (+) and ill-typed (−) uses of variables b of the five types Shop, Shop<Car>, Shop<?>, Shop<? extends Car>, and Shop<? super Car>. Note that Shop is the raw type underlying Shop<T>.

Operation \ Type of b	Shop	Shop<Car>	Shop<?>	Shop<? extends Car>	Shop<? super Car>
b = new Shop<Object>()	+	−	+	−	+
b = new Shop<Vehicle>()	+	−	+	−	+
b = new Shop<Car>()	+	+	+	+	+
b = new Shop<Sedan>()	+	−	+	+	−
b.sellTo(object)	+	−	−	−	−
b.sellTo(vehicle)	+	−	−	−	−
b.sellTo(car)	+	+	−	−	+
b.sellTo(sedan)	+	+	−	−	+
Object o = b.buyFrom()	+	+	+	+	+
Vehicle v = b.buyFrom()	−	+	−	+	−
Car c = b.buyFrom()	−	+	−	+	−
Sedan s = b.buyFrom()	−	−	−	−	−
b.sellTo(b.buyFrom())	+	+	−	−	−

For a variable b of raw type Shop, the sellTo method will accept any object at all, as would Shop<Object>. (But a new Shop<Car>() could not be assigned to a variable of type Shop<Object>). Although Car is a subclass of Object, Shop<Car> is not a subclass of Shop<Object>; see section 21.4.

For a Shop<Car>, the sellTo-method will accept a Car or any subclass such as Sedan, and the object returned by the buyFrom-method can be considered a Car or any superclass, such as Vehicle.

For a Shop<?>, the sellTo-method will accept neither Car nor Sedan nor Vehicle (because the actual element type T might be completely unrelated to these types; say, type Painting), and the object returned by the buyFrom-method could be assigned to a variable of type Object, but not Vehicle nor Car nor Sedan (again because the actual element type T might be completely unrelated to these types).

For a Shop<? extends Car>, the sellTo-method will accept neither Car nor Sedan nor Vehicle (because the actual element type T might be a subtype of Car unrelated to Sedan, say, Convertible). The object returned by the buyFrom-method can be considered a Car or any superclass, such as Vehicle.

For a Shop<? super Car>, the sellTo-method will accept a Car or any subclass such as Sedan, and the object returned by the buyFrom-method can be considered an Object, but not Vehicle nor Car nor Sedan (because the actual element type T might be a superclass of Vehicle, such as Mobile).

The expression b.sellTo(b.buyFrom()) is well-typed when b has type Shop or Shop<Car>, but ill-typed in the other cases, although a object returned by buyFrom would always be a suitable argument for sellTo.

21.10   The Raw Type

For every generic type there is an underlying *raw type*. For a generic class C<T1, ..., Tn> the raw type is a non-generic class C that is a supertype of all type instances C<t1, ..., tn> of the generic class C<T1, ..., Tn>. For a generic interface I<T1, ..., Tn> the raw type is an interface I that is a superinterface of all type instances I<t1, ..., tn> of the generic interface I<T1, ..., Tn>.

The raw type C is derived from the generic class declaration by *erasure* as follows:

- If Ti is a type parameter of C<T1, ..., Tn> without a constraint, then any use of Ti in the body of class C is replaced by Object.

- If Ti is a type parameter of C<T1, ..., Tn> with constraints c_1 & c_2 & ... & c_n, then any use of Ti in the body of class C is replaced by c_1.

For this reason one sometimes sees constraints of the form Ti extends Object & c_2 & ... & c_n that begin with an apparently superfluous occurrence of Object.

21.11   The Implementation of Generic Types and Methods

Generic types and methods in Java resemble C++ type templates and function templates, as well as generic types and methods in the C# programming language. However, generic types and methods in Java have been designed to allow programs that use generics to run on the same non-generic Java Virtual Machine as older Java programs. This design has several implications:

- Only reference types, not primitive types, can be used as generic type arguments. Thus a type parameter T must be instantiated with type Integer, not type int, and int values must be wrapped as Integer objects. This so-called boxed representation carries a certain overhead in execution time and space because Integer objects must be allocated on the heap to wrap int values, extra memory accesses are needed, and the int values must be unboxed before performing arithmetic or comparisons.

- There is a single type in the run-time system common to all the type instances C<t1, ..., tn> of a generic type C<T1, ..., Tn>, namely, the raw type C. In particular, all object instances of all type instances have the same field layout and contain the same bytecode instructions.

  Thus at run-time, the type instances Pair<String, Integer> and Pair<Date, String> in example 118 are actually represented by the same raw type Pair with fields of type Object. This loses some optimization opportunities that exist for C++ templates and for C# generic types and methods.

  On the other hand, the existence of the raw type makes it easy for new Java generic types to interoperate with legacy non-generic types; this is more difficult in C# programs.

- Overloading resolution of a method m or constructor does not take type arguments in m's parameter types into account and does not distinguish generic and raw types in m's parameter types. For example, these three methods are not considered distinct, and at most one of them can be declared in a given scope:

```
void m(List xs) { ... }
void m(List<Integer> xs) { ... }
void m(List<String> xs) { ... }
```

- At run-time there is no information about the actual type arguments of a generic type or method. So type parameters can be used only to a limited extent in reflection and not at all in instanceof tests.

Example 131 Implementation by Type Erasure
The type erasure of example 123 is shown below. In other words, the JVM bytecode generated from that example is identical to that generated from the Java code below.

```
class Hold {
  private Object contents;
  public void set(Object x) { contents = x; }      // Note: no cast
  public Object get() { return contents; }
}
...
Hold h = new Hold();
h.set("foo");                      // Succeeds at run-time
h.get();                           // Succeeds at run-time
Integer i = (Integer)h.get();      // Legal, but fails at run-time
```

Example 132 Java Generics Limitation: Cannot Create Array with Generic Element Type
In declarations of fields, variables, parameters, and return types, one can freely use array types whose element types are type parameters such as T, or type instances such as C<T> or C<Integer>. However, one cannot create (using new) an array whose element type is a type parameter or any kind of constructed type.

This is because Java (and C#) considers array type s[] to be a subtype of t[] whenever s and t are reference types and s is a subtype of t. This is safe only if at every array assignment arr[i] = e, it is checked that the run-time of e is a subtype of the actual element type of arr (section 8.1). This requires a representation of the element type to exist at run-time for every array. Since Java generics are implemented by type erasure, there exists no precise representation of the types T or C<T> or C<Integer> at run-time, so this information cannot be associated with an array type such as T[], and therefore the array element assignment check cannot be performed accurately. Therefore the creation of such arrays is rejected by the compiler.

By contrast, the type ArrayList<s> is *not* a subtype of ArrayList<t> when s is a subtype of t. Hence no check is needed at run-time when storing objects in the array list, and there is no need for a run-time representation of the array list's element type.

```
class F<T> {
  public void M() {
    T[] tarr;                       // Legal declaration
    G<T>[] ctarr;                   // Legal declaration
    G<Integer>[] ciarr;             // Legal declaration
    // tarr = new T[5];             // Illegal generic array creation
    // ctarr = new G<T>[5];         // Illegal generic array creation
    // ciarr = new G<Integer>[5];   // Illegal generic array creation

    ArrayList<T> tlist;             // Legal declaration
    ArrayList<G<T>> ctlist;         // Legal declaration
    ArrayList<G<Integer>> cilist;   // Legal declaration
    tlist = new ArrayList<T>();     // Legal array list creation
    ctlist = new ArrayList<G<T>>(); // Legal array list creation
    cilist = new ArrayList<G<Integer>>(); // Legal array list creation
  }
}
```

22   Generic Collections and Maps

The Java class library package `java.util` provides collection classes and map (or dictionary) classes:

- A *collection*, described by generic interface Collection<T> (section 22.1), is used to group and handle many distinct *elements* of type T as a whole.
- A *list*, described by generic interface List<T> (section 22.2), is a collection whose elements can be traversed in insertion order. Implemented by the generic classes LinkedList<T> (for linked lists, double-ended queues, and stacks) and ArrayList<T> (for dynamically extensible arrays and stacks).
- A *set*, described by generic interface Set<T> (section 22.3), is a collection that cannot contain duplicate elements. Implemented by the generic classes HashSet<T> and LinkedHashSet<T>.

  A *sorted set*, described by generic interface SortedSet<T> (section 22.4), is a set whose elements are ordered: either the elements implement method `compareTo` specified by interface Comparable<T>, or the set's ordering is given explicitly by an object of type Comparator<T> (section 22.9). Implemented by generic class TreeSet<T>.

- A *map*, described by generic interface Map<K,V> (section 22.5), represents a mapping from a key of type K to at most one value of type V for each key. Implemented by the generic classes HashMap<K,V>, IdentityHashMap<K,V>, and LinkedHashMap<K,V>.

  A *sorted map*, described by generic interface SortedMap<K,V> (section 22.6), is a map whose keys are ordered, as for SortedSet<K>. Implemented by class TreeMap<K,V>.

The standard interfaces, intermediate abstract classes, and concrete implementation classes are shown below. User-defined implementation classes can be conveniently defined as subclasses of the abstract classes; see the Java class library documentation on package `java.util`. Solid arrows denote the subinterface and subclass relations, and dashed arrows indicate the "implements" relation between a class and an interface.

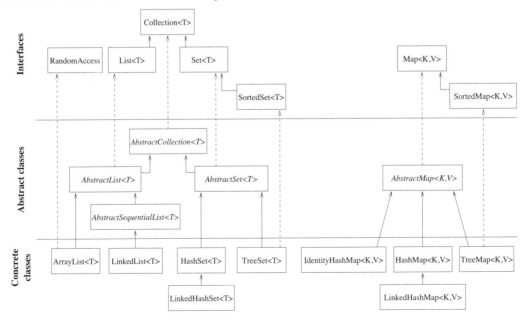

Example 133 Using the Concrete Collection and Map Classes

Here we create instances of five concrete collection classes with element type String and add some elements to them. For each collection, we call method `traverse` from example 141 to print its elements.

We also create instances of three concrete map classes with keys and values of type String and add some entries to them. For each map, we call `traverse` separately on its set of keys and its collection of values.

Note that TreeSet, which implements SortedSet, guarantees that the elements will be traversed in the order specified by the `compareTo` method (section 22.9) of the elements, and LinkedHashSet guarantees that the elements will be traversed in insertion order, whereas HashSet provides no order guarantees. Similarly, a TreeMap guarantees traversal in key order, and LinkedHashMap guarantees traversal in key insertion order (`J K M L`), whereas HashMap provides no order guarantees.

```java
import java.util.*;

class CollectionAll {
  public static void main(String[] args) {
    List<String> list1 = new LinkedList<String>();
    list1.add("list"); list1.add("dup"); list1.add("x"); list1.add("dup");
    traverse(list1);                    // Must print: list dup x dup
    List<String> list2 = new ArrayList<String>();
    list2.add("list"); list2.add("dup"); list2.add("x"); list2.add("dup");
    traverse(list2);                    // Must print: list dup x dup
    Set<String> set1 = new HashSet<String>();
    set1.add("set"); set1.add("dup"); set1.add("x"); set1.add("dup");
    traverse(set1);                     // May print:  x dup set
    SortedSet<String> set2 = new TreeSet<String>();
    set2.add("set"); set2.add("dup"); set2.add("x"); set2.add("dup");
    traverse(set2);                     // Must print: dup set x
    LinkedHashSet<String> set3 = new LinkedHashSet<String>();
    set3.add("set"); set3.add("dup"); set3.add("x"); set3.add("dup");
    traverse(set3);                     // Must print: set dup x
    Map<String,String> m1 = new HashMap<String,String>();
    m1.put("map", "J"); m1.put("dup", "K"); m1.put("x", "M"); m1.put("dup", "L");
    traverse(m1.keySet());              // May print:  x dup map
    traverse(m1.values());             // May print:  M L J
    SortedMap<String,String> m2 = new TreeMap<String,String>();
    m2.put("map", "J"); m2.put("dup", "K"); m2.put("x", "M"); m2.put("dup", "L");
    traverse(m2.keySet());             // Must print: dup map x
    traverse(m2.values());             // Must print: L J M
    LinkedHashMap<String,String> m3 = new LinkedHashMap<String,String>();
    m3.put("map", "J"); m3.put("dup", "K"); m3.put("x", "M"); m3.put("dup", "L");
    traverse(m3.keySet());             // Must print: map dup x
    traverse(m3.values());             // Must print: J L M
  }

  static void traverse(Collection<String> coll) { ... }
}
```

22.1   Interface Collection<T>

The Collection<T> interface extends the Iterable<T> interface (section 22.7) and describes these methods:

- `boolean add(T o)` adds element o to the collection; returns `true` if the element was added, `false` if the collection disallows duplicates and contains an element equal to o already.

- `boolean addAll(Collection<? extends T> coll)` adds all elements of `coll` to the collection; returns `true` if any element was added.

- `void clear()` removes all elements from the collection.

- `boolean contains(T o)` returns `true` if any element of the collection equals o.

- `boolean containsAll(Collection<?> coll)` returns `true` if the collection has all `coll`'s elements.

- `boolean isEmpty()` returns `true` if the collection has no elements.

- `Iterator<T> iterator()` returns an iterator (section 22.7) over the elements of the collection.

- `boolean remove(Object o)` removes a single instance of element o from the collection; returns `true` if the collection contained such an element.

- `boolean removeAll(Collection<?> coll)` removes all those elements that are also in `coll`; returns `true` if any element was removed. After this operation, no element equals an element of `coll`.

- `default boolean removeIf(Predicate<E> p)` removes, in iteration order, those elements x for which `p.test(x)` is true; returns true if any element was removed.

- `boolean retainAll(Collection<?> coll)` retains only those elements that are also in `coll`; returns `true` if any element was removed. After this operation, every element equals some element of `coll`.

- `int size()` returns the number of elements in the collection.

- `default Stream<T> parallelStream()` returns a possibly parallel stream of this collection's elements.

- `default Stream<T> stream()` returns a sequential stream containing the elements of this collection.

- `Object[] toArray()` returns a new array containing all elements of the collection.

- `<T> T[] toArray(T[] a)` works like the preceding, but the returned array's element type is the same as the element type of the given array a. Moreover, the elements are returned in the given array a if `a.length >= size()`, otherwise in a newly created array.

The element type T must be a reference type, so values of primitive type such as int must be boxed (as Integer) when inserted and unboxed when retrieved; in Java this is done automatically (section 5.4).

A *view* of a collection co1 is another collection co2 that refers to the same underlying data structure. As a consequence, modifications to co1 immediately affect co2, and modifications to co2 immediately affect co1.

An *unmodifiable collection* does not admit modification: the operations add, clear, remove, set, and so on throw UnsupportedOperationException. The utility class Collections (section 22.11) provides static methods to create an unmodifiable view of a given collection.

A *synchronized collection* is thread-safe: several concurrent threads can safely access and modify it. For efficiency, the standard collection classes are not synchronized, and concurrent modification of a collection may make its internal state inconsistent. The utility class Collections (section 22.11) provides static methods to create a synchronized view of a given collection. All concurrent access to a collection should go through its synchronized view.

22.2 Interface List<T> and Its Implementations LinkedList<T> and ArrayList<T>

The List<T> interface extends the Collection<T> interface with operations for position-based access using indexes $0, 1, 2, \ldots$ and gives more precise specifications of some methods:

- `boolean add(T o)` adds element o at the end of the list. Returns true.

- `void add(int i, T o)` adds element o at position i, increasing the index of any element to the right by 1. Throws IndexOutOfBoundsException if `i<0` or `i>size()`.

- `boolean addAll(int i, Collection<? extends T> coll)` adds all elements of `coll` to the list, starting at position i; returns `true` if any element was added. Throws IndexOutOfBoundsException if `i<0` or `i>size()`.

- `boolean equals(Object o)` returns `true` if o is a List with equal elements in the same order.

- `T get(int i)` returns the element at index i; throws IndexOutOfBoundsException if `i<0` or `i>=size()`.

- `int hashCode()` returns the hash code of the list, which is a function of the hash codes of the elements and their order in the list.

- `int indexOf(Object o)` returns the least index i for which the element at position i equals o; returns -1 if the list does not contain such an element.

- `int lastIndexOf(Object o)` returns the greatest index i for which the element at position i equals o; returns -1 if the list does not contain such an element.

- `ListIterator<T> listIterator()` returns a bidirectional list iterator; see section 22.8.

- `T remove(int i)` removes the element at position i and returns it; or throws IndexOutOfBounds-Exception if `i<0` or `i>=size()`.

- `T set(int i, T o)` sets the element at position i to o and returns the element previously at position i; throws IndexOutOfBoundsException if `i<0` or `i>=size()`.

- `List<T> subList(int from, int to)` returns a list of the elements at positions `from..(to-1)`, as a view of the underlying list. Throws IndexOutOfBoundsException if `from<0` or `from>to` or `to>size()`.

The LinkedList<T> class implements all the operations described by the List interface and has the following constructors. The implementation is a doubly linked list, so elements can be accessed, added, and removed efficiently at either end of the list. It therefore provides additional methods for position-based get, add, and remove called `addFirst`, `addLast`, `getFirst`, `getLast`, `removeFirst`, and `removeLast`. The latter four throw NoSuchElementException if the list is empty.

- `LinkedList()` creates a new empty LinkedList<T>.

- `LinkedList(Collection<T> coll)` creates a new list containing the elements from `coll`'s iterator.

The ArrayList<T> class implements all the operations described by the List interface and has the following constructors. The implementation uses an underlying array (expanded as needed to hold the elements), which permits efficient position-based access anywhere in the list. Class ArrayList implements the RandomAccess interface just to indicate that element access by index is guaranteed to be fast, in contrast to LinkedList. The ArrayList class provides all the functionality provided originally (pre-Java 1.2) by the Vector class, which is a subclass of AbstractList and implements List and RandomAccess.

- `ArrayList()` creates a new empty ArrayList<T>.

- `ArrayList(Collection<T> coll)` creates a new list containing the elements from `coll`'s iterator.

22.3   Interface Set<T> and Its Implementations HashSet<T> and LinkedHashSet<T>

The Set<T> interface describes the same methods as the Collection<T> interface. The methods add and addAll must make sure that a set contains no duplicates: no two equal elements and at most one null element. Also, the methods equals and hashCode have more precise specifications for Set<T> objects:

- boolean equals(Object o) returns true if o is a Set with the same number of elements, and every element of o is also in this set.
- int hashCode() returns the hash code of the set: the sum of the hash codes of its non-null elements.

For Set arguments, addAll computes set union, containsAll computes set inclusion, removeAll computes set difference, and retainAll computes set intersection (example 152).

The HashSet<T> class implements the Set<T> interface and has the following constructors. Operations on a HashSet rely on the equals and hashCode methods of the element objects.

- HashSet() creates an empty set.
- HashSet(Collection<T> coll) creates a set containing the elements of coll, without duplicates.

The LinkedHashSet<T> class is a subclass of HashSet<T> and works the same way but additionally guarantees that its iterator traverses the elements in insertion order (rather than the unpredictable order provided by HashSet).

22.4   Interface SortedSet<T> and Implementation TreeSet<T>

The SortedSet<T> interface extends the Set<T> interface. Operations on a SortedSet<T> rely on the natural ordering of the elements defined by their compareTo method, or on an explicit Comparator<T> object provided when the set was created (section 22.9), as for TreeSet<T> below.

- Comparator<? super T> comparator() returns the Comparator associated with this sorted set, or null if it uses the natural ordering (section 22.9) of the elements.
- T first() returns the least element; throws NoSuchElementException if the set is empty.
- SortedSet<T> headSet(T to) returns the set of all elements strictly less than to. The resulting set is a view of the underlying set.
- T last() returns the greatest element; throws NoSuchElementException if the set is empty.
- SortedSet<T> subSet(T from, T to) returns the set of all elements greater than or equal to from and strictly less than to. The resulting set is a view of the underlying set.
- SortedSet<T> tailSet(T from) returns the set of all elements greater than or equal to from. The resulting set is a view of the underlying set.

The TreeSet<T> class implements the SortedSet<T> interface and has the following constructors. The implementation uses balanced binary trees, so all operations are guaranteed to be efficient.

- TreeSet() creates an empty set, ordering elements using their compareTo method.
- TreeSet(Collection<? extends T> coll) creates a set containing the elements of coll, without duplicates, ordering elements using their compareTo method.
- TreeSet(Comparator<? super T> cmp) creates an empty set, ordering elements using cmp.
- TreeSet(SortedSet<T> s) creates a set containing the elements of s, ordering elements as in s.

Example 134 Set Membership Test Using HashSet or Binary Search
Imagine that we want to exclude Java reserved names (chapter 2) from the concordance built in example 139, so we need a fast way to recognize such names. Method isKeyword1 uses a HashSet built from a 53-element array of Java keywords, whereas method isKeyword2 uses binary search in the sorted array. The HashSet is two to five times faster in this case.

```
class SetMembership {
  final static String[] keywordarray =
    { "abstract", "assert", "boolean", "break", "byte", ..., "while" };
  final static Set<String> keywords
    = new HashSet<String>(Arrays.asList(keywordarray));

  static boolean isKeyword1(String id)
  { return keywords.contains(id); }

  static boolean isKeyword2(String id)
  { return Arrays.binarySearch(keywordarray, id) >= 0; }
}
```

Example 135 Using a LinkedHashSet to Remove Duplicates While Maintaining Element Order
Method unique takes an array of strings and returns a new array with the same strings in the same order but without duplicates. For instance, the array might hold names of files to be recompiled in a particular order, but possibly with the same file appearing multiple times. Clearly the order should be maintained, but all occurrences except the first one should be removed. This is simply and efficiently done using a LinkedHash-Set<String>, whereas a HashSet<String> would return the file names in some arbitrary order.

The call toArray(new String[]) creates a new array with element type String, and copies the elements of uniqueFiles to that array; see section 22.1.

```
public static String[] unique(String[] filenames) {
  LinkedHashSet<String> uniqueFiles = new LinkedHashSet<String>();
  for (String filename : filenames)
    uniqueFiles.add(filename);
  return uniqueFiles.toArray(new String[0]);
}
```

Example 136 Using a TreeSet to Show a Range of File Names in Alphabetic Order
When file names are stored in a TreeSet, then one can efficiently extract a subrange of file names, and iteration over the set or a subrange will produce the file names in alphabetical (sorted) order. For instance, to extract all file names that begin with P or Q or R or S, one can compute filenames.subSet("P", "T"), the set of those strings greater than or equal to "P", and strictly less than "T".

```
SortedSet<String> filenames = new TreeSet<String>();
File cwd = new File(".");                 // Current working directory
for (File f : cwd.listFiles())
  filenames.add(f.getName());
for (String filename : filenames.subSet("P", "T"))
  System.out.println(filename);
```

22.5   Interface Map<K,V> and Implementation HashMap<K,V>

The Map<K,V> interface describes the following methods. A map can be considered a collection of entries, where an *entry* is a pair (k,v) of a key k of type K and a value v of type V. Both K and V must be reference types, so values of primitive type such as int must be boxed when inserted and unboxed when retrieved. In Java this is done automatically (section 5.4). A map can contain no two entries with the same key.

- void clear() removes all entries from this map.
- boolean containsKey(Object k) returns true if the map has an entry with key k.
- boolean containsValue(Object v) returns true if the map has an entry with value v.
- Set<Map.Entry<K,V>> entrySet() returns a set view of the map's entries; each entry has type Map.Entry<K,V> (see below).
- boolean equals(Object o) returns true if o is a Map with the same entry set.
- V get(Object k) returns the value v in the entry (k, v) with key k, if any; otherwise null.
- int hashCode() returns the hash code for the map, computed as the sum of the hash codes of the entries returned by entrySet().
- boolean isEmpty() returns true if this map contains no entries; that is, if size() is zero.
- Set<K> keySet() returns a set view of the keys in the map.
- V put(K k, V v) modifies the map so that it contains the entry (k, v); returns the value previously associated with key k, if any; else returns null.
- void putAll(Map<? extends K, ? extends V> map) copies all entries from map to this map.
- V remove(Object k) removes the entry for key k from the map, if any; returns the value previously associated with k, if any; else returns null.
- int size() returns the number of entries, which equals the number of keys, in the map.
- Collection<V> values() returns a collection view of the values in the map.

The Map.Entry<K,V> interface (example 142) describes operations on map entries:

- K getKey() returns the key in this entry.
- V getValue() returns the value in this entry.

The HashMap<K,V> class implements the Map<K,V> interface and has the following constructors. Operations on a HashMap rely on the equals and hashCode methods of the key objects.

- HashMap() creates an empty HashMap.
- HashMap(Map<? extends K, ? extends V> map) creates a HashMap<K,V> containing the same entries as map.

The LinkedHashMap<K,V> class is a subclass of HashMap<K,V> and works the same way but additionally guarantees that its iterator traverses the entries in key insertion order (rather than the unpredictable order provided by HashMap).

The IdentityHashMap<K,V> class implements Map<K,V> but compares keys using reference equality (==) instead of the equals method, and computes hash values using System.identityHashCode instead of hashCode.

Example 137 Storing the Result of a Database Query

This method executes a database query, using classes from the `java.sql` package. It returns the result of the query as an ArrayList with one element for each row in the result. Each row is stored as a HashMap, mapping a result field name to an object (e.g., an Integer or String) holding the value of that field in that row. This is a simple and useful way to separate the database query from the processing of the query result (but it may be too inefficient if the query result is very large). The row list returned by `getRows` could be printed by method `printNameAndMsg`.

```
static ArrayList<Map<String,Object>> getRows(Connection conn, String query)
  throws SQLException
{
  Statement stmt = conn.createStatement();
  ResultSet rset = stmt.executeQuery(query);
  ResultSetMetaData rsmd = rset.getMetaData();
  int columncount = rsmd.getColumnCount();
  ArrayList<Map<String,Object>> queryResult = new ArrayList<Map<String,Object>>();
  while (rset.next()) {
    Map<String,Object> row = new HashMap<String,Object>();
    for (int i=1; i<=columncount; i++)
      row.put(rsmd.getColumnName(i), rset.getObject(i));
    queryResult.add(row);
  }
  return queryResult;
}
static void printNameAndMsg(Collection<Map<String,Object>> coll) {
  for (Map<String,Object> row : coll)
    System.out.println(row.get("name") + ": " + row.get("msg"));
}
```

Example 138 From Weekday Name to Weekday Number Using a HashMap

Method `wdayno5` behaves the same as those in examples 72 and 80 but uses a HashMap to map a string to an integer instead of `if` statements or a `while` loop. A HashMap is often faster, especially when the number of strings is large. The HashMap is initialized once using a static initializer block (section 9.13) and should be private to prevent accidental modification. There is an implicit unboxing from Integer to `int` in `wdayno5`.

```
class C {
  private static final HashMap<String,Integer> wdayNumber = new HashMap<String,Integer>();
  static { // Static initializer block, executed once
    int wdayno = 0;
    String[] wdays =
      { "Monday", "Tuesday", "Wednesday", "Thursday", "Friday", "Saturday", "Sunday" };
    for (String wday : wdays)
      wdayNumber.put(wday, wdayno++);
  }
  public static int wdayno5(String wday) {
    Integer res = wdayNumber.get(wday);
    return res == null ? -1 : res;
  }
  ...
}
```

22.6   Interface SortedMap<K,V> and Implementation TreeMap<K,V>

The SortedMap<K,V> interface extends the Map<K,V> interface. Operations on a SortedMap rely on the natural ordering of the keys defined by their `compareTo` method or on an explicit Comparator<K> object provided when the map was created (section 22.9), as for TreeMap<K,V> below.

- `Comparator<? super K> comparator()` returns the Comparator associated with this sorted map, or `null` if it uses the natural ordering (section 22.9) of the keys.
- `K firstKey()` returns the least key in this sorted map; throws NoSuchElementException if the map is empty.
- `SortedMap<K,V> headMap(K to)` returns the sorted map of all entries whose keys are strictly less than `to`. The resulting map is a view of the underlying map.
- `K lastKey()` returns the greatest key in this sorted map; throws NoSuchElementException if the map is empty.
- `SortedMap<K,V> subMap(K from, K to)` returns the sorted map of all entries whose keys are greater than or equal to `from` and strictly less than `to`. The resulting map is a view of the underlying map.
- `SortedMap<K,V> tailMap(K from)` returns the sorted map of all entries whose keys are greater than or equal to `from`. The resulting map is a view of the underlying map.

The TreeMap<K,V> class implements the SortedMap<K,V> interface and has the following constructors. The implementation uses balanced ordered binary trees, so all operations are guaranteed to be efficient.

- `TreeMap()` creates an empty map, ordering entries using the `compareTo` method of the keys.
- `TreeMap(Map<? extends K, ? extends V>)` creates a map containing the entries of `map`, ordering entries using the `compareTo` method of the keys.
- `TreeMap(Comparator<? super K> cmp)` creates an empty map, ordering entries using `cmp` on the keys.
- `TreeMap(SortedMap<? extends K, ? extends V> s)` creates a map containing the entries of `s`, ordering entries as in `s`.

Example 139 Building a Concordance

This method reads words (alphanumeric tokens) from a text file and creates a concordance, which shows for each word the line numbers of its occurrences. The resulting concordance `index` is a SortedMap from String to SortedSet of Integer. Example 142 shows how to print the resulting concordance.

```
static SortedMap<String,SortedSet<Integer>> buildIndex(String filename)
  throws IOException
{
  Reader r = new BufferedReader(new FileReader(filename));
  StreamTokenizer stok = new StreamTokenizer(r);
  stok.quoteChar('"'); stok.ordinaryChars('!', '/');
  stok.nextToken();
  SortedMap<String,SortedSet<Integer>> index = new TreeMap<String,SortedSet<Integer>>();
  while (stok.ttype != StreamTokenizer.TT_EOF) {
    if (stok.ttype == StreamTokenizer.TT_WORD) {
      SortedSet<Integer> ts;
      if (index.containsKey(stok.sval))        // If word has a set, get it
        ts = index.get(stok.sval);
      else {
        ts = new TreeSet<Integer>();           // Otherwise create one
        index.put(stok.sval, ts);
      }
      ts.add(stok.lineno());
    }
    stok.nextToken();
  }
  return index;
}
```

Example 140 Obtaining a Submap

A date book is a sorted map whose keys are Time objects (example 145). Using `tailMap` we can extract that part of the date book that concerns times on or after 12:00:

```
SortedMap<Time,String> datebook = new TreeMap<Time,String>();
datebook.put(new Time(12, 30), "Lunch");
datebook.put(new Time(15, 30), "Afternoon coffee break");
datebook.put(new Time( 9,  0), "Lecture");
datebook.put(new Time(13, 15), "Board meeting");
SortedMap<Time,String> pm = datebook.tailMap(new Time(12, 0));
for (Map.Entry<Time,String> entry : pm.entrySet())
  System.out.println(entry.getKey() + " " + entry.getValue());
```

22.7   Going through a Collection: Interfaces Iterator<T> and Iterable<T>

The interfaces Iterator<T> and Iterable<T> provide a convenient way to go through the elements of a collection or the entries of a map. Namely, an Iterator<T> has methods `hasNext` and `next` to go through a sequence of elements, and an Iterable<T> has a method `iterator` that returns a new Iterator<T>.

The elements of an iterable are usually traversed using the enhanced `for` statement (section 12.5.2) as shown in examples 141 and 142, but one can also explicitly get an iterator from the iterable and then use that in a `while` or `for` loop, as shown in examples 79 and 82.

The Iterator<T> interface from package `java.util` describes the following methods:

- `default void forEachRemaining(Consumer<T> cons)` calls `cons.accept(x)` on each remaining element x, in iteration order.

- `boolean hasNext()` returns `true` if a call to `next()` will return a new element.

- `T next()` returns the next element and advances past that element, if any; throws NoSuchElementException if there is no next element.

- `void remove()` removes the last element returned by the iterator; throws IllegalStateException if no element has been returned by the iterator yet, or if the element has been removed already. If element removal is not supported, it throws UnsupportedOperationException.

There are primitive-type specialized versions PrimitiveIterator.Of{Double,Int,Long} of the interface Iterator<T> for efficiency; see section 23.3. Such primitive-type iterators are produced by method `iterator()` on the numeric streams {Double,Int,Long}Stream. The interfaces PrimitiveIterator.Of{Double,Int,Long} have Iterator<T>'s methods `forEachRemaining`, `hasNext`, `next`, and `remove`, as well as the following, obviously with {Int,Long} instead of Double for PrimitiveIterator.Of{Int,Long}:

- `default void forEachRemaining(DoubleConsumer cons)` calls `cons.accept(x)` on each remaining element x, in iteration order, passing x as a non-wrapped `double`.

- `double nextDouble()` returns the next element as a non-wrapped `double`.

The Iterable<T> interface from package `java.lang` has the following methods:

- `Iterator<T> iterator()` returns a new iterator for this iterable.

- `default void forEach(Consumer<T> cons)` calls `cons.accept(x)` on each collection element x, in iteration order.

All collections are directly iterable because the interface Collection<T> has superinterface Iterable<T> . The entries of a map can be iterated over because interface Map<K,V> describes a method `entrySet` that returns a Set<Map.Entry<K,V>>, which implements Iterable<Map.Entry<K,V>>.

An iterator obtained from a List will traverse the elements in the order of the list. An iterator obtained from SortedSet, or from the keys or values of a SortedMap, will traverse the elements in the order of the set elements or the map keys. An iterator obtained from a HashSet will traverse the elements in some unpredictable order.

When iterating over a collection or map, the underlying collection should not be modified except through the iterator's `remove` method. If it is modified in any other way, the result is unpredictable. In fact, the concrete classes ArrayList, LinkedList, HashMap, HashSet, TreeMap, and TreeSet produce fail-fast iterators: if the underlying collection is structurally modified (except by the iterator's `remove` method) after an iterator has been obtained, then a ConcurrentModificationException is thrown by the next call to `hasNext` or `next`.

Example 141 Iteration over an Iterable Collection
This method uses the enhanced `for` statement (section 12.5.2) to iterate over a collection `coll` and print its elements. The method is called in example 133. Examples 79 and 82 make explicit use of an iterator.

```
static void traverse(Collection<String> coll) {
  for (String elem : coll)
    System.out.print(elem + " ");
  System.out.println();
}
```

Example 142 Printing a Concordance Using Iterables
The map `index` is assumed to be a concordance as created in example 139. Method `printIndex` prints an alphabetical list of the words, and for each word, its line numbers. The foreach statements (section 12.5.2) create one iterator to go through the words, and for each word, a separate iterator to go through its line numbers.

```
static void printIndex(SortedMap<String,SortedSet<Integer>> index) {
  for (Map.Entry<String,SortedSet<Integer>> entry : index.entrySet()) {
    System.out.print(entry.getKey() + ": ");
    SortedSet<Integer> lineNoSet = entry.getValue();
    for (int lineno : lineNoSet)
      System.out.print(lineno + " ");
    System.out.println();
  }
}
```

Example 143 A Method Returning an Iterable
A call `fromTo(m,n)` returns an Iterable<Integer> that can produce an Iterator<Integer> that can produce the integers from m to n. Examples 78, 79, and 82 show some ways to use the iterable. It is created as an instance of a local class FromToIterable whose `iterator` method creates an instance of the local class FromToIterator. The same can be done using anonymous inner classes in the style of example 44, or much clearer and simpler, using a Java 8.0 lambda expression (section 11.13) and a stream (chapter 24) as shown last.

```
public static Iterable<Integer> fromTo(final int m, final int n) {
  class FromToIterator implements Iterator<Integer> {        // local class
    private int i = m;
    public boolean hasNext() { return i <= n; }
    public Integer next() {
      if (i <= n)
        return i++;
      else
        throw new NoSuchElementException();
    }
    public void remove() { throw new UnsupportedOperationException(); }
  }
  class FromToIterable implements Iterable<Integer> {        // local class
    public Iterator<Integer> iterator() { return new FromToIterator(); }
  }
  return new FromToIterable();
}
public static Iterable<Integer> fromToStream(final int m, final int n) {
  return () -> IntStream.rangeClosed(m, n).iterator();
}
```

22.8   Interface ListIterator<T>

The ListIterator<T> interface from package `java.util` extends interface Iterator<T> and permits insertion, update, and bidirectional traversal of an underlying list·

- void `add(T o)` inserts the element o just before the list cursor, that is, between the elements that would be returned by calls to `previous` and `next`. If at the head or end of the list, it inserts the element before the head or after the end. A subsequent call to `previous` will return the new element.

- boolean `hasPrevious()` returns true if a call to `previous()` would return an element.

- int `nextIndex()` returns the list index of the element that would be returned by a call to `next`.

- T `previous()` returns the element after the list cursor (if any) and moves the cursor one element closer to the head of the list. Throws NoSuchElementException if the cursor cannot be moved back.

- int `previousIndex()` returns the list index of the element that would be returned by a call to `previous`.

22.9   Equality, Hash Codes, and Comparison

The elements of a collection must have a sensible `equals` method. If the elements have a sensible `hashCode` method, they can be used as HashSet elements or HashMap keys. If they have a `compareTo` method as described by the `java.lang.Comparable` interface, they can be used as TreeSet elements or TreeMap keys.

All classes have default implementations of the `equals` and `hashCode` methods, inherited from class Object. Most classes should override them to provide sensible notions of equality and hash codes. If a class overrides either method, it should override also the other one, satisfying the requirements below.

The primitive type wrapper classes (section 5.4) and the String class all have sensible `equals`, `hashCode`, and `compareTo` methods, and so can be used as elements of collections and as keys in maps.

- boolean `equals(Object o)` determines the equality of two objects. It is used by ArrayList, LinkedList, HashSet, and HashMap. It should satisfy `o.equals(o)`; *not* `o.equals(null)`; if `o1.equals(o2)`, then also `o2.equals(o1)`; and if `o1.equals(o2)` and `o2.equals(o3)`, then also `o1.equals(o3)` for non-null o1, o2, and o3.

- int `hashCode()` returns the hash code of an object. It is used by HashSet and HashMap. It should satisfy that if `o1.equals(o2)`, then `o1.hashCode()==o2.hashCode()`.

The generic interface Comparable<T> from package `java.lang` describes a single method:

- int `compareTo(T o)` performs a three-way comparison of two objects: `o1.compareTo(o2)` is negative if o1 is less than o2, zero if o1 and o2 are equal, and positive if o1 is greater than o2.

  It is called the *natural ordering* of elements and is used, for instance, by TreeSet and TreeMap unless a Comparator was given when the set or map was created. It should satisfy that `o1.compareTo(o2)==0` whenever `o1.equals(o2)`.

Example 144 A Comparator for the Integer Class

```
class IntegerComparator implements Comparator<Integer> {
  public int compare(Integer v1, Integer v2) {
    return v1 < v2 ? -1 : v1 > v2 ? +1 : 0;
} }
```

Example 145 A Time Class Implementing Comparable<Time>
A Time object represents the time of day 00:00–23:59. The method call t1.compareTo(t2) returns a negative number if t1 is before t2, a positive number if t1 is after t2, and zero if they are the same time.

```
class Time implements Comparable<Time> {
  public final int hh, mm;           // 24-hour clock
  public Time(int hh, int mm) { this.hh = hh; this.mm = mm; }
  public int compareTo(Time t) {
    return hh != t.hh ? hh - t.hh : mm - t.mm;
  }
  public boolean equals(Object o) { ... }       // See below
  public int hashCode() { return 60 * hh + mm; }
}
```

Example 146 An equals Method for the Time Class
First, equals in example 145 should quickly deal with the frequent case of comparing an object to itself. Next, if o is null, or if the run-time class of this is different from the run-time class of o, the result must be false. Finally, if o is non-null and has the same run-time class as this, then compare the fields for equality.

It is a common mistake to use argument type Time instead of Object. But then the method will not be called (by the hashset implementation, for instance) because it does not override equals(Object).

```
public boolean equals(Object o) {                // Note: Object, not Time
  if (this == o)                                 // Fast and frequent case
    return true;
  if (o == null || this.getClass() != o.getClass()) // null or different classes
    return false;
  Time t = (Time)o;                              // Now, o instanceof Time
  return hh == t.hh && mm == t.mm;
}
```

Example 147 A Comparator for the String Class
The concordance in example 139 uses the built-in compareTo method of String, which orders all uppercase letters before all lowercase letters: "Create" before "add" before "create". The Comparator class below puts strings that differ only in case next to each other: "add" before "Create" before "create".

To use it in example 139, replace new TreeMap<String,SortedSet<Integer>>() in that example by new TreeMap<String,SortedSet<Integer>>(new IgnoreCaseComparator()).

It is often preferable to specify the ordering separately by a comparator rather than using the default comparer of a comparable class, especially if several different comparators may be relevant.

```
class IgnoreCaseComparator implements Comparator<String> {
  public int compare(String s1, String s2) {
    int res = s1.compareToIgnoreCase(s2);
    return res != 0 ? res : s1.compareTo(s2);
  }
}
```

22.10　The Comparator<T> Interface

Functional interface Comparator<T> from the `java.util` package has single abstract method `compare` and many methods useful in connection with collections and sorting of streams and arrays:

- `abstract int compare(T o1, T o2)` performs a three-way comparison of two objects: it is negative if o1 is less than o2, zero if o1 and o2 are equal, and positive if o1 is greater than o2. It can be used to define non-standard element orderings when creating TreeSets and TreeMaps (see example 147). It should satisfy that `compare(o1, o2)==0` whenever `o1.equals(o2)`.

- `static <T,U extends Comparable<U>> Comparator<T> comparing(Function<T,U> f)` returns a comparator that transforms given keys by `f` and compares the results by natural order, as in `f.apply(x).compareTo(f.apply(y))`

- `static <T,U> Comparator<T> comparing(Function<T,U> f, Comparator<U> cmp)` returns a comparator `(x, y) -> cmp.compare(f.apply(x), f.apply(y))` that transforms given keys by `f` and compares the results by `cmp`. Primitive-type specialized versions `comparing{Double,Int,Long}` take a first argument of type To{Double,Int,Long}Function<T> but no comparator argument.

- `boolean equals(Object otherComparator)` overrides `equals` from Object. A comparator can override it to specify when it is equivalent to a given `otherComparator`. That is, `cmp1.equals(cmp2)` may return true if for all objects o1 and o2, the sign of `cmp1(o1,o2)` is the same as that of `cmp2(o1,o2)`.

- `static <T extends Comparable<T>> Comparator<T> naturalOrder()` returns a natural order comparator, equivalent to `(x, y) -> x.compareTo(y)`.

- `static <T> Comparator<T> nullsFirst(Comparator<T> cmp)` returns a null-friendly comparator that is like `cmp` but orders `null` before any non-`null` value.

- `static <T> Comparator<T> nullsLast(Comparator<T> cmp)` returns a null-friendly comparator that is like `cmp` but orders `null` after any non-`null` value.

- `default Comparator<T> reversed()` returns a reverse ordering comparator, equivalent to `(x, y) -> compare(y,x)`.

- `static <T extends Comparable<T>> Comparator<T> reverseOrder()` returns a reverse natural order comparator, equivalent to `(x, y) -> y.compareTo(x)`.

- `default Comparator<T> thenComparing(Comparator<T> cmp)` returns a lexicographic-order comparator that first compares using `this.compare(x,y)`, then using `cmp.compare(x,y)`.

- `default <U extends Comparable<U>> Comparator<T> thenComparing(Function<T,U> f)` returns a lexicographic-order comparator that first compares using `this.compare(x,y)`, then using `f.apply(x).compareTo(f.apply(y))`.

- `default <U> Comparator<T> thenComparing(Function<T,U> f, Comparator<U> cmp)` returns a lexicographic-order comparator that first compares using `this.compare(x,y)`, then using `cmp.compare(f.apply(x), f.apply(y))`.

There are also primitive-type specialized methods `thenComparing{Double, Int, Long}` that take arguments of type To{Double,Int,Long}Function<T>.

Example 148 Comparators on Strings

An array of strings can be sorted in many other ways than the natural letter ordering, by passing a suitable comparator to sorting methods on a stream (or an array; see section 8.4):

```
String[] words = { "car", "ape", "act", ... };
Comparator<String> shortestThenLetters
  = Comparator.comparing(String::length)
  .thenComparing(Comparator.<String>naturalOrder());
Comparator<String> longestThenLetters
  = Comparator.comparing(String::length)
  .reversed()
  .thenComparing(Comparator.<String>naturalOrder());
// Stream sort by natural letter order:
Stream.of(words).sorted(Comparator.<String>naturalOrder()).forEach(System.out::println);
// Stream sort by reverse natural letter order:
Stream.of(words).sorted(Comparator.<String>naturalOrder()).forEach(System.out::println);
// Stream sort by word length:
Stream.of(words).sorted(Comparator.comparing(String::length)).forEach(System.out::println);
// Stream sort by increasing word length, then letters:
Stream.of(words).sorted(shortestThenLetters).forEach(System.out::println);
// Stream sort by decreasing word length, then letters:
Stream.of(words).sorted(longestThenLetters).forEach(System.out::println);
```

Example 149 Comparators for Sorting Records

Consider a simple class of Address records:

```
class Address {
  public final String street, postcode;
  public final int number;
  public Address(String street, int number, String postcode) { ... }
  public String toString() {
    return String.format("%s #%d in %s", street, number, postcode);
  }
}
```

Using static and default methods on the Comparator interface, one can easily sort a stream (or an array; see section 8.4) of addresses as one pleases:

```
// (1) Stream sort by street name:
Stream.of(addresses).sorted(cmpStreet).forEach(System.out::println);
// (2) Stream sort by street name, reversed:
Stream.of(addresses).sorted(cmpStreetReverse).forEach(System.out::println);
// (3) Stream sort lexicographically by street name and then house number:
Stream.of(addresses).sorted(cmpStreetThenNumber).forEach(System.out::println);
// (4) Array sort lexicographically by street name and house number:
Arrays.sort(addresses, cmpStreetThenNumber);
Stream.of(addresses).forEach(System.out::println);
```

22.11   The Utility Class Collections

Class java.util.Collections provides static utility methods. The methods binarySearch, max, min, and sort also have versions that take an extra Comparator<? super T> argument and use it to compare elements.

There are static methods similar to synchronizedList and unmodifiableList for creating a synchronized or unmodifiable view (section 22.1) of a Collection, Set, SortedSet, Map, or SortedMap.

- static <T extends Comparable<? super T>> int binarySearch(List<? extends T> lst, T k) returns an index i>=0 for which lst.get(i) is equal to k, if any; otherwise returns i<0 such that (-i-1) would be the proper position for k. This is fast for ArrayList but slow for LinkedList. The list lst must be sorted, as by sort(lst).

- static <T> void copy(List<? super T> dst, List<? extends T> src) adds all elements from src to dst, in order.

- static <T> Enumeration<T> enumeration(Collection<T> coll) returns an enumeration of coll.

- static <T> void fill(List<? super T> lst, T o) sets all elements of lst to o.

- static <T extends Comparable<? super T>> T max(Collection<? extends T> coll) returns the greatest element of coll. Throws NoSuchElementException if coll is empty.

- static <T extends Comparable<? super T>> min(Collection<? extends T> coll) returns the least element of coll. Throws NoSuchElementException if coll is empty.

- static <T> List<T> nCopies(int n, T o) returns an unmodifiable list with n copies of o.

- static <T> boolean replaceAll(List<T> lst, T o1, T o2) replaces all elements equal to o1 by o2 in lst; returns true if an element was replaced.

- static void reverse(List<?> lst) reverses the order of the elements in lst.

- static <T> Comparator<T> reverseOrder() returns a comparator that is the reverse of the natural ordering implemented by the compareTo method of elements or keys.

- static void rotate(List<?> lst, int d) rotates lst right by d positions, so -1 rotates left by one position. Rotates a sublist if applied to a sublist view (section 22.2).

- static void shuffle(List<?> lst) randomly permutes the elements of lst.

- static void shuffle(List<?> lst, Random rnd) randomly permutes the elements of lst using rnd to generate random numbers.

- static <T> Set<T> singleton(T o) returns an unmodifiable set containing only o.

- static <T> List<T> singletonList(T o) returns an unmodifiable list containing only o.

- static <K,V> Map<K,V> singletonMap(K k, V v) returns an unmodifiable map containing only the entry (k, v).

- static <T extends Comparable<? super T>> void sort(List<T> lst) sorts lst using merge-sort and the natural element ordering. This sorting algorithm is stable and is fast on all Lists.

- static void swap(List<?> lst, int i, int j) exchanges the list elements at positions i and j. It throws IndexOutOfBoundsException unless 0 <= i, j and i, j < lst.size().

- static List<T> synchronizedList(List<T> lst) returns a synchronized view of lst.

- static List<T> unmodifiableList(List<T> lst) returns an unmodifiable view of lst.

Example 150 Understanding the Type of the `Collections.binarySearch` Method

The generic method `binarySearch` has a type parameter T whose constraint involves a wildcard:

```
static <T extends Comparable<? super T>> int binarySearch(...)
```

The constraint says that type T must be a subtype of `Comparable<? super T>`. In other words, T or a supertype of T must have a `compareTo` method, and that method's argument type must be T or a supertype of T; in any case, that method can take a T object as argument.

For instance, assume that class Vehicle from example 130 implements Comparable<Vehicle>. Then the subclass Car also implements Comparable<Vehicle>, and so when T is Car, the unknown type that the wildcard (?) stands for could be Vehicle, satisfying the constraint on T.

Continuing with this scenario, consider the wildcard type in the `lst` parameter of `binarySearch`:

```
static ... int binarySearch(List<? extends T> lst, T k)
```

This means that `lst` may be any List whose element type is a subtype of T (which we assumed to be Car). For instance, that subtype could be Sedan from example 130. Taken together this means that method `binarySearch` can be applied to an argument `lst` of type List<Car> and an argument k of type Sedan, just because objects of their superclass Vehicle are comparable to themselves.

Note that if the signature of `binarySearch` were more straightforward and less permissive, such as,

```
static <T extends Comparable<T>> int binarySearch(List<T> lst, T k)
```

then one could not apply the method to arguments of type List<Car> and Sedan. However, it could still be applied to List<Vehicle> and Sedan, because Vehicle implements Comparable<Vehicle>, and Sedan is a subclass of Vehicle.

Example 151 Understanding the Type of the `Collections.copy` Method

The generic method `copy` uses two wildcards in its parameters:

```
static <T> void copy(List<? super T> dst, List<? extends T> src)
```

The parameter `dst` must be a List whose element type is a supertype of T, and the parameter `src` must be a List whose element type is a subtype of T. Thus even when T is Car, the `dst` could have type List<Vehicle> and the `src` could have type List<Sedan>, where the types Vehicle, Car, and Sedan are from example 130. Note that different occurrences of the wildcard (?) may stand for different unknown types, for instance, Vehicle and Sedan.

The use of two wildcards rather than one in the type for `copy` provides a pleasant symmetry, or lack of bias towards either `dst` or `src`. But in fact this signature, with only one wildcard, would permit basically the same method calls:

```
static <U> void copy(List<? super U> dst, List<U> src)
```

In this case the type argument U must be instantiated to the subtype of T used for the `src` parameter in the previous signature.

22.12   Choosing the Right Collection Class or Map Class

The proper choice of a collection or map class depends on the operations you need to perform on it, and how frequent those operations are. There is no universal best choice.

- LinkedList (section 22.2) or ArrayList (section 22.2 and example 137) should be used for collecting elements for sequential iteration in index order, allowing duplicates.

- HashSet (section 22.3 and example 134) and HashMap (section 22.5 and example 137) are good default choices when random access by element or key is needed, and sequential access in element or key order is not needed. LinkedHashSet (example 135) and LinkedHashMap additionally guarantee sequential access (using their iterators) in element or key insertion order.

- TreeSet (section 22.4 and examples 136 and 139) or TreeMap (section 22.6 and example 139) should be used for random access by element or key as well as for iteration in element or key order.

- LinkedList, not ArrayList, should be used for worklist algorithms (example 152), queues, double-ended queues, and stacks.

- ArrayList, not LinkedList, should be used for random access get(i) or set(i, o) by index.

- HashSet or HashMap should be used for sets or maps whose elements or keys are collections, because the collection classes implement useful hashCode methods (example 153).

- For maps whose keys are small non-negative integers, use ordinary arrays (chapter 8).

The running time, or *time complexity*, of an operation on a collection is usually given in O notation, as a function of the size n of the collection. Thus $O(1)$ means *constant time*, $O(\log n)$ means *logarithmic time* (time proportional to the logarithm of n), and $O(n)$ means *linear time* (time proportional to n). For accessing, adding, or removing an element, these roughly correspond to *very fast*, *fast*, and *slow*.

In the following table, n is the number of elements in the collection, i is an integer index, and d is the distance from an index i to the nearest end of a list, that is, $\min(i, n-i)$. Thus adding or removing an element of a LinkedList is fast near both ends of the list, where d is small, but for an ArrayList, it is fast only near the back end, where $n-i$ is small. The subscript a indicates *amortized complexity*: over a long sequence of operations, the average time per operation is $O(1)$, although any single operation could take time $O(n)$.

Operation	LinkedList	ArrayList	HashSet LinkedHashSet	TreeSet	HashMap LinkedHashMap	TreeMap
add(o) (last)	$O(1)$	$O(1)_a$	$O(1)_a$	$O(\log n)$		
add(i,o)	$O(d)$	$O(n-i)_a$				
addFirst(o)	$O(1)$					
put(k,v)					$O(1)_a$	$O(\log n)$
remove(o)	$O(n)$	$O(n)$	$O(1)$	$O(\log n)$	$O(1)$	$O(\log n)$
remove(i)	$O(d)$	$O(n-i)$				
removeFirst()	$O(1)$					
contains(o)	$O(n)$	$O(n)$	$O(1)$	$O(\log n)$		
containsKey(o)					$O(1)$	$O(\log n)$
containsValue(o)					$O(n)$	$O(n)$
indexOf(o)	$O(n)$	$O(n)$				
get(i)	$O(d)$	$O(1)$				
set(i,o)	$O(d)$	$O(1)$				
get(o)					$O(1)$	$O(\log n)$

Example 152 A Worklist Algorithm

Some algorithms use a *worklist*, containing subproblems still to be solved. For instance, given a set ss of sets of Integers, compute its intersection closure: the least set tt such that ss is a subset of tt and such that for any two sets s and t in tt, their intersection s ∩ t is also in tt. For instance, if ss is $\{\{2,3\},\{1,3\},\{1,2\}\}$, then tt is $\{\{2,3\},\{1,3\},\{1,2\},\{3\},\{2\},\{1\},\{\}\}$.

The set tt may be computed by putting all elements of ss in a worklist, then repeatedly selecting an element s from the worklist, adding it to tt, and for every set t already in tt, adding the intersection of s and t to the worklist if not already in tt. When the worklist is empty, tt is intersection-closed.

The epsilon closure of a state of a nondeterministic finite automaton (NFA) may be computed using the same approach; see the full program text underlying example 153.

```
static <T> Set<Set<T>> intersectionClose(Set<Set<T>> ss) {
  LinkedList<Set<T>> worklist = new LinkedList<Set<T>>(ss);
  Set<Set<T>> tt = new HashSet<Set<T>>();
  while (!worklist.isEmpty()) {
    Set<T> s = worklist.removeLast();
    for (Set<T> t : tt) {
      Set<T> ts = new TreeSet<T>(t);
      ts.retainAll(s);                  // ts is the intersection of t and s
      if (!tt.contains(ts))
        worklist.add(ts);
    }
    tt.add(s);
  }
  return tt;
}
```

Example 153 Using Sets as Keys in a HashMap

The standard algorithm for turning an NFA into a deterministic finite automaton (DFA) creates composite automaton states that are sets of integers. It is preferable to replace such composite states by simple integers. Method mkRenamer takes as argument a collection of composite states and returns a renamer, which is a map from composite states (Set of Integer) to simple states (Integer).

Method rename takes as arguments a renamer and a transition (which is a Map from Set of Integer to Map from String to Set of Integer) and performs the actual renaming, returning a renamed transition. The method is included here to show that type instances can be arbitrarily complex.

```
static Map<Set<Integer>,Integer> mkRenamer(Collection<Set<Integer>> states) {
  Map<Set<Integer>,Integer> renamer = new HashMap<Set<Integer>,Integer>();
  for (Set<Integer> k : states)
    renamer.put(k, renamer.size());
  return renamer;
}

static Map<Integer,Map<String,Integer>>
  rename(Map<Set<Integer>,Integer> renamer,
         Map<Set<Integer>,Map<String,Set<Integer>>> trans)
{
  Map<Integer,Map<String,Integer>> newtrans = new HashMap<Integer,Map<String,Integer>>();
  ...
  return newtrans;
}
```

23   Functional Interfaces (Java 8.0)

Java supports functional programming through functional interfaces (section 23.2), lambda expressions (section 11.13), and method reference expressions (section 11.14).

23.1   Functional Programming

Functional programming has many uses, especially in connection with streams (chapter 24) and parallel processing of arrays (section 8.4). It goes back to Lisp (1960), and more recent functional languages include ML, Scheme, OCaml, Haskell, F#, and Scala. Some characteristics of functional programming are as follows:

- Functional programming uses immutable data structures (in which all fields are final and refer only to immutable data) instead of objects with mutable state. In example 154, the call `list1.insert(1, 12)` produces a new list instead of updating the existing `list1`. This may seem to cause excessive allocation of data, but much less than one might think because immutability permits sharing between new and old data. A major advantage is that immutable data structures are automatically thread-safe and require no synchronization when used from multiple threads. See example 176.

- Functional programming performs most iteration using (recursive) function calls instead of `for` loops, `while` loops, and the like. This would lead to deep method call stacks if the implementations did not optimize tail calls, that is, calls performed as the last action of the calling function. Since the Java implementation does not optimize tail calls, it is often better to use loops instead of recursion. In example 154, method `getNodeRecursive` might be replaced by a loop.

- Functional programming often uses higher-order functions, that is, functions that take as argument parameters of function type or return results of function type. In the former case, the higher-order function may embody a general behavior such as data structure traversal, and its function-type argument may represent the specific action to be taken on each data element. Higher-order function `map` in example 154 takes a function argument f and applies it to every list element. Higher-order function `less` in example 158 returns a function that can convert numbers less than `limit*limit` into English numerals.

- Some functional programming languages (including ML, Haskell, F#, and Scala) use pattern matching to make choices, instead of nested `if` and `switch` statements; this achieves great clarity and some guarantee against missed cases. Java does not support pattern matching.

Many operations on streams (chapter 24) and parallel operations on arrays (section 8.4) require their function arguments to be side-effect free for the operations to make sense. A function f is *side-effect free*, or *pure*, if it does not modify or rely on any modifiable state; in particular, two calls `f.apply(v1)` and `f.apply(v2)` where v1 and v2 are equal values must produce the same result. But note that in an object-oriented setting, where object fields are mutable by default, it is not obvious what "equal values" and "same result" really means. Also, the Java compiler cannot check that a function has no side effects, so the correctness of functional and parallel programming must rely on care and conventions.

Some operations, such as `reduce` on streams and `parallelPrefix` on arrays, further require their BinaryOperator arguments to be associative. A binary operator op is *associative* if for arguments x, y, and z, it holds that `op.apply(op.apply(x,y),z)` equals `op.apply(x,op.apply(y,z))`. Writing `op.apply(x,y)` using infix notation as $x \otimes y$, it means that $(x \otimes y) \otimes z$ must equal $x \otimes (y \otimes z)$. Typical associative operators are numeric addition (+) and multiplication (*), `max`, `min`, string concatenation (+), logical conjunction (&&) and disjunction (||), bitwise "and" (&), bitwise "or" (|), bitwise "xor" (^), set union, and set intersection. Non-associative operators include numeric subtraction (-), division (/) and average, and set difference.

Example 154 Functional Programming with Immutable Lists
Class FunList<T> represents immutable lists of T values, using immutable Node<T> objects. All operations produce a new list instead of updating existing ones, so any number of operations on the same list could proceed concurrently without synchronization. A new list may share nodes with existing ones; list1–list4 all share the three node objects holding 9, 13, and 0. This is harmless because nodes are immutable.

Thanks to recursion and immutability, the methods are simple. Thus insert(i, item, xs) says: If i==0, put item in a new node and let its tail be node list xs; otherwise put the first element of xs in a new node, and let its tail be the result of inserting item at position i-1 in the rest of list xs. Similarly map(f, xs) says: If xs is the empty list (null), the result is an empty list; otherwise create a node to hold the result of applying f to the first element of xs, and let its tail be the result of mapping f over the rest of xs.

```
class FunList<T> {
  final Node<T> first;
  protected static class Node<U> {
    public final U item;
    public final Node<U> next;
    public Node(U item, Node<U> next) { this.item = item; this.next = next; }
  }
  public FunList(Node<T> xs) { this.first = xs; }
  public int getCount() { ... }
  public T get(int i) { return getNodeRecursive(i, first).item; }
  protected static <T> Node<T> getNodeRecursive(int i, Node<T> xs) {    // Could use loop instead
    return i == 0 ? xs : getNodeRecursive(i-1, xs.next);
  }
  public static <T> FunList<T> cons(T item, FunList<T> list) { return list.insert(0, item);  }
  public FunList<T> insert(int i, T item) { return new FunList<T>(insert(i, item, this.first)); }
  protected static <T> Node<T> insert(int i, T item, Node<T> xs) {
    return i == 0 ? new Node<T>(item, xs) : new Node<T>(xs.item, insert(i-1, item, xs.next));
  }
  public FunList<T> removeAt(int i) { return new FunList<T>(removeAt(i, this.first)); }
  protected static <T> Node<T> removeAt(int i, Node<T> xs) {
    return i == 0 ? xs.next : new Node<T>(xs.item, removeAt(i-1, xs.next));
  }
  public FunList<T> reverse() { ... }
  public FunList<T> append(FunList<T> ys) { ... }
  public <U> FunList<U> map(Function<T,U> f) { return new FunList<U>(map(f, first)); }
  protected static <T,U> Node<U> map(Function<T,U> f, Node<T> xs) {
    return xs == null ? null : new Node<U>(f.apply(xs.item), map(f, xs.next));
  }
  public <U> U reduce(U x0, BiFunction<U,T,U> op) { ... }
}
...
FunList<Integer> empty = new FunList<>(null),
  list1 = cons(9, cons(13, cons(0, empty))),          // 9 13 0
  list2 = cons(7, list1),                             // 7 9 13 0
  list3 = cons(8, list1),                             // 8 9 13 0
  list4 = list1.insert(1, 12),                        // 9 12 13 0
  list5 = list2.removeAt(3),                          // 7 9 13
  list6 = list5.reverse(),                            // 13 9 7
  list7 = list5.append(list5);                        // 7 9 13 7 9 13
FunList<Double> list8 = list5.map(i -> 2.5 * i);      // 17.5 22.5 32.5
double sum = list8.reduce(0.0, (res, item) -> res + item);  // 72.5
```

23.2 Generic Functional Interfaces

A *functional interface* is an interface that has a single abstract method, such as `apply`, `test`, or `accept`, and possibly some default and static methods. A concrete instance of a functional interface represents a function, namely the implementation of the interface's single abstract method. Functions are especially useful in connection with stream pipelines (chapter 24) and parallel processing of arrays (section 8.4).

The generic functional interfaces from package `java.util.function` are listed in the table opposite, along with the corresponding function type notation, as used in many other languages. The arrow (->) indicates a function type, and the star (*) indicates a product or pair type. More precisely, `T -> R` is the type of a function that takes arguments of type `T` and returns results of type `R`, and `T * U` is the type of a pair of a value of type `T` and a value of type `U`. These can be combined, so `T * U -> R` is the type of a function that takes two arguments of type `T` and `U` and returns a result of type `R`.

Conceptually, the most important functional interface is Function<T,R>, the type of a function that takes an argument of type T and returns a result of type R, corresponding to the function type `T -> R`. The interface's single abstract method is `R apply(T x)`.

Thus Function<String,Integer> is the type of a function that takes a String argument and returns an Integer result. A value of such a function type can be produced in numerous ways, usually from a lambda expression (section 11.13) or a method reference expression (section 11.14), as shown in example 155.

There are other functional interfaces, such as Comparator<T> from package `java.util`; see section 22.10.

23.3 Primitive-Type Specialized Functional Interfaces

The table's list of functional interfaces is very long, but many of them are just *primitive-type specialized* versions of the more generic functional interfaces Function<T,R> and so on, in particular for R and T being Double, Integer, and Long. The primitive-type specialized interfaces exist purely for efficiency reasons. The problem is that Java's generic types, such as Function<T,R>, can take only reference type arguments such as Integer and Long, not primitive type arguments such as `int` and `long`; see section 21.11. But calling a function represented by an instance of Function<Integer,Long> means calling the method `Long apply(Integer x)`, and this involves checking and unwrapping the Integer argument and subsequent wrapping of the `long` result as a Long object, which is inefficient. Using instead the `long applyAsLong(int x)` method on an instance of the primitive-type specialized interface IntToLongFunction avoids this run-time overhead. But it also makes the list of functional interfaces bulky and daunting to look at; and it could be even worse, had the Java class library included versions for Byte, Character, Float, and Short, which it sensibly does not.

Interface	Sec.	Function Type	Single Abstract Method Signature
		One-Argument Functions and Predicates	
Function<T,R>	23.5	`T -> R`	`R apply(T)`
UnaryOperator<T>	23.6	`T -> T`	`T apply(T)`
Predicate<T>	23.7	`T -> boolean`	`boolean test(T)`
Consumer<T>	23.8	`T -> void`	`void accept(T)`
Supplier<T>	23.9	`void -> T`	`T get()`
Runnable		`void -> void`	`void run()`
		Two-Argument Functions and Predicates	
BiFunction<T,U,R>	23.10	`T * U -> R`	`R apply(T, U)`
BinaryOperator<T>	23.11	`T * T -> T`	`T apply(T, T)`
BiPredicate<T,U>	23.7	`T * U -> boolean`	`boolean test(T, U)`
BiConsumer<T,U>	23.8	`T * U -> void`	`void accept(T, U)`
		Primitive-Type Specialized Versions of the Generic Functional Interfaces	
DoubleToIntFunction	23.5	`double -> int`	`int applyAsInt(double)`
DoubleToLongFunction	23.5	`double -> long`	`long applyAsLong(double)`
IntToDoubleFunction	23.5	`int -> double`	`double applyAsDouble(int)`
IntToLongFunction	23.5	`int -> long`	`long applyAsLong(int)`
LongToDoubleFunction	23.5	`long -> double`	`double applyAsDouble(long)`
LongToIntFunction	23.5	`long -> int`	`int applyAsInt(long)`
DoubleFunction<R>	23.5	`double -> R`	`R apply(double)`
IntFunction<R>	23.5	`int -> R`	`R apply(int)`
LongFunction<R>	23.5	`long -> R`	`R apply(long)`
ToDoubleFunction<T>	23.5	`T -> double`	`double applyAsDouble(T)`
ToIntFunction<T>	23.5	`T -> int`	`int applyAsInt(T)`
ToLongFunction<T>	23.5	`T -> long`	`long applyAsLong(T)`
ToDoubleBiFunction<T,U>	23.10	`T * U -> double`	`double applyAsDouble(T, U)`
ToIntBiFunction<T,U>	23.10	`T * U -> int`	`int applyAsInt(T, U)`
ToLongBiFunction<T,U>	23.10	`T * U -> long`	`long applyAsLong(T, U)`
DoubleUnaryOperator	23.6	`double -> double`	`double applyAsDouble(double)`
IntUnaryOperator	23.6	`int -> int`	`int applyAsInt(int)`
LongUnaryOperator	23.6	`long -> long`	`long applyAsLong(long)`
DoubleBinaryOperator	23.11	`double * double -> double`	`double applyAsDouble(double, double)`
IntBinaryOperator	23.11	`int * int -> int`	`int applyAsInt(int, int)`
LongBinaryOperator	23.11	`long * long -> long`	`long applyAsLong(long, long)`
DoublePredicate	23.7	`double -> boolean`	`boolean test(double)`
IntPredicate	23.7	`int -> boolean`	`boolean test(int)`
LongPredicate	23.7	`long -> boolean`	`boolean test(long)`
DoubleConsumer	23.8	`double -> void`	`void accept(double)`
IntConsumer	23.8	`int -> void`	`void accept(int)`
LongConsumer	23.8	`long -> void`	`void accept(long)`
ObjDoubleConsumer<T>	23.8	`T * double -> void`	`void accept(T, double)`
ObjIntConsumer<T>	23.8	`T * int -> void`	`void accept(T, int)`
ObjLongConsumer<T>	23.8	`T * long -> void`	`void accept(T, long)`
BooleanSupplier	23.9	`void -> boolean`	`boolean getAsBoolean()`
DoubleSupplier	23.9	`void -> double`	`double getAsDouble()`
IntSupplier	23.9	`void -> int`	`int getAsInt()`
LongSupplier	23.9	`void -> long`	`long getAsLong()`

23.4   Covariance and Contravariance in Functional Interfaces

In general, whenever a method `void m(Function<T,R> f)` expects an argument f whose type is a functional interface such as `Function<T,R>`, it is acceptable to provide an actual function f that accepts an argument of a supertype of T and produces a result of a subtype of R. One says that function types are *contravariant* in their argument types and *covariant* in their result type. In Java's type system this flexibility is expressed using wildcard type arguments; see section 21.9 and example 157. Thus the more flexible signature of method m would be described like this: `void m(Function<? super T, ? extends R> f)`.

However, this makes the descriptions of methods that take functional arguments considerably more verbose and harder to read. Hence in most cases, this book uses the simple form `Function<T,R>` rather than the more general `Function<? super T, ? extends R>`; we do this in particular for the stream methods in section 24.3. Similarly, we write `Comparator<T>` instead of `Comparator<? super T>`, write `Predicate<T>` instead of `Predicate<? super T>`, and so on. Respecting the method signatures as shown will always work, but the actual Java library implementation is more accommodating.

23.5   Interface Function<T,R>

The functional interface Function<T,R> describes one-argument functions of type `T -> R`, that is, those that take an argument of type T and return a result of type R. It has a single abstract method `apply` and some default and static methods:

- abstract `R apply(T x)` is the function represented by an object implementing the interface.
- default `Function<T,V> andThen(Function<R,V> after)` returns a function that applies function after to the result of this function, that is, `(T x) -> after.apply(this.apply(x))`.
- default `Function<V,R> compose(Function<V,T> before)` returns a function that applies this function to the result of function before, that is, `(V x) -> this.apply(before.apply(x))`.
- static `Function<T,T> identity()` returns the identity function `(T x) -> x` on type T.

The primitive-type specialized interfaces {Double,Long,Int}Function and To{Double,Long,Int}Function and {Double,Long,Int}To{Double,Long,Int}Function have only the abstract methods shown on page 125; not the default methods `andThen` and `compose` because that would require many overloads; see example 162.

23.6   Interface UnaryOperator<T>

The functional interface UnaryOperator<T> extends Function<T,T> and describes one-argument functions of type `T -> T` that take an argument of type T and return a result of the same type T. It has the single abstract method `apply`, the default methods `andThen` and `compose` described by Function<T,T>, and a static method:

- abstract `T apply(T x)` is the unary operator represented by an implementation of the interface.
- default `Function<T,V> andThen(Function<T,V> after)` returns a function that applies function after to the result of this unary operator, that is, `x -> after.apply(this.apply(x))`.
- default `Function<V,T> compose(Function<V,T> before)` returns a function that applies this unary operator to the result of function before, that is, `x -> this.apply(before.apply(x))`.
- static `UnaryOperator<T> identity()` returns the identity unary operator `x -> x` on type T.

There are primitive-type specialized interfaces {Double,Int,Long}UnaryOperator with the same default and static methods and with single abstract methods named `applyAs{Double, Int, Long}`; see page 125.

Example 155 Some Ways to Obtain a Function<String,Integer>

A value of type Function<String,Integer>, that is, a function from String to Integer, can be obtained in many ways, as shown by the definitions of fsi1–fsi7 below, where fsi1–fsi4 parse a string as an integer, and fsi5–fsi7 return a string's length. The lambda (section 11.13) and method reference (section 11.14) notation are more compact than the anonymous inner class notation used for fsi7, but the resulting function values are invoked the same way, as fsi1.apply("4711"). Compile-time type inference finds the correct Integer constructor overload in the fsi4 case and the correct length method in the fsi5 case.

```
Function<String,Integer>
  fsi1 = s -> Integer.parseInt(s),          // lambda with parameter s
  fsi2 = (String s) -> Integer.parseInt(s), // same, with explicit parameter type
  fsi3 = Integer::parseInt,                  // reference to static method Integer.parseInt
  fsi4 = Integer::new,                       // reference to constructor Integer(String)
  fsi5 = s -> s.length(),                    // lambda with parameter s
  fsi6 = String::length,                     // reference to instance method s.length()
  fsi7 = new Function<String,Integer>() {    // anonymous inner class (Java 1.1)
         public Integer apply(String s) {
           return s.length();
         }};
```

Example 156 Multiple Traversals of a Stream

With function interfaces one can encapsulate general behaviors in methods that take function-type arguments in a type-safe manner. For instance, method traverse1 below encapsulates the notion of transforming a stream xs with element type T, first by a function f of type T->U and then by a function g of type U->V; the result is a stream with element type V.

Function traverse2 computes exactly the same result but makes only one "traversal" of the stream, applying the composed function f.andThen(g) to each element. Java's stream implementation may in fact automatically fuse the double traversal into a single one.

```
public static <T,U,V> Stream<V> traverse1(Stream<T> xs, Function<T,U> f, Function<U,V> g) {
  return xs.map(f).map(g);
}
public static <T,U,V> Stream<V> traverse2(Stream<T> xs, Function<T,U> f, Function<U,V> g) {
  return xs.map(f.andThen(g));
}
```

Example 157 Wildcard Types for a More Accommodating Method Signature

Method traverse2 from example 156 cannot be applied to a stream xs of type Stream<Long>, a function f of type Function<Number,String>, and a function g of type Function<Object,Integer> because the types do not match. Type Number is different from Long, and type Object is different from String. However, since Number is a supertype of Long, and Object is a supertype of String, the function composition should actually work. Using wildcard types (section 21.9) we can safely give traverse3 below a more accommodating signature, and then the application traverse3(xs, f, g) works:

```
public static <T,U,V> Stream<V> traverse3(Stream<T> xs, Function<? super T, ? extends U> f,
                                                         Function<? super U, ? extends V> g) {
  return xs.map(f.andThen(g));
}
// Stream<Double> res = traverse2(xs, f, g);          // Type error!
Stream<Integer> res = traverse3(xs, f, g);
```

23.7   Interfaces Predicate<T> and BiPredicate<T,U>

The functional interface Predicate<T> describes one-argument predicates of type `T -> boolean`, that is, functions that take an argument of type T and return a truth value. It has the single abstract method `test` and some default and static methods:

- `abstract boolean test(T x)` is the predicate represented by an object implementing the interface.
- `default Predicate<T> and(Predicate<T> p)` returns a predicate that is a short-circuiting logical conjunction ("and") of this predicate and p, that is, `x -> this.test(x) && p.test(x)`.
- `static <T> Predicate<T> isEqual(Object y)` returns a predicate that tests whether its argument equals y, that is, `x -> Objects.equals(y,x)`.
- `default Predicate<T> negate()` returns a predicate that represents the logical negation ("not") of this predicate, that is, `x -> !this.test(x)`.
- `default Predicate<T> or(Predicate<T> other)` returns a predicate that is a short-circuiting logical disjunction ("or") of this predicate and p, that is, `x -> this.test(x) || p.test(x)`.

The primitive-type specialized interfaces {Double,Int,Long}Predicate have the same methods except `isEqual`.

The functional interface BiPredicate<T,U> describes two-argument predicates and has a single abstract method (and also the default methods but not the `isEqual` method of Predicate<T>):

- `abstract boolean test(T x, U y)` is the predicate represented by the interface implementation.

23.8   Interfaces Consumer<T> and BiConsumer<T,U>

The functional interface Consumer<T> describes one-argument consumers of type `T -> void`, that is, functions that take an argument of type T and return nothing. It has a single abstract method and a default method:

- `abstract void accept(T x)` is the consumer represented by an object implementing the interface.
- `default Consumer<T> andThen(Consumer<T> after)` returns a Consumer<T> that performs `this.accept(x)` followed by `after.accept(x)`.

The primitive-type specialized interfaces {Double,Int,Long}Consumer have corresponding default methods.

The functional interface BiConsumer<T,U> describes two-argument consumers and has a single abstract method (and also a corresponding default method `andThen`):

- `abstract void accept(T x, U y)` is the consumer represented by the interface implementation.

The primitive-type specialized interfaces Obj{Double,Int,Long}Consumer have corresponding abstract methods; see page 125.

23.9   Interface Supplier<T>

The functional interface Supplier<T> describes one-argument suppliers of type `void -> T`, that is, functions that take no arguments and produce a result of type T. It has the single abstract method `get`:

- `abstract T get()` is the supplier represented by an implementation of the interface.

The primitive-type specialized interfaces {Boolean,Double,Int,Long}Supplier have corresponding abstract methods, named getAs{Boolean,Double,Int,Long}; see page 125.

Example 158 Converting Numbers to English Numerals

The conversion of a long integer to an English numeral, such as converting 2,147,483,647 to "two billion one hundred forty-seven million four hundred eighty-three thousand six hundred forty-seven", follows a simple pattern, captured by method `less` below. Method `less` returns a function (n -> ...) of type LongFunction<String> and is called four times to define functions `less1K`, ..., `less1G`, where the latter handles numbers in the range $\pm 10^{12}$ and is called by method `toEnglish`. To extend the range to $\pm 10^{15}$, or 1,000 trillion, simply define an appropriate fifth function `less1T` using `less` and `less1G`, and call `less1T` from `toEnglish`.

```
private static final String[] ones = { "", "one", "two", ..., "nineteen" },
                              tens = { "twenty", "thirty", ..., "ninety" };
private static String after(String d, String s) { return s.equals("") ? "" : d + s; }
private static String less100(long n) {
  return n<20 ? ones[(int)n] : tens[(int)n/10-2] + after("-", ones[(int)n%10]);
}
private static LongFunction<String> less(long limit, String unit, LongFunction<String> conv) {
  return n -> n<limit ? conv.apply(n)
                      : conv.apply(n/limit) + " " + unit + after(" ", conv.apply(n%limit));
}
private static final LongFunction<String>
  less1K = less(          100, "hundred",  Numerals::less100),
  less1M = less(        1_000, "thousand", less1K),
  less1B = less(    1_000_000, "million",  less1M),
  less1G = less(1_000_000_000, "billion",  less1B);
public static String toEnglish(long n) {
  return n==0 ? "zero" : n<0 ? "minus " + less1G.apply(-n) : less1G.apply(n);
}
```

Example 159 Consumer Arguments

The `forEach` method on Stream<T> takes as argument a Consumer<T> and applies it to each element of the stream. To print some strings we use method reference `System.out::println` as a Consumer<String>:

```
Stream<String> ss = Stream.of("Hoover", "Roosevelt", "Truman", "Eisenhower", "Kennedy");
ss.forEach(System.out::println);
```

Example 160 Using a Supplier to Generate Infinite Streams of Natural Numbers or Fibonacci Numbers

The stream `nats` of natural numbers $0, 1, \ldots$ may be produced functionally as in example 165. Or use `generate` with an IntSupplier whose state `next` is held inside the anonymous inner class, as in `nats2` below. Or the IntSupplier may be a lambda expression () -> next[0]++ whose state is in next[0] as in `nats3`:

```
IntStream nats2 = IntStream.generate(new IntSupplier() {
    private int next = 0;
    public int getAsInt() { return next++; }
  });
final int[] next = { 0 };                      // next is final, its element mutable by the lambda
IntStream nats3 = IntStream.generate(() -> next[0]++);
```

The stateful `generate` approach is particularly useful when the next element depends not just on the preceding element, as in the Fibonacci number sequence. Here the lambda expression is a Supplier<BigInteger>:

```
final BigInteger[] fib = { BigInteger.ZERO, BigInteger.ONE };  // fib final, elements mutable
Stream<BigInteger> fibonaccis =
  Stream.generate(() -> { BigInteger f1=fib[1]; fib[1]=fib[0].add(fib[1]); return fib[0]=f1; });
```

23.10   Interface BiFunction<T,U,R>

The functional interface BiFunction<T,U,R> describes two-argument functions of type T * U -> R, that is, those that take two arguments of type T and U and return a result of type R. It has a single abstract method apply and a default method:

- abstract R apply(T x, U y) is the function represented by an object implementing the interface.

- default BiFunction<T,U,V> andThen(Function<R,V> after) returns a function that applies function after to the result of this function, that is, (x, y) -> after.apply(this.apply(x,y)).

The primitive-type specialized interfaces To{Double,Long,Int}BiFunction have only their single abstract methods, named applyAs{Double,Int,Long}; see page 125.

23.11   Interface BinaryOperator<T>

The functional interface BinaryOperator<T> extends the interface BiFunction<T,T,T> and describes two-argument functions of type T * T -> T, that is, those that take two arguments of type T and return a result of the same type T. It has the single abstract method apply and the default method andThen described by BiFunction<T,T,T>, as well as two static methods:

- abstract T apply(T x, T y) is the binary operator represented by an implementation of the interface.

- default BiFunction<T,T,V> andThen(Function<T,V> after) returns a function that applies function after to the result of this function, that is, (x, y) -> after.apply(this.apply(x,y)).

- static <T> BinaryOperator<T> maxBy(Comparator<T> cmp) returns a BinaryOperator<T> that returns the greatest of two T elements as defined by the comparator cmp.

- static <T> BinaryOperator<T> minBy(Comparator<T> cmp) returns a BinaryOperator<T> that returns the smallest of two T elements as defined by the comparator cmp.

The primitive-type specialized interfaces {Double,Int,Long}BinaryOperator have only their single abstract methods, named applyAs{Double,Int,Long}; see page 125. The static methods max and min from class Math (chapter 18) may sometimes be used instead of the missing maxBy and minBy.

Example 161 Some Ways to Obtain a ToIntFunction<String>
Example 155 shows how to create a function of type Function<String,Integer>, but sometimes it is better to use a primitive-type specialized value of type ToIntFunction<String>, which produces an unboxed int. Exactly the same definitions can be used, except that the value assigned to `fsi7` must use the correct interface and method name, different from those in example 155—which shows that lambda expressions and method references are easier to use than anonymous inner classes.

```
ToIntFunction<String>
  fsi1 = s -> Integer.parseInt(s),          // lambda with parameter s
  fsi2 = (String s) -> Integer.parseInt(s), // same, with explicit parameter type
  fsi3 = Integer::parseInt,                 // reference to static method Integer.parseInt
  fsi4 = Integer::new,                      // reference to constructor Integer(String)
  fsi5 = s -> s.length(),                   // lambda with parameter s
  fsi6 = String::length,                    // reference to instance method s.length()
  fsi7 = new ToIntFunction<String>() {      // anonymous inner class (Java 1.1)
         public int applyAsInt(String s) {
           return s.length();
         }};
```

The `fs1–fs6` assignments work because a function-value expression such as `s -> Integer.parseInt(s)` does not have a type in itself. Instead, the Java compiler performs type inference and inserts boxing and unboxing operations to match the type of the variable assigned. Thus the same function-value expression can be assigned to variables of type ToIntFunction<String> as well as Function<String,Integer>. However, there is no subtype relation or conversion between those two types, so the assignment g = f, where f does have a type in itself, will be rejected by the compiler:

```
Function<String,Integer> f = s -> Integer.parseInt(s);
// ToIntFunction<String> g = f;              // Type error!
```

Example 162 Why No `andThen` Method on Primitive-Type Specialized Interfaces?
Some of the primitive-type specialized interfaces such as {Double,Long,Int}Function do not have methods such as `andThen` and `compose` found on the corresponding generic interface. Presumably the reason is that there would be an excessive number of plausible overloads. For instance, IntFunction<R> might be expected to have these five overloads of `andThen`, and four overloads of `compose`, but has none of them:

```
// Hypothetic methods on IntFunction<R>:
default IntFunction<V> andThen(Function<R,V> after)
default IntUnaryOperator andThen(ToIntFunction<R> after)
default IntToDoubleFunction andThen(ToDoubleFunction<R> after)
default IntToLongFunction andThen(ToLongFunction<R> after)
default IntPredicate andThen(Predicate<R> after)
```

Example 163 A Functional Interface for Variable-Arity Functions
This interface describes functions that take a variable number of arguments via a parameter array (section 9.9) but may not be type-safe. By declaring fsas1–fsas3 from example 64 as VarargFunction<String,String> instead of Function<String[],String>, they can all be called as `fsas1.apply("abc", "DEF")` and so on.

```
interface VarargFunction<T,R> extends Function<T[],R> {
  public abstract R apply(T... xs);
}
```

24   Streams for Bulk Data (Java 8.0)

A *stream* represents a number of data elements, or bulk data, though usually not explicitly stored in the manner of an array or collection. A stream is typically processed by a pipeline, built from a *stream generator*, several *intermediate stream operations*, and a single *terminal stream operation*. A stream generator produces a stream, an intermediate operation consumes and produces a stream, and a terminal operation only consumes a stream. This approach supports mostly functional data processing and in particular enables parallel computation in a painless and safe manner.

A stream is often lazily generated and lazily processed, and the creation and processing of stream elements are driven by the terminal operation's pull (demand) at the end of the pipeline rather than the stream generator's push at the beginning of the pipeline. So only a small fraction of the stream's elements are actually stored in memory at any given time. In fact, a lazily created stream may be infinite, although some operations such as count() would never terminate on such a stream. Moreover, some intermediate operations, such as consecutive map transformations, may be fused, so that intermediate results are actually never stored at all. This makes functional stream pipelines very fast, sometimes faster than the "obviously best" imperative code; see example 167.

For instance, while it seems that xs.map(f).map(g) will perform two traversals of the stream xs, transforming the elements first by function f and then by function g, this can be implemented behind the scenes by a single traversal xs.map(f.andThen(g)) applying the composition of f and g; see example 156.

A stream may be *sequential* or *parallel*. On a sequential stream, intermediate and terminal operations will be performed sequentially, on a single thread. On a parallel stream, intermediate and terminal operations may be performed in parallel on multiple threads.

A stream may be *ordered* or *unordered*. For an ordered stream, intermediate operations such as filter(p) and map(f) respect the element order and produce a stream with elements in the expected order, even if the stream is parallel. For an unordered stream, there is no such guarantee, so some parallel intermediate operations may be more efficient on unordered streams.

Also note that on a parallel stream, even an ordered one, there is no guaranteed order in which the functional arguments f and p are applied to the stream's elements: the only guarantee is that the resulting stream's elements appear in the expected order.

For example, the result of IntStream.range(0,5).parallel().map(x -> x*2).toArray() is guaranteed to be an array containing the elements [0, 2, 4, 6, 8], but the function (x -> x*2) may be applied to element 3 before element 2, or vice versa, or at the exact same time.

Regardless whether the stream is ordered or unordered, the terminal operation forEach does not respect the element order for parallel streams.

Since operations on a parallel stream may be evaluated on multiple threads and in an unpredictable order, the functions passed to stream operations should be *stateless*: they must not depend on any state that may change during the pipeline computation, not even state internal to the function. Example 172 uses a predicate that is not stateless and therefore does not work on parallel streams.

A stream's elements can be consumed only once; trying to use a stream twice will throw IllegalStateException. In this respect Java streams are very different from Haskell's lazy lists, for instance.

When a stream is created from a source such as an array, collection, or file, that source must not be modified while the stream is being used; otherwise the results are unpredictable, and exceptions may be thrown. The functions passed to stream operations should be *non-interfering*: they must not modify the stream's source.

Example 164 Creating Finite Streams
A finite sequential stream can be created by enumerating its elements, from an array, or from a collection such as a set:

```
IntStream is = IntStream.of(2, 3, 5, 7, 11, 13);

String[] a = { "Hoover", "Roosevelt", "Truman", "Eisenhower", "Kennedy" };
Stream<String> presidents = Arrays.stream(a);

Collection<String> coll = new HashSet<String>();
coll.add("Denmark"); coll.add("Norway"); coll.add("Sweden");
Stream<String> countries = coll.stream();
```

Example 165 Creating an Infinite Stream of Prime Numbers
One can create an infinite sequential stream `nats` of the natural numbers by starting with 0 and adding 1 to each successive element, using the `iterate` method. One can then create an infinite stream `primes` of prime numbers (a natural number divisible only by 1 and itself) by filtering the stream of natural numbers. Simple and efficient.

```
IntStream nats = IntStream.iterate(0, x -> x+1);
IntStream primes = nats.filter(x -> isPrime(x));
```

Example 166 Creating a Finite Stream of Prime Numbers
The simplest way to create a finite sequential stream of the first n prime numbers is to create an infinite stream, as in example 165, and then `limit` it to the first n elements:

```
public static IntStream primes2(int n) {
  return IntStream.iterate(0, x -> x+1).filter(x -> isPrime(x)).limit(n);
}
```

Example 167 Counting Prime Numbers: Sequential Stream, Imperative Loop, and Parallel Stream
One can count the prime numbers less than 10 million by this stream pipeline. It generates the integers between 0 and 10 million, tests whether each of them is a prime, throws away the non-primes, and counts the rest:

```
IntStream.range(0, 10_000_000).filter(i -> isPrime(i)).count()
```

Since the numbers are lazily generated, this uses very little memory, and in fact the above stream expression is just as fast as a classic efficient-looking imperative loop:

```
int count = 0;
for (int i=0; i<10_000_000; i++)
  if (isPrime(i))
    count++;
```

The real advantage of the stream pipeline is that it is trivial to parallelize: just insert `.parallel()`, then the prime number testing and counting will exploit any available parallel processor cores. The parallelized version below is four times faster than the imperative loop on a 4-core laptop, and sixteen times faster than the imperative loop on a 32-core server. Parallelizing the imperative loop is vastly more cumbersome and not more efficient.

```
IntStream.range(0, 10_000_000).parallel().filter(i -> isPrime(i)).count()
```

24.1   Creating Streams

There are many ways to create a stream:

- By explicit enumeration of elements, using the variable-arity static method `Stream.of(T ...)`, which creates a sequential ordered stream, or `Stream.empty()`, which creates a stream with no elements.

- From an array, using the static methods `Arrays.stream(T[])` and `Arrays.stream(T[],from,to)` from class Arrays (section 8.4), both of which create a sequential Stream<T>. There are primitive-type specialized overloads `Arrays.stream(double[])` and `Arrays.stream(double[],from,to)` that create a sequential DoubleStream, and similar ones for IntStream and LongStream.

- From a collection, using the Collection<T> default method `coll.stream()`, which creates a sequential Stream<T>, or default method `coll.parallelStream()`, which creates a possibly parallel Stream<T>.

- By static generator methods on Stream<T> such as `iterate(x0, f)` and `generate(supp)`, or from IntStream's and LongStream's static methods `range(from,to)` and `rangeClosed(from,to)`.

- By imperative generation of stream elements, using a stream builder; see section 24.2.

- From a BitSet (package `java.util`) using method `stream()`, which returns an IntStream of the numbers in the set; see examples 175 and 176.

- From a random number generator of class Random, using methods `ints(n)`, `ints()`, `ints(a,b)`, or `ints(n,a,b)`, which produce an IntStream of n random integers, or infinitely many random integers, possibly limited to the range `a..(b-1)`; or using corresponding methods called `doubles` and `longs` to generate a DoubleStream or LongStream.

- From a BufferedReader using the `lines()` method, which generates a Stream<String>; see example 170.

24.2   Stream Builders

The Stream.Builder<T> interface from `java.util.stream` extends the Consumer<T> interface (section 23.8) and can be used to build a sequential stream using imperative programming. A stream builder computes the stream elements eagerly, so it cannot create an infinite stream, and it may do more work than necessary in case only some of the generated elements are ever consumed.

The Stream.Builder<T> interface has two abstract methods and a default one:

- `void accept(T x)` adds an element to the stream being built.

- `default Stream.Builder<T> add(T x)` works exactly as `accept(x)` but in addition returns the stream builder to allow chained calls, as in `sb.add(2).add(3).add(5)`.

- `Stream<T> build()` builds the stream and moves the stream builder to the built state. After this call, any call to `accept` or `add` will throw IllegalStateException.

The primitive-type specialized interfaces {Double,Int,Long}Stream.Builder extend the DoubleConsumer, IntConsumer, and LongConsumer interfaces (section 23.8) and have the same methods as listed above, with corresponding specialized argument and return types.

Example 168 Using a Stream Builder to Create a Stream of Prime Numbers
One can use a stream builder to create a stream of the first n prime numbers as shown below. This will compute the prime numbers eagerly, that is, before anything is consumed from the stream. The functional way to generate such a stream is much more elegant, more efficient, and parallelizable if desired; see example 166.

```
public static IntStream primes4(int n) {
  IntStream.Builder isb = IntStream.builder();
  int p = 2, count = 0;
  while (count < n) {
    if (isPrime(p)) {
      isb.accept(p);
      count++;
    }
    p++;
  }
  return isb.build();
}
```

Example 169 Using a Stream Builder to Collect Pattern Matches
The regular expression urlPattern below matches a link a href="link" in a web page. Using a stream builder, one can create a stream of Links whose elements are pairs (url, link) of the web page url and each link found in the web page. The stream is built eagerly: all links must be found before the stream can be used.

```
public static Stream<Link> scanLinks(Webpage page) {
  Matcher urlMatcher = urlPattern.matcher(page.contents);
  Stream.Builder<Link> links = Stream.<Link>builder();
  while (urlMatcher.find()) {
    String link = urlMatcher.group(1);
    links.accept(new Link(page.url, link));
  }
  return links.build();
}
final static Pattern urlPattern = Pattern.compile("a href=\"(\\p{Graph}*)\"");
```

Example 170 Reading a Stream of Lines from a BufferedReader
A stream of the text lines making up a web page can be obtained by reading the web page through a Buffered-Reader (section 26.13) and creating a lazy sequential Stream<String> from the web page. The consumer of the stream determines how much of the web page will actually be read via the network. It might be tempting to close the BufferedReader before returning the stream of lines, but this is wrong and likely would throw an UncheckedIOException. The BufferedReader will be in use as long as lines are consumed from the stream, and only when the stream gets closed may the reader and input stream be closed too.

```
public static Stream<String> getPageLines(String url) {
  try {
    InputStreamReader isr = new InputStreamReader(new URL(url).openStream());
    BufferedReader reader = new BufferedReader(isr);
    return reader.lines();
  } catch (IOException exn) {
    return Stream.<String>empty();
  }
}
```

24.3   Methods on Streams

Interface Stream<T> from package `java.util.stream` has methods for creating, further processing, or consuming streams. In the descriptions below, the elements of a stream are denoted x1, x2, ..., and in general xi. For brevity we have simplified some types in the method signatures, as explained in section 23.4.

- `boolean allMatch(Predicate<T> p)` returns true if `p.test(xi)` is true for all elements, else false.
- `boolean anyMatch(Predicate<T> p)` returns true if `p.test(xi)` is true for some element, else false.
- `static <T> Stream.Builder<T> builder()` returns a builder for a Stream<T>; see section 24.2.
- `void close()` closes this stream, causing all close handlers for this stream pipeline to be called.
- `R collect(Collector<? super T,A,R> coltor)` performs a mutable reduction operation on the stream using the collector; see section 24.6. Interfaces {Double,Int,Long}Stream do not have this method.
- `R collect(Supplier<R> supp, BiConsumer<R,T> accumulate, BiConsumer<R,R> combine)` performs a mutable reduction operation using the collector components; see section 24.6 and example 186.
- `static <T> Stream<T> concat(Stream<? extends T> xs, Stream<? extends T> ys)` creates a lazy stream whose elements are the elements of xs followed by the elements of ys.
- `long count()` returns the number of elements in this stream.
- `Stream<T> distinct()` returns a stream without duplicate elements, as determined by `x.equals(y)`.
- `static <T> Stream<T> empty()` returns an empty sequential stream.
- `Stream<T> filter(Predicate<T> p)` returns a stream of the xi for which `p.test(xi)` is true.
- `Optional<T> findAny()` returns an Optional containing some element from the stream if non-empty; otherwise returns an empty Optional (see section 25).
- `Optional<T> findFirst()` returns an Optional containing the first element from the stream if non-empty; otherwise returns an empty Optional.
- `<R> Stream<R> flatMap(Function<T,Stream<R>> f)` returns a stream whose elements result from computing `f.apply(x1)`, `f.apply(x2)`, ... to produce a sequence of streams, and flattening the resulting streams into one. The primitive-type specialized methods `flatMapTo{Double,Int,Long}` correspondingly produce streams of type {Double,Int,Long}Stream.
- `void forEach(Consumer<T> cons)` performs `cons.accept(xi)` on the elements xi of this stream.
- `void forEachOrdered(Consumer<T> cons)` performs `cons.accept(xi)` on the elements xi of this stream, in encounter order.
- `static <T> Stream<T> generate(Supplier<T> supp)` returns an infinite sequential unordered stream resulting from the call sequence `supp.get()`, `supp.get()`, ... where supp is possibly stateful. Note that unlike for iterators (section 22.7), there is no way to indicate end-of-stream.
- `boolean isParallel()` returns true if this is a parallel stream, otherwise false.
- `static <T> Stream<T> iterate(T x0, UnaryOperator<T> f)` returns an infinite sequential ordered stream whose elements ri are r0 = x0, r1 = f.apply(r0), r2 = f.apply(r1), ...
- `Iterator<T> iterator()` returns an iterator for the elements of this stream.
- `Stream<T> limit(long n)` returns a stream consisting of at most the first n elements of this stream.

Example 171 Using Stream Methods to Find and Print Web Page Links

This example reads web pages from the net, scans the first 200 lines of each web page for links, discards duplicate links and prints the unique ones, using streams and functional programming to cleanly separate these tasks. Method `getPage` from example 181 returns a Webpage object consisting of a URL and a string holding the first 200 lines of the page contents. Method `scanLinks` from example 169 scans a (partial) web page for hyperlinks and returns a stream of Links. The stream method `flatMap` calls `scanLinks` on many web pages to obtain many Link streams and then flattens all those into a single Link stream. The stream method `distinct` discards duplicates from the Link stream. The stream method `forEach` prints the links as they are produced.

```
String[] allUrls = { "http://www.itu.dk", ... };

Stream<String> urls = Stream.<String>of(allUrls);
Stream<Webpage> pages = urls.map(url -> getPage(url, 200));
Stream<Link> links = pages.flatMap(page -> scanLinks(page));
Stream<Link> uniqueLinks = links.distinct();
uniqueLinks.forEach(System.out::println);  // Calls Link.toString()
```

Example 172 Checking Sortedness of a Sequential Stream

To check whether a sequential ordered stream is sorted, one can use the stream method `allMatch` together with a stateful predicate as shown below. Each application of the predicate `x -> { ... }` compares a stream element `x` to its predecessor. The singleton array `last[0]` holds that predecessor; we cannot use a plain `int` variable for that purpose because variables captured in a Java lambda expression must be effectively final, that is, immutable (section 9.11). This method does not work on a parallel stream because the predicate is stateful.

```
static boolean isSorted2(IntStream xs) {
  final int[] last = { Integer.MIN_VALUE };
  return xs.allMatch(x -> { int old = last[0]; last[0] = x; return old <= x; } );
}
```

Example 173 Making a Stream of English Numerals

Using function `toEnglish` from example 158 one can create a (practically) infinite stream of the English numerals "zero", "one", "two", ..., "thirteen million nine hundred eighty-nine thousand four hundred twenty-two", and so on. One can also generate a stream of "logorithms", where the logorithm of a number n is the number of letters in its numeral (we believe this tongue-in-cheek concept is attributable to Martin Gardner).

```
Stream<String> numerals
  = LongStream.iterate(0, x -> x+1).mapToObj(Numerals::toEnglish);
IntStream logorithms = numerals.mapToInt(String::length);
System.out.println(logorithms.limit(1_000_000).max());
```

Example 174 Versatility of Streams

Streams are very versatile. For instance, if we can lazily generate a stream of solutions to the 8-queens problem (example 176), then we can later decide whether we want to print all solutions, the number of solutions, the first 20 solutions, or an arbitrary solution, as shown below. With a more imperative approach, we would typically have to decide beforehand how to use the results.

```
queens(8).forEach(System.out::println);
System.out.println(queens(8).count());
queens(8).limit(20).forEach(System.out::println);
System.out.println(queens(8).findAny());
```

Methods on interface Stream<T> continued:

- `Stream<R> map(Function<T,R> f)` returns a stream with elements `f.apply(x1)`, `f.apply(x2)`, ... The primitive-type specialized methods `mapTo{Double,Int,Long}` correspondingly produce streams of type {Double,Int,Long}Stream.

- `Optional<T> max(Comparator<T> cmp)` returns the stream's maximal element according to `cmp`, or an absent Optional if there are no elements.

- `Optional<T> min(Comparator<T> cmp)` returns the stream's minimal element according to `cmp`, or an absent Optional if there are no elements.

- `boolean noneMatch(Predicate<T> p)` returns true if `p.test(xi)` is false for all elements, else false.

- `static <T> Stream<T> of(T... vs)` returns a sequential ordered stream whose elements are the `vs`.

- `static <T> Stream<T> of(T x)` returns a sequential Stream containing the single element x.

- `Stream<T> onClose(Runnable handler)` returns a stream with the same elements but an additional close handler. When closing the stream, the close handlers are executed in the order they were added.

- `Stream<T> parallel()` returns a parallel stream with the same elements as this stream.

- `Stream<T> peek(Consumer<T> cons)` returns a stream consisting of the same elements x1, x2, ... as this stream, additionally performing actions `cons.accept(x1)`, `cons.accept(x2)`, ... as the elements are being consumed from the resulting stream. Use it for debugging purposes only.

- `Optional<T> reduce(BinaryOperator<T> op)` computes the reduction of the stream's elements using the associative operator `op`. More precisely, writing `op.apply(x,y)` as infix $x \otimes y$, returns an Optional containing the value $x_1 \otimes x_2 \otimes \ldots \otimes x_n$, computed in some order, if the stream is non-empty; otherwise returns an empty Optional.

- `T reduce(T x0, BinaryOperator<T> op)` computes the reduction of x0 and the stream's elements using the associative operator `op`. More precisely, writing `op.apply(x,y)` as infix $x \otimes y$, the method returns $x_0 \otimes x_1 \otimes x_2 \otimes \ldots \otimes x_n$, computed in some order.

- `U reduce(U r0, BiFunction<U,T,U> op, BinaryOperator<U> comb)` computes the reduction of the stream's elements, using the provided identity r0, accumulation function `op`, and combiner `comb`. More precisely, writing `op.apply(r,x)` as infix $r \otimes x$ and writing the combiner `comp.apply(r,s)` as infix $r \oplus s$, returns $(r_0 \otimes x_{11} \otimes \ldots \otimes x_{1m}) \oplus \ldots \oplus (r_0 \otimes x_{k1} \otimes \ldots \otimes x_{km})$, computed in some order, where the `xij` represents some partitioning of the stream's elements into segments. It must hold that $r_0 \otimes x$ equals x, that $r \oplus (r_0 \otimes x)$ equals $r \otimes x$ for all x and r, and $\oplus$ must be associative. The primitive-type specialized {Double,Int,Long}Stream interfaces do not have this overload.

- `Stream<T> sequential()` returns a sequential stream with the same elements as this stream.

- `Stream<T> skip(long n)` returns a stream of the remaining elements after discarding the n first ones.

- `Stream<T> sorted()` returns a stream consisting of the elements of this stream, sorted in natural order.

- `Stream<T> sorted(Comparator<T> cmp)` returns a stream consisting of the elements, sorted by `cmp`.

- `Spliterator<T> spliterator()` returns a spliterator for the elements of this stream.

- `Object[] toArray()` returns an array containing the elements of this stream.

- `T[] toArray(IntFunction<T[]> alloc)` returns an array containing the elements of this stream, using `alloc.apply(n)` to allocate the returned array as well as any intermediate arrays.

- `Stream<T> unordered()` returns an unordered stream with the same elements as this stream.

Example 175 Generating a Stream of Permutations
The stream of all permutations of n numbers $0\ldots(n-1)$ can be generated by maintaining a partially generated permutation as an integer list `tail`, and a set `todo` of the numbers not yet used in the permutation. If `todo` is empty, `tail` is a permutation of all n numbers. Otherwise recursively generate those permutations that can be obtained by removing an element `r` from `todo` and putting it in front of `tail`. To create all n-permutations, start with an empty `tail`, and a `todo` set containing the numbers $0\ldots(n-1)$.

Class IntList represents immutable integer lists; see example 182. The `boxed()` operation turns an IntStream into a Stream<Integer> so one can apply `flatMap` to obtain a Stream<IntList>; the `flatMap` method on IntStream produces only IntStreams. The call `minus(todo, r)` returns a new BitSet with r removed.

```
public static Stream<IntList> perms(BitSet todo, IntList tail) {
  if (todo.isEmpty())
    return Stream.of(tail);
  else
    return todo.stream().boxed().flatMap(r -> perms(minus(todo, r), new IntList(r, tail)));
}
public static Stream<IntList> perms(int n) {
  BitSet todo = new BitSet(n); todo.flip(0, n); return perms(todo, null);
}
```

Example 176 Generating a Stream of Solutions to the n-Queens Problem
We now augment the permutation generator (example 175) to generate solutions to the n-queens problem: How to place n queens on an n-by-n chessboard so all queens are safe from each other. A 3-permutation such as $[1,0,2]$ can be considered a safe placement of 3 rooks on a 3-by-3 chessboard, in rows 1, 0, and 2 of columns 0, 1, and 2. So a solution to the n-queens problem is a permutation further constrained by considering diagonals: Filter away those r values from `todo` that, if put in front of `tail`, would constitute an unsafe queen's position that could attack some queen in the columns represented by `tail`.

This solution is simple, quite fast, versatile (example 174), and trivial to parallelize because all operations are purely functional. Putting `.parallel()` after `filter` gives a speed-up of 3.5 on a 4-core i7 processor.

```
public static Stream<IntList> queens(BitSet todo, IntList tail) {
  if (todo.isEmpty())
    return Stream.of(tail);
  else
    return todo.stream()
      .filter(r -> safe(r, tail)).boxed()          // could use .parallel() here
      .flatMap(r -> queens(minus(todo, r), new IntList(r, tail)));
}
public static boolean safe(int mid, IntList tail) { return safe(mid+1, mid-1, tail); }
public static boolean safe(int d1, int d2, IntList tail) {
  return tail==null || d1!=tail.item && d2!=tail.item && safe(d1+1, d2-1, tail.next);
}
```

Example 177 A Stream Can Be Consumed Only Once
A stream can be consumed only once, so one cannot find the standard deviation of a DoubleStream `ds` by separately computing its mean and the sum of its squares; instead compute both in one traversal, as in example 180.

```
DoubleSummaryStatistics stats = ds.summaryStatistics();
// Fails with IllegalStateException: stream has already been operated upon or closed:
double sqsum = ds.map(x -> x*x).sum();
double sdev = Math.sqrt(sqsum/stats.getCount() - stats.getAverage()*stats.getAverage());
```

24.4　Numeric Streams: DoubleStream, IntStream, and LongStream

Numeric streams may be represented by primitive-type specialized interfaces {Double,Int,Long}Stream for efficiency; see section 23.3. They have additional methods `average()`, `max()`, `min()`, `sum()`, and `mapToObject`. The argument and result types of their Stream<T> methods are appropriately primitive-type specialized. For instance, the `iterator()` methods return PrimitiveIterator.Of{Double,Int,Long} objects (section 22.7), and the `generate` method's signatures in IntStream and Stream<T> look like this:

```
static IntStream generate(IntSupplier supp)
static Stream<T> generate(Supplier<T> supp)
```

In addition to the general stream methods (section 24.3), DoubleStream has these methods:

- `Stream<Double> boxed()` returns a stream of this stream's elements, each boxed as a Double object.
- `DoubleSummaryStatistics summaryStatistics()` returns statistics for this stream; see section 24.5.

In addition to the general stream methods (section 24.3), IntStream has these methods:

- `DoubleStream asDoubleStream()` returns a stream of this stream's elements converted to `double`.
- `LongStream asLongStream()` returns a stream of this stream's elements converted to `long`.
- `Stream<Integer> boxed()` returns a stream of this stream's elements, each boxed as an Integer object.
- `static IntStream range(int a, int b)` returns the `int` stream `[a..(b-1)]`, empty if a>=b.
- `static IntStream rangeClosed(int a, int b)` returns the `int` stream `[a..b]`, empty if a>b.
- `IntSummaryStatistics summaryStatistics()` returns statistics for this stream; see section 24.5.

In addition to the general stream methods (section 24.3), LongStream has these methods:

- `DoubleStream asDoubleStream()` returns a stream of this stream's elements converted to `double`.
- `Stream<Long> boxed()` returns a stream of this stream's elements, each boxed as a Long object.
- `static LongStream range(long a, long b)` returns the `long` stream `[a..(b-1)]`, empty if a>=b.
- `static LongStream rangeClosed(long a, long b)` returns `long` stream `[a..b]`, empty if a>b.
- `LongSummaryStatistics summaryStatistics()` returns statistics for this stream; see section 24.5.

24.5　Summary Statistics for Numeric Streams

The classes {Double,Int,Long}SummaryStatistics from package `java.util` represent summary statistics of a numeric stream. The classes have `get` methods that return count, min, max, sum, and average (mean); see example 178. The min, max, and sum have the same type as the stream elements, except that the sum of an IntStream is a `long`. The average is always a `double`.

Class DoubleSummaryStatistics implements the DoubleConsumer interface and, in addition to the `get` methods shown in example 178, has these methods to collect the statistics:

- `void accept(double x)` records value x in the summary information.
- `void combine(DoubleSummaryStatistics other)` combines the `other` statistics into this one.

The IntSummaryStatistics and LongSummaryStatistics classes have corresponding methods. These methods can be passed to a stream's `collect` method to compute the statistics (example 179), and they can be overridden to collect more comprehensive statistics (example 180).

Example 178 Summary Statistics for Numeric Streams
The summary statistics for a `double` stream can be computed and printed like this, with the printed output inserted as a comment:

```
DoubleStream ds = DoubleStream.of(2, 4, 4, 4, 5, 5, 7, 9);
DoubleSummaryStatistics stats = ds.summaryStatistics();
System.out.printf("count=%d, min=%g, max=%g, sum=%g, mean=%g%n",
                  stats.getCount(), stats.getMin(), stats.getMax(),
                  stats.getSum(), stats.getAverage());
// count=8, min=2.00000, max=9.00000, sum=40.0000, mean=5.00000
```

Example 179 Computing Summary Statistics Using Collector Functions
The DoubleSummaryStatistics object `stats` computed in example 178 can equivalently be computed like this, using the collector components (section 24.6) of the DoubleSummaryStatistics class:

```
DoubleSummaryStatistics stats
  = ds.collect(DoubleSummaryStatistics::new,
               DoubleSummaryStatistics::accept,
               DoubleSummaryStatistics::combine);
```

Example 180 Extending Double Summary Statistics with Standard Deviation
By creating a subclass BetterDoubleStatistics of the DoubleSummaryStatistics class, one can also compute the standard deviation in the same traversal of a stream of `doubles`. Note that this cannot be done by multiple traversals (first compute the usual summary statistics, then compute the sum of squares of the stream) because a stream can be consumed only once; see example 177.

The BetterDoubleStatistics class computes the sum of squares in addition to whatever is done by superclass DoubleSummaryStatistics and adds a method `getSdev` to compute the standard deviation afterwards:

```
class BetterDoubleStatistics extends DoubleSummaryStatistics {
  private double sqsum = 0.0;
  @Override
  public void accept(double d) {
    super.accept(d);
    sqsum += d * d;
  }
  public void combine(BetterDoubleStatistics other) {
    super.combine(other);
    sqsum += other.sqsum;
  }
  public double getSdev() {
    double mean = getAverage();
    return Math.sqrt(sqsum/getCount() - mean*mean);
  }
}
...
DoubleStream ds = DoubleStream.of(2, 4, 4, 4, 5, 5, 7, 9);
BetterDoubleStatistics stats
  = ds.collect(BetterDoubleStatistics::new,
               BetterDoubleStatistics::accept,
               BetterDoubleStatistics::combine);
// count=8, min=2.00000, max=9.00000, sum=40.0000, mean=5.00000, sdev=2.00000
```

24.6   Collectors on Streams

In some cases, it is difficult to make the functional stream reduce operations efficient enough. This holds, for instance, for massive string concatenation (where repeated use of `s1+s` has quadratic execution time); for creating a collection, list, or set from a stream; and for various grouping and binning operations. In those cases, a *mutable reduction operation* using a so-called collector may be more efficient. However, functional reductions should be preferred where possible, because the mutable reduction operations are easier to get wrong and often see much less speed-up (or even considerable slow-down) on parallel streams than the functional operations.

A collector `coltor` is an instance of interface Collector<T,A,R> that can process a stream `xs` of type Stream<T>, using an internal accumulator of type A, and producing a result of type R.

Stream method `xs.collect(coltor)` applies the collector to the stream `xs`, performing the mutable reduction operation and returning a result of type R. Utility class Collectors in package `java.util.stream` defines many useful collectors, listed below.

Stream method `xs.collect(Supplier<R> supp, BiConsumer<R,T> accu, BiConsumer<R,R> comb)` supports custom mutable reduction operations, producing a final result of type R. Function `supp()` generates a result container; function `accu(rc, x)` is called to process stream element x and add it to result container `rc`; and function `comb(rc1,rc2)` is called to combine the state of result container `rc2` into `rc1`; see examples 179, 180, and 186.

Some more advanced features of collectors are not described in this book; see the Java class library documentation [2].

Below we list the static methods in class Collectors that produce often used collectors. For readability we have simplified some of the wildcard types in the signatures, as described in section 23.4. We use the parameter names `coltor` for collector, `fin` for finisher, `rc` for result container, `comb` for combiner, `cons` for consumer, and `cfier` for classifier.

- `Collector<T,?,Double> averagingDouble(ToDoubleFunction<T> f)` computes the arithmetic mean, or average, of `f.apply(xi)`. There are similarly named methods for Int and Long.

- `Collector<T,A,RR> collectingAndThen(Collector<T,A,R> coltor, Function<R,RR> fin)` collects by `coltor` and then applies finisher `fin` to the result container.

- `Collector<T,?,Long> counting()` counts the number of elements.

- `Collector<T,?,Map<K,List<T>>> groupingBy(Function<T,K> cfier)` groups elements `xi` into lists by the value of key `cfier.apply(xi)`.

- `Collector<T,?,Map<K,D>> groupingBy(Function<T,K> cfier, Collector<? super T,A,D> coltor)` groups elements `xi` into lists by the value of key `cfier.apply(xi)`, then performs reduction operation `coltor` on the set of values `xi` associated with each key.

  There is also an overload with an additional argument of type Supplier<Map<K,D>> to produce the map used. There are concurrent versions of these methods also, named `groupingByConcurrent`; these produce a ConcurrentMap.

  Two `partitioningBy` methods work like the methods above but take a Predicate<T> instead of a Function<T,K> and produce a map whose only keys are `true` and `false`.

Example 181 Using a Collector to Join Lines into a Page

Method `getPageLines` from example 170 produces a lazy stream of the lines of a web page. We can join the first `maxLines` lines into a single string using the stream methods `limit` and `collect`, where the latter is applied to the predefined `joining` collector that efficiently joins strings.

```
public static Webpage getPage(String url, int maxLines) {
  String contents =
    getPageLines(url).limit(maxLines).collect(Collectors.joining());
  return new Webpage(url, contents);
}
```

Example 182 Using a Collector and IntStream to Print an Integer List

Class IntList is used in examples 175 and 176 to represent immutable integer lists, which we would like to print in the format [1, 3, 0, 2] within square brackets and with comma-separated numbers. We could cleverly define `toString` using a StringBuilder, but a simpler and more general idea is to define a method `stream` to convert IntList to IntStream and then use a predefined collector to format the IntStream as a string.

```
class IntList {
  public final int item;
  public final IntList next;
  public IntList(int item, IntList next) { this.item = item; this.next = next; }
  public static IntStream stream(IntList xs) {
    IntStream.Builder sb = IntStream.builder();
    while (xs != null) {
      sb.accept(xs.item);
      xs = xs.next;
    }
    return sb.build();
  }
  public String toString() {
    return stream(this).mapToObj(String::valueOf).collect(Collectors.joining(",", "[", "]"));
  }
}
```

Example 183 Using Stream Functions to Generate a van der Corput Sequence

A van der Corput sequence is an infinite sequence $\frac{1}{2}, \frac{1}{4}, \frac{3}{4}, \frac{1}{8}, \frac{5}{8}, \frac{3}{8}, \frac{7}{8}, \ldots$ that is dense in the interval $[0,1]$ and evenly distributed over it. The infinite sequence is typically used in (financial) simulations. A 2 billion element approximation of the sequence may be generated lazily using stream functions: for every bit count b in range $1 \ldots 31$ and for every i in range $2^{b-1} \ldots 2^b - 1$, compute the bit-reversal of integer i and divide by 2^b.

Example 186 uses collectors to test that the generated numbers are evenly distributed over $[0,1]$; and example 24 uses array sort to show that they are dense in $[0,1]$.

```
public static DoubleStream vanDerCorput() {
  return IntStream.range(1, 31).asDoubleStream().flatMap(b -> bitReversedRange((int)b));
}

private static DoubleStream bitReversedRange(int b) {
  final long bp = Math.round(Math.pow(2, b));
  return LongStream.range(bp/2, bp).mapToDouble(i -> (double)(bitReverse((int)i)>>>(32-b))/bp);
}
private static int bitReverse(int i) { ... /* reverse the bits in i */ ...}
```

Static methods on class Collectors that generate collectors continued:

- `Collector<CharSequence,?,String> joining()` concatenates the input elements `xi` into a string.
- `Collector<CharSequence,?,String> joining(CharSequence delim)` concatenates the input elements `xi`, separated by `delim`, into a string.
- `Collector<CharSequence,?,String> joining(CharSequence delim, CharSequence pre, CharSequence suf)` concatenates the input elements `xi`, separated by `delim`, into a string starting with `pre` and ending with `suf`.
- `Collector<T,?,R> mapping(Function<T,U> f, Collector<? super U,A,R> coltor)` applies `f` to each element `xi` and then uses `coltor` to perform a reduction of the `f.apply(xi)` values.
- `Collector<T,?,Optional<T>> maxBy(Comparator<T> cmp)` produces an optional maximal element according to `cmp`, or absent if no elements.
- `Collector<T,?,Optional<T>> minBy(Comparator<T> cmp)` produces an optional minimal element according to `cmp`, or absent if no elements.
- `Collector<T,?,Optional<T>> reducing(BinaryOperator<T> op)` performs a reduction of the elements using `op`. More precisely, writing `op.apply(x,y)` as infix $x \otimes y$, returns an Optional containing the value $x1 \otimes x2 \otimes \ldots \otimes xn$ if the stream is non-empty; otherwise returns an empty Optional.
- `Collector<T,?,T> reducing(T x0, BinaryOperator<T> op)` performs a reduction of `x0` and the elements using `op`. More precisely, writing `op.apply(x,y)` as infix $x \otimes y$, returns $x0 \otimes x1 \otimes x2 \otimes \ldots \otimes xn$.
- `Collector<T,?,U> reducing(U e, Function<T,U> f, BinaryOperator<U> op)` performs a reduction of transformed elements using `op`. More precisely, writing `op.apply(x,y)` as infix $x \otimes y$, returns an Optional containing the value `f.apply(x1)` $\otimes$ `f.apply(x2)` $\otimes \ldots \otimes$ `f.apply(xn)` if the stream is non-empty; otherwise returns an empty Optional.
- `Collector<T,?,DoubleSummaryStatistics> summarizingDouble(ToDoubleFunction<T> f)` applies function `f` to each element and returns summary statistics for the resulting values; see section 24.5. There are similarly named methods for Int and Long.
- `Collector<T,?,Double> summingDouble(ToDoubleFunction<T> f)` applies function `f` to each element and returns the sum of the values. There are similarly named methods for Int and Long.
- `Collector<T,?,C> toCollection(Supplier<C> collectionFactory)` accumulates the elements into a new collection of type `<C extends Collection<T>>` created by the `collectionFactory`.
- `Collector<T,?,List<T>> toList()` accumulates the elements into a new list.
- `Collector<T,?,Map<K,U>> toMap(Function<T,K> fk, Function<T,U> fv)` accumulates the elements into a new map whose key-value pairs are `(fk.apply(xi), fv.apply(xi))`; throws IllegalStateException unless `fk.apply(xi)` is distinct for all elements `xi`.
- `Collector<T,?,Map<K,U>> toMap(Function<T,K> fk, Function<T,U> fv, BinaryOperator<U> merge)` accumulates the elements into a map whose key-value pairs are `(fk.apply(xi), xival)` where `xiVal` is the result `fv.apply(xi1)` $\otimes \ldots \otimes$ `fv.apply(xin)` of merging the fv-values of all `xij` for which `fk.apply(xij)` equals `fk.apply(xi)`, where $x \otimes y$ is `merge.apply(x,y)`.

  There is also an overload with an additional argument of type `Supplier<Map<K,U>>` to produce the map used. There are also `toConcurrentMap` versions of the two preceding methods that produce concurrent maps, more efficient on parallel streams.
- `Collector<T,?,Set<T>> toSet()` accumulates the elements into a new set.

Example 184 Generating a Stream of Lists of Prime Factors
An infinite stream of lists of prime factors can be generated by mapping as suitable method `factorList` on the infinite stream $[2, 3, \ldots]$. This is used in example 185.

```
public static List<Integer> factorList(int p) { ... }
public static Stream<List<Integer>> allFactorLists() {
  return IntStream.iterate(2, x -> x+1).mapToObj(Streams::factorList);
}
```

The computed lists of prime factors for the 11 numbers $2 \ldots 12$ look like this:

```
[2] [3] [2, 2] [5] [2, 3] [7] [2, 2, 2] [3, 3] [2, 5] [11] [2, 2, 3]
```

Example 185 Collectors for Grouping and Counting
Using a collector, one can group the lists of prime factors from example 184 by their length, that is, number p of prime factors. The grouping is represented by a map from p to the factor lists of length p, so group 1 contains the prime numbers, as shown below.

Moreover, instead of storing all factor lists, one can count them using another collector, to obtain a map from the prime factor count p to the number of numbers with that many prime factors; so $3 = 1273$ below means that 1273 numbers between 2 and 5001 have 3 prime factors.

```
Map<Integer, List<List<Integer>>> factorGroups =
  allFactorLists().limit(11).collect(Collectors.groupingBy(List::size));
// {1=[[2], [3], [5], [7], [11]], 2=[[2, 2], [2, 3], [3, 3], [2, 5]], 3=[[2, 2, 2], [2, 2, 3]]}
Map<Integer, Long> factorGroupSizes =
  allFactorLists().limit(5000).collect(Collectors.groupingBy(List::size, Collectors.counting()));
// {1=669, 2=1366, 3=1273, 4=832, 5=452, 6=224, 7=104, 8=47, 9=22, 10=7, 11=3, 12=1}
```

Example 186 Grouping and Counting on a DoubleStream
Example 183 shows how to generate a van der Corput sequence. To test that the generated numbers are indeed evenly distributed over $[0, 1]$ we put the numbers into 10 equally large bins and count them; there should be equally many numbers in each bin. We do this by calling the DoubleStream's three-argument `collect` method with a Supplier<int[]>, an ObjDoubleConsumer<int[]>, and a BiConsumer<int[],int[]> that directly collect the bin counts in a 10-element integer array. Generating and binning the first 100 million van der Corput numbers using this method takes 0.9 seconds using a single CPU core.

Alternatively, we could have used `.boxed()` to obtain a Stream<Double> and applied the one-argument `collect` method to a predefined collector, as in example 185. But the boxing of every `double` makes that approach slower by a factor of five.

```
final int bins = 10;
int[] binFrequenciesArray =
  vanDerCorput().limit(100_000_000).
  collect(() -> new int[bins],
          (a, x) -> { a[(int)(bins * x)]++; },
          (a1, a2) -> { for (int i=0; i<a1.length; i++) a1[i] += a2[i]; });
Arrays.stream(binFrequenciesArray).forEach(k -> System.out.printf("%d ", k));
// 10000002 10000001 10000000 10000000 9999997 10000002 10000001 10000000 10000000 9999997
```

25   Class Optional<T> (Java 8.0)

An instance of class Optional<T> from package `java.util` represents a value that is either *absent* (missing, empty) or *present*, and in the latter case contains a non-null value of type T. Class Optional<T> can be used to make it clearer that an operation may not return a result, instead of letting it silently return `null`. For instance, the `findAny` method on interface Stream<T> has type

```
Optional<T> findAny()
```

which makes it clear that sometimes `findAny` cannot produce a result, namely, when the stream is empty.

Class Optional<T> has these methods:

- `static <T> Optional<T> empty()` returns an absent (empty) Optional.

- `Optional<T> filter(Predicate<T> p)` returns a present Optional containing v if a value v is present and `p.test(v)` is true; otherwise returns an absent Optional.

- `Optional<U> flatMap(Function<T,Optional<U>> f)` returns `f.apply(v)` if a value v is present; otherwise returns an absent Optional.

- `T get()` returns the value if present; otherwise throws NoSuchElementException.

- `void ifPresent(Consumer<T> cons)` invokes `cons.accept(v)` on the value v if present; otherwise does nothing.

- `boolean isPresent()` returns true if there is a value present; otherwise false.

- `Optional<U> map(Function<T,U> f)` returns a present Optional containing res provided a value v is present in this Optional and res = `f.apply(v)` is non-null; otherwise returns an absent Optional.

- `static <T> Optional<T> of(T x)` returns a present Optional containing x if non-null; otherwise throws NullPointerException.

- `static <T> Optional<T> ofNullable(T x)` returns a present Optional containing x if x is non-null; otherwise returns an absent Optional.

- `T orElse(T other)` returns the value if present; `other` if not. Hence it behaves just like `isPresent()` `? get() : other`.

- `T orElseGet(Supplier<T> supp)` returns the value if present; otherwise the result of `supp.get()`.

- `T orElseThrow(Supplier<Throwable> exn)` returns the value if present; otherwise throws the exception created by `exn.get()`.

Note that the methods `empty`, `filter`, `flatMap`, `map`, and `of` exist on the Stream<T> interface also, and indeed conceptually an Optional<T> can be thought of as a stream with zero or one element. The `ifPresent` method on an Optional is the same as `forEach` on a stream.

There are primitive-type specialized classes OptionalDouble, OptionalInt, and OptionalLong for representing results of type `double`, `int`, or `long` that may be absent; this is particularly useful since a value of primitive types cannot itself be `null`. These classes have methods `empty`, `getAs{Double,Int,Long}`, `ifPresent`, `isPresent`, `of`, `orElse`, `orElseGet`, and `orElseThrow`, with correspondingly primitive-type specialized argument and result types.

Example 187 Replacing Multiple Kinds of Failure with Optional

Assume we need to (1) read a field `"area"` off a web form, (2) parse the field value as a `double`, (3) compute its square root, and then print either the result or an error message. This illustrates Java's three ways to indicate the absence of a result: (1) returning `null`, if the field is missing from the web form; (2) throwing an exception, if the string cannot be parsed as a `double`; and (3) returning a `NaN`, if taking the square root of a negative number. Code fragment (A) below gives the messy error-handling code necessary in this case.

Code fragments (B) and (C) show two ways to do the same using class Optional and its methods. However, this assumes that suitable Option-returning versions of methods `parseDouble` and `sqrt` are available, but the Java class libraries currently have only a few such methods outside the streams framework.

```java
// Alternative (A): Handling three kinds of error indication explicitly:
String areaString = form.get("area"), toPrint = "No value";
if (areaString != null) {
  try {
    double areaValue = Double.parseDouble(areaString);
    double result = Math.sqrt(areaValue);
    if (!Double.isNaN(result))
      toPrint = String.valueOf(result);
  } catch (NumberFormatException exn) { }
}
System.out.println(toPrint);
// Alternative (B): Using Optional, assuming suitable Option-returning methods exist:
Optional<String> areaString = Optional.<String>ofNullable(form.get("area"));
Optional<Double> areaValue = areaString.flatMap(s -> parseDouble(s));
Optional<Double> result = areaValue.flatMap(v -> sqrt(v));
System.out.println(result.map(String::valueOf).orElse("No value"));
// Alternative (C): As (B) but without naming the intermediate results:
String toPrint = Optional.<String>ofNullable(form.get("area"))
                         .flatMap(s -> parseDouble(s))
                         .flatMap(v -> sqrt(v))
                         .map(String::valueOf)
                         .orElse("No value");
System.out.println(toPrint);
```

Example 188 Optional Stream Element

One can use method `findAny` on the stream `queens(n)` of solutions to the *n*-queens problem (example 176), to obtain an arbitrary solution, provided there is one. The result is an Optional<IntList>.

The first few lines of output are shown as comments. They show that the *n*-queens problem has no solution for *n* equal to 2 and 3 (so the Optional is empty), but does have a solution for *n* equal to 1, 4, and 5.

```java
for (int n=1; n<=17; n++) {
  Optional<IntList> solution = queens(n).findAny();
  System.out.printf("%4d-queens solution: %s%n", n, solution);
}
//  1-queens solution: Optional[[0]]
//  2-queens solution: Optional.empty
//  3-queens solution: Optional.empty
//  4-queens solution: Optional[[1, 3, 0, 2]]
//  5-queens solution: Optional[[4, 1, 3, 0, 2]]
//  ...
```

26   Input and Output

Sequential input and output uses objects called *IO streams*, not to be confused with streams for bulk data (chapter 24). There are two kinds of IO streams: *character streams* and *byte streams*, also called text streams and binary streams. Character streams are used for input from text files and human-readable output to text files, printers, and so on, using 16-bit Unicode characters [1]. Byte streams are used for compact and efficient input and output of primitive data (`int`, `double`, ...) as well as objects and arrays, in machine-readable form.

There are separate classes for handling character streams and byte streams. The classes for character input and output are called Readers and Writers. The classes for byte input and output are called InputStreams and OutputStreams. This chapter describes input and output using the `java.io` package. Java provides additional facilities in package `java.nio`, not described here.

One can create subclasses of the IO stream classes, overriding inherited methods to obtain specialized IO stream classes. We shall not further discuss how to do that here.

The four IO stream class hierarchies are shown in the following table, with related input and output classes shown on the same line. The table shows, for instance, that BufferedReader and FilterReader are subclasses of Reader, and that LineNumberReader is a subclass of BufferedReader. Abstract classes are shown in *italics*.

	Input Streams	Output Streams
Character Streams	*Reader*	*Writer*
	BufferedReader	BufferedWriter
	LineNumberReader	
	FilterReader	*FilterWriter*
	PushBackReader	
	InputStreamReader	OutputStreamWriter
	FileReader	FileWriter
	PipedReader	PipedWriter
		PrintWriter
	CharArrayReader	CharArrayWriter
	StringReader	StringWriter
Byte Streams	*InputStream*	*OutputStream*
	ByteArrayInputStream	ByteArrayOutputStream
	FileInputStream	FileOutputStream
	FilterInputStream	FilterOutputStream
	BufferedInputStream	BufferedOutputStream
	DataInputStream	DataOutputStream
	PushBackInputStream	
		PrintStream
	ObjectInputStream	ObjectOutputStream
	PipedInputStream	PipedOutputStream
	SequenceInputStream	
	RandomAccessFile	

The classes DataInputStream, ObjectInputStream, and RandomAccessFile implement the interface DataInput, and the classes DataOutputStream, ObjectOutputStream, and RandomAccessFile implement the interface DataOutput (section 26.11).

The class ObjectInputStream implements interface ObjectInput, and class ObjectOutputStream implements interface ObjectOutput (section 26.12).

26.1 Creating an IO Stream from Another One

An IO stream may be created either outright (e.g., a FileInputStream may be created and associated with a named file on disk, for reading from that file) or from an existing IO stream to provide additional features (e.g., a BufferedInputStream may be created from a FileInputStream, for more efficient input). In any case, an input stream or reader has an underlying source of data to read from, and an output stream or writer has an underlying sink of data to write to. The following figure shows how IO streams may be defined in terms of existing IO streams, or in terms of other data.

The IO stream classes are divided along two lines: character streams (top) versus byte streams (bottom), and input streams (left) versus output streams (right). The arrows show what IO streams can be created from other streams. For instance, the arrow from InputStream to InputStreamReader shows that one can create an InputStreamReader from an InputStream. The arrow from Reader to BufferedReader shows that one can create a BufferedReader from a Reader. Since an InputStreamReader is a Reader, one can create a BufferedReader from an existing InputStream (such as `System.in`) in two steps, as shown in example 189. On the other hand, there is no way to create a PipedOutputStream from a File or a file name; a PipedOutputStream must be created outright, or from an existing PipedInputStream, and similarly for other pipes (section 26.16).

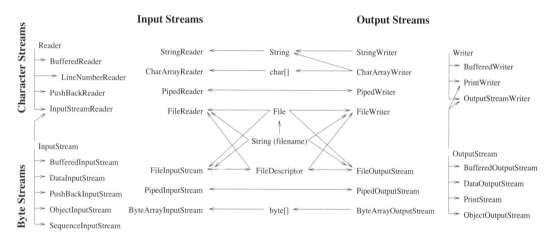

Example 189 A Complete Input-Output Example

```java
import java.io.*;
class BasicIOExample {
  public static void main(String[] args) throws IOException {
    BufferedReader r = new BufferedReader(new InputStreamReader(System.in));
    int count = 0;
    String s = r.readLine();
    while (s != null && !s.equals("")) {
      count++;
      s = r.readLine();
    }
    System.out.println("You entered " + count + " nonempty lines");
} }
```

26.2   Kinds of Input and Output Methods

The following table summarizes the naming conventions for methods of the input and output classes as well as their main characteristics, such as their end-of-stream behavior.

Method Name	Effect
read	Inputs characters from a Reader (section 26.4) or inputs bytes from an InputStream (section 26.9). It *blocks*, that is, does not return, until some input is available; returns -1 on end-of-stream.
write	Outputs characters to a Writer (section 26.5) or outputs bytes to an OutputStream (section 26.10).
format	Uses a formatting string to convert values to textual representation and then outputs that representation to a PrintWriter or PrintStream (section 7.1).
print	Converts a value (int, double, ..., Object) to textual representation and outputs it to a PrintWriter or PrintStream (section 26.6).
println	Same as print but outputs a newline after printing.
printf	Same as format (section 7.1).
read*t*	Inputs a value of primitive type *t* from a DataInput stream (section 26.11). Blocks until some input is available; throws EOFException on end-of-stream.
write*t*	Outputs a primitive value of primitive type *t* to a DataOutput stream (section 26.11).
readObject	Deserializes objects from an ObjectInput stream (section 26.12). Blocks until some input is available; throws ObjectStreamException on end-of-stream.
writeObject	Serializes objects to an ObjectOutput stream (section 26.12).
skip(n)	Skips at most n bytes (from InputStreams) or n characters (from Readers). If n>0, blocks until some input is available; if n<0, throws IllegalArgumentException; returns 0 on end-of-stream.
flush	Writes any buffered data to the underlying IO stream, then flushes it. The effect is to make sure that all data have actually been written to the file system or the network.
close	Flushes and closes the IO stream, then flushes and closes all underlying IO streams. Further operations on the IO stream, except close, will throw IOException. Buffered writers and output streams should be explicitly closed or flushed to make sure that all data have been written; otherwise output data may be lost, even in the case of normal program termination.

26.3   Imports, Exceptions, Thread Safety

A program using the input and output classes may contain the import declaration

```
import java.io.*;
```

Most input and output operations can throw an exception of class IOException or one of its subclasses, all of which are checked exceptions (chapter 15). Hence a method doing input or output must either do so in a try-catch block (section 12.6.6) or have the declaration throws IOException (section 9.8).

The standard implementation of input-output is thread-safe: multiple concurrent threads (chapter 20) can safely read from or write to the same IO stream without corrupting it. However, the Java class library documentation is not explicit on this point, so probably one should avoid using the same IO stream from multiple threads, or else explicitly synchronize on the IO stream.

Example 190 Input-Output: Twelve Examples in One

This example illustrates input and output with human-readable text files; input and output of primitive values with binary files; input and output of arrays and objects with binary files; input and output of primitive values with random access binary files; input and output using strings and string builders; output to standard output and standard error; and input from standard input.

These brief examples do not use buffering, but input and output from files, sockets, and so on should use buffering for efficiency (section 26.13).

```java
// Write numbers and words on file "f.txt" in human-readable form:
PrintWriter pwr = new PrintWriter(new FileWriter("f.txt"));
pwr.print(4711); pwr.print(' '); pwr.print("cool"); pwr.close();
// Read numbers and words from human-readable text file "f.txt":
StreamTokenizer stok = new StreamTokenizer(new FileReader("f.txt"));
int tok = stok.nextToken();
while (tok != StreamTokenizer.TT_EOF)
  { System.out.println(stok.sval); tok = stok.nextToken(); }
// Write primitive values to a binary file "p.dat":
DataOutputStream dos = new DataOutputStream(new FileOutputStream("p.dat"));
dos.writeInt(4711); dos.writeChar(' '); dos.writeUTF("cool"); dos.close();
// Read primitive values from binary file "p.dat":
DataInputStream dis = new DataInputStream(new FileInputStream("p.dat"));
System.out.println(dis.readInt()+"|"+dis.readChar()+"|"+ dis.readUTF());
// Write an object or array to binary file "o.dat":
ObjectOutputStream oos = new ObjectOutputStream(new FileOutputStream("o.dat"));
oos.writeObject(new int[] { 2, 3, 5, 7, 11 }); oos.close();
// Read objects or arrays from binary file "o.dat":
ObjectInputStream ois = new ObjectInputStream(new FileInputStream("o.dat"));
int[] ia = (int[])(ois.readObject());
System.out.println(ia[0]+","+ia[1]+","+ia[2]+","+ia[3]+","+ia[4]);
// Read and write parts of file "raf.dat" in arbitrary order:
RandomAccessFile raf = new RandomAccessFile("raf.dat", "rw");
raf.writeDouble(3.1415); raf.writeInt(42);
raf.seek(0); System.out.println(raf.readDouble() + " " + raf.readInt());
// Read from a String s as if it were a text file:
Reader r = new StringReader("abc");
System.out.println("abc: " + (char)r.read() + (char)r.read() + (char)r.read());
// Write to a StringBuilder as if it were a text file:
Writer sw = new StringWriter();
sw.write('d'); sw.write('e'); sw.write('f');
System.out.println(sw.toString());
// Write characters to standard output and standard error:
System.out.println("std output"); System.err.println("std error");
// Read characters from standard input (the keyboard):
System.out.print("Type some characters and press Enter: ");
BufferedReader bisr = new BufferedReader(new InputStreamReader(System.in));
String response = bisr.readLine();
System.out.println("You typed: '" + response + "'");
// Read a byte from standard input (the keyboard):
System.out.print("Type one character and press Enter: ");
byte b = (byte)System.in.read();
System.out.println("First byte of your input is: " + b);
```

26.4 Sequential Character Input: Readers

The abstract class Reader and its subclasses (all having names ending in Reader) are used for character-oriented sequential input. In addition to the classes shown here, see BufferedReader (section 26.13) and LineNumber-Reader (example 195). The Reader class has the following methods:

- `void close()` flushes and closes the IO stream and any underlying IO stream. Any subsequent operation, except `close`, will throw IOException.
- `void mark(int limt)` marks the current input position, permitting at least `limt` characters to be read before calling `reset`.
- `boolean markSupported()` is `true` if the reader supports setting of marks and resetting to latest mark.
- `int read()` reads one character (with code 0 – 65535) and returns it. Blocks until input is available, end-of-stream is reached (and then returns −1), or an error occurs (and then throws IOException).
- `int read(char[] b)` reads at most `b.length` characters into `b` and returns the number of characters read. Blocks until at least one character is available unless `b.length` is 0. Returns −1 on end-of-stream.
- `int read(char[] b, int i, int n)` works like the preceding, but reads into `b[i..(i+n-1)]`. Throws IndexOutOfBoundsException if `i<0` or `n<0` or `i+n>b.length`.
- `boolean ready()` returns `true` if the next `read` or `skip` will not block.
- `void reset()` resets the IO stream to the position of the latest call to `mark`.
- `int skip(int n)` skips at most `n` characters and returns the number of characters skipped; returns 0 on end-of-stream.

26.4.1 Reading Characters from a Byte Stream: InputStreamReader and Character Encoding

An InputStreamReader is a reader (a character input stream) that reads from a byte input stream, assembling bytes into characters using a character encoding. It performs buffered input from the underlying IO stream. An InputStreamReader has the same methods as a Reader (section 26.4), and also these constructors and method:

- `InputStreamReader(InputStream is)` creates an InputStreamReader from `is`, using the platform's standard character encoding to convert bytes to characters.
- `InputStreamReader(InputStream is, String enc)` creates an InputStreamReader that uses character encoding `enc`, for instance `"US-ASCII"` or `"ISO-8859-1"` (Latin1) or `"UTF-8"` or `"UTF-16"` or `"UTF-16BE"` (big-endian 16-bit) or `"UTF-16LE"` (little-endian 16-bit) or `"Cp1252"` (MS Windows).
- `String getEncoding()` returns the canonical name of the character encoding used by this reader.

26.4.2 Sequential Character Input from a File: FileReader

A FileReader is a buffered character input stream associated with a (sequential) file and equivalent to an InputStreamReader created from a FileInputStream. It has the same methods as InputStreamReader, as well as these constructors:

- `FileReader(String name)` creates a character input stream associated with the named file. Throws FileNotFoundException if the file does not exist, is a directory, or cannot be opened for other reasons.
- `FileReader(File file)` creates a character input stream from the given file in the file system.
- `FileReader(FileDescriptor fd)` creates a character input stream from the file descriptor.

26.5 Sequential Character Output: Writers

The abstract class Writer and its subclasses (all having names ending in Writer) are used for character-oriented sequential output. They have the following methods:

- `void close()` flushes and closes the IO stream.
- `void flush()` actually writes data to the underlying IO stream or file, and then flushes that.
- `void write(char[] b)` writes the contents of character array `b`.
- `void write(char[] b, int i, int n)` writes `n` characters from `b` starting at position `i`; throws IndexOutOfBoundsException if `i<0` or `n<0` or `i+n>b.length`.
- `void write(int c)` writes a single character, namely, the two low-order bytes of `c`.
- `void write(String s)` writes string `s`.
- `void write(String s, int i, int n)` writes `n` characters from `s` starting at position `i`; throws StringIndexOutOfBoundsException if `i<0` or `n<0` or `i+n>s.length`.

26.5.1 Writing Characters to a Byte Stream: OutputStreamWriter

An OutputStreamWriter is a writer (character output stream) that writes to a byte output stream, converting characters to bytes using a character encoding. It performs buffered output to the underlying IO stream. An OutputStreamWriter has the same methods as a Writer (section 26.5), as well as these constructors and method:

- `OutputStreamWriter(OutputStream os)` creates an OutputStreamWriter that writes to IO stream `os` using the platform's default character encoding.
- `OutputStreamWriter(OutputStream os, String enc)` creates an OutputStreamWriter that writes to IO stream `os` using the character encoding specified by `enc`; see section 26.4.1 for some valid `enc` values, and example 200 for a typical use.
- `String getEncoding()` returns the canonical name of the character encoding used by this writer.

26.5.2 Sequential Character Output to a File: FileWriter

A FileWriter is a buffered character output stream associated with a (sequential) file, equivalent to an OutputStreamWriter created from a FileOutputStream. It has the same methods as OutputStreamWriter as well as these constructors:

- `FileWriter(String name)` creates a character output stream and associates it with the named file in the file system. If the file exists, then it truncates the file; otherwise it tries to create a new empty file. Throws FileNotFoundException if the named file is a directory or cannot be opened or created for some other reason.
- `FileWriter(String file, boolean append)` works like the previous method, but if `append` is `true`, it does not truncate the file: instead output will be appended to the existing file contents.
- `FileWriter(File file)` works like the previous method, but creates the writer from `file`.
- `FileWriter(FileDescriptor fd)` works like the previous method, but creates the writer from `fd`.

26.6   Printing Primitive Data to a Character Stream: PrintWriter

The class PrintWriter is used to output primitive data to text files in human-readable form. Unlike the methods of other Writers, those of PrintWriter never throw IOException but set the error status. The PrintWriter class has all the methods of Writer as well as these constructors and methods:

- PrintWriter(OutputStream os) creates a PrintWriter that prints to IO stream os, without autoflush.
- PrintWriter(OutputStream os, boolean flush) creates a PrintWriter that prints to output stream os; if flush is true, then it flushes the writer after every call to println.
- PrintWriter(Writer wr) creates a PrintWriter that prints to the writer wr, without autoflush.
- PrintWriter(Writer wr, boolean flush) creates a PrintWriter that prints to the writer wr; if flush is true, then it flushes the writer after every call to println.
- boolean checkError() flushes the IO stream, then returns true if an error has ever occurred.
- void print(boolean b) prints the boolean b, that is, true or false.
- void print(char c) prints the character c.
- void print(char[] cs) prints the characters in cs.
- void print(double d) prints the double d.
- void print(float f) prints the float f.
- void print(int i) prints the integer i.
- void print(long l) prints the long integer l.
- void print(Object o) prints the object o using o.toString().
- void print(String s) prints the string s.
- void println() prints a single newline.
- void println(e) works like print(e) followed by println().

26.6.1   Standard Output: `System.out` and `System.err` Are PrintStreams

The standard output stream System.out and standard error stream System.err are PrintStreams. PrintStream is a subclass of OutputStream but in addition has methods print and println for character-based output, just as PrintWriter does. These methods convert characters to bytes using the default encoding; to use another encoding enc, write to a PrintWriter created by new PrintWriter(new OutputStreamWriter(System.out, enc)) as in example 200. Some possible values for enc are shown in section 26.4.1. The methods of a PrintStream never throw IOException but set the error status; use checkError() to test the error status.

26.7   The Appendable Interface and the CharSequence Interface

The java.lang.Appendable interface (implemented by PrintStream, StringBuilder, StringBuffer, and the Writer classes) describes three method overloads, all of which return a reference to the Appendable:

- append(char c) adds character c to the appendable.
- append(CharSequence cseq) adds all characters from cseq to the appendable.
- append(CharSequence cseq, int i, int j) adds characters i..j-1 from cseq.

The java.lang.CharSequence interface (implemented by String, StringBuilder, and StringBuffer) has methods charAt(int), length, subSequence(int,int), and toString; they behave as for String in chapter 7.

Example 191 Printing Numbers to a Text File

Simulate 1,000 rolls of a die and print the outcome to the text file `dice.txt`, 20 numbers to a line:

```
PrintWriter pw = new PrintWriter(new FileWriter("dice.txt"));
for (int i=1; i<=1000; i++) {
  int die = (int)(1 + 6 * Math.random());
  pw.print(die); pw.print(' ');
  if (i % 20 == 0) pw.println();
}
pw.println();
pw.close();                 // Without this, the output file may be empty
```

Example 192 Printing an HTML Table

This example generates a temperature conversion table in HTML. The Fahrenheit temperature f corresponds to the Celsius temperature $c = 5 \cdot (f - 32)/9$. The number of fractional digits is controlled by a formatting string. The HTML TABLE tag is used to control the alignment of numbers into columns.

To print a conversion table in text format in a fixed-pitch font, replace the second `pw.format` call by `pw.format("%10d%10.1f%n", f, c)` and delete the other HTML-generating statements.

```
PrintWriter pw = new PrintWriter(new FileWriter("temperature.html"));
pw.println("<TABLE BORDER><TR><TH>Fahrenheit<TH>Celsius</TR>");
for (int f=100; f<=400; f+=10) {
  double c = 5 * (f - 32.0) / 9;
  pw.format("<TR ALIGN=RIGHT><TD>%d<TD>%.1f%n", f, c);
}
pw.println("</TABLE>");
pw.close();                 // Without this, the output file may be empty
```

Example 193 Using the Appendable Interface

The Expr abstract syntax for simple expressions below has a method `output` that writes the expression in text form to the given Appendable. That way the expression can be formatted to a StringBuilder, as a string; to standard output; and to other character streams far more efficiently than by using `toString` methods.

```
abstract class Expr {
  public abstract void output(Appendable sink) throws IOException;
}
class Cst extends Expr { ... }
class Add extends Expr {
  Expr e1, e2;
  public Add(Expr e1, Expr e2) { this.e1 = e1; this.e2 = e2; }
  public void output(Appendable sink) throws IOException {
    sink.append('('); e1.output(sink); sink.append('+');
    e2.output(sink); sink.append(')');
} }
...
Expr expr = ...;
expr.output(System.out); System.out.println();     // To standard output
StringBuilder sb = new StringBuilder();             // To StringBuilder
expr.output(sb);
String s = sb.toString();                           // To String
Writer wr = new FileWriter("expr.txt");
expr.output(wr); wr.append('\n');                   // To text file
```

26.8   Reading Primitive Data from a Character Stream: StreamTokenizer

Reading words and numbers from a character stream is more complicated than printing them, so there is no text input counterpart to PrintWriter. Instead create a StreamTokenizer from a Reader.

A StreamTokenizer collects characters into tokens. Characters are classified as white space (separating tokens), number characters (making up a number token), word characters (making up a word token), quote characters (delimiting a string token), end-line comment characters (initiating a comment extending to end-of-line), or ordinary characters (none of the preceding).

A StreamTokenizer can be created and configured using this constructor and these methods and fields:

- StreamTokenizer(Reader r) creates a StreamTokenizer that reads from IO stream r.
- void commentChar(int ch) tells the tokenizer that ch is an end-line comment character.
- void eolIsSignificant(boolean b) tells the tokenizer to consider newline as a separate token of type TT_EOL, not as white space, if b is true.
- void ordinaryChars(int c1, int c2) tells the tokenizer that any character in the range c1..c2 (inclusive) is an ordinary character: a single-character token, with ttype set to the character code.
- void parseNumbers() tells the tokenizer to recognize number tokens. A number token is a "word" beginning with a decimal digit (0..9) or a decimal point (.) or a minus sign (-), and consisting only of these three kinds of characters, so numbers in scientific notation 6.02e23 are not recognized. A number token has type TT_NUMBER.
- void quoteChar(int ch) tells the tokenizer that character ch is a string delimiter. When this character is encountered, ttype is set to ch, and sval is set to the string's contents: the characters strictly between ch and the next occurrence of ch or newline or end-of-stream.
- void resetSyntax() makes all characters ordinary; see ordinaryChars.
- void whitespaceChars(int c1, int c2) tells the tokenizer that all characters in the range c1..c2 (inclusive) are white space also, that is, token separators.
- void wordChars(int c1, int c2) tells the tokenizer that all characters in the range c1..c2 (inclusive) are word characters also.

Class StreamTokenizer has these methods and fields for reading values:

- int lineno() returns the current line number, counting from 1.
- int nextToken() reads the next (or first) token and returns its type.
- double nval is the number value of the current number token (when ttype is TT_NUMBER).
- String sval is the string value of the current word token (when ttype is TT_WORD), or the string body of the current string token (when ttype is a quote character).
- int ttype is the type of the current token. The type may be StreamTokenizer.TT_NUMBER, indicating a number; or StreamTokenizer.TT_WORD, indicating a word; or StreamTokenizer.TT_EOL, indicating a newline; or StreamTokenizer.TT_EOF, indicating end-of-stream (no more tokens); or a quote character, indicating a string (in quotes); or any other character, indicating that character as a token by itself.

While a StreamTokenizer is useful for reading fairly simple text files, more structured text files should be read using regular expressions (package java.util.regex, see [2]), a proper lexer and parser (see common textbooks for compiler courses), or special-purpose libraries (e.g., for XML).

Example 194 Reading Numbers from a Text File

A StreamTokenizer `stok` is created from a buffered file reader and told to recognize number tokens. Tokens are read until end-of-stream, and the number tokens are added together, whereas non-number tokens are printed to standard output. The buffering of input is important: it makes the program more than twenty times faster.

```
static void sumfile(String filename) throws IOException {
  Reader r = new BufferedReader(new FileReader(filename));
  StreamTokenizer stok = new StreamTokenizer(r);
  stok.parseNumbers();
  double sum = 0;
  stok.nextToken();
  while (stok.ttype != StreamTokenizer.TT_EOF) {
    if (stok.ttype == StreamTokenizer.TT_NUMBER)
      sum += stok.nval;
    else
      System.out.println("Nonnumber: " + stok.sval);
    stok.nextToken();
  }
  System.out.println("The file sum is " + sum);
}
```

Example 195 Reading Numbers from a Text File, Line by Line

A StreamTokenizer `stok` is created from a LineNumberReader and told to recognize number tokens and new-lines. Tokens are read until end-of-stream, and the sum of the number tokens is computed line by line. The line number is set to count from 1 (default is 0). Class LineNumberReader is a subclass of BufferedReader and therefore is already buffered. Using a LineNumberReader is somewhat redundant, since StreamTokenizer itself provides a `lineno()` method.

```
static void sumlines(String filename) throws IOException {
  LineNumberReader lnr = new LineNumberReader(new FileReader(filename));
  lnr.setLineNumber(1);
  StreamTokenizer stok = new StreamTokenizer(lnr);
  stok.parseNumbers();
  stok.eolIsSignificant(true);
  stok.nextToken();
  while (stok.ttype != StreamTokenizer.TT_EOF) {
    int lineno = lnr.getLineNumber();
    double sum = 0;
    while (stok.ttype != StreamTokenizer.TT_EOL) {
      if (stok.ttype == StreamTokenizer.TT_NUMBER)
        sum += stok.nval;
      stok.nextToken();
    }
    System.out.println("Sum of line " + lineno + " is " + sum);
    stok.nextToken();
  }
}
```

26.9   Sequential Byte Input: InputStream

The abstract class InputStream and its subclasses (all of whose names end in InputStream) are used for byte-oriented sequential input. They have the following methods:

- `int available()` returns the number of bytes that can be read or skipped without blocking.
- `void close()` closes the IO stream.
- `void mark(int limt)` marks the current input position, permitting at least `limt` bytes to be read before calling `reset`.
- `boolean markSupported()` returns `true` if the IO stream supports `mark` and `reset`.
- `int read()` reads one byte (0...255) and returns it, blocking until input is available; returns −1 on end-of-stream.
- `int read(byte[] b)` reads at most `b.length` bytes into `b`, blocking until at least one byte is available; then returns the number of bytes actually read. Returns −1 on end-of-stream.
- `int read(byte[] b, int i, int n)` reads at most `n` bytes into `b` at position `i`, blocking until at least one byte is available, and returns the number of bytes actually read. Returns −1 on end-of-stream. Throws IndexOutOfBoundsException if `i<0` or `n<0` or `i+n>b.length`.
- `void reset()` repositions the IO stream to the position at which the `mark` method was last called.
- `long skip(long n)` skips at most `n` bytes, blocking until a byte is available, and returns the number of bytes actually skipped. Returns 0 if end-of-stream is reached before input is available.

The standard input `System.in` is an InputStream; to read characters from it, create an InputStreamReader using `new InputStreamReader(System.in)`; see example 190.

26.9.1   Sequential Byte Input from File: FileInputStream

A FileInputStream is an InputStream that reads sequentially from an existing file on the file system. It has the same methods as InputStream (section 26.9), as well as these constructors and method:

- `FileInputStream(String name)` creates a byte input stream and associates it with file `name` in the file system. Throws FileNotFoundException if the file does not exist, is a directory, or cannot be opened.
- `FileInputStream(File file)` works like the preceding, but associates the IO stream with `file`.
- `FileInputStream(FileDescriptor fd)` works the same, but associates the IO stream with `fd`.
- `FileDescriptor getFD()` returns the file descriptor associated with this IO stream.

26.9.2   Sequential Binary Input of Primitive Data: DataInputStream

Class DataInputStream provides methods for machine-independent sequential binary input of Java primitive types such as `int` and `double`. The class implements the DataInput interface (section 26.11) and in addition provides this constructor and static method:

- `DataInputStream(InputStream is)` creates a DataInputStream that reads from IO stream `is`.
- `static String readUTF(DataInput di)` reads a Java UTF-8 encoded string from IO stream `di`.

Class DataInputStream also has a `readLine` method, which is deprecated. To read lines of text from a DataInputStream, create an InputStreamReader (section 26.4.1) from it instead.

26.10   Sequential Byte Output: OutputStream

The abstract class OutputStream and its subclasses (all of whose names end in OutputStream) are used for byte-oriented sequential output. It has the following methods:

- `void close()` closes the output stream.
- `void flush()` flushes the output stream and forces any buffered output bytes to be written to the underlying IO stream or file, then flushes that.
- `void write(byte[] b)` writes `b.length` bytes from `b` to the output stream.
- `void write(byte[] b, int i, int n)` writes `n` bytes from `b` starting at offset `i` to the output stream. Throws IndexOutOfBoundsException if `i<0` or `n<0` or `i+n>b.length`.
- `void write(int b)` writes the byte `b` (0...255) to the output stream.

26.10.1   Sequential Byte Output to a File: FileOutputStream

A FileOutputStream is an OutputStream that writes sequentially to a file on the file system. It has the same methods as OutputStream (section 26.10) and these constructors and additional method:

- `FileOutputStream(String name)` creates a byte output stream and associates it with the named file in the file system. If the file exists, then it is truncated; otherwise, an attempt is made to create the file. Throws FileNotFoundException if the file is a directory or cannot be opened or created for some other reason.
- `FileOutputStream(String name, boolean append)` works like the preceding, but if `append` is `true`, then does not truncate the file: instead output will be appended to any existing file contents.
- `FileOutputStream(File file)` works like the preceding but associates the IO stream with `file`.
- `FileOutputStream(FileDescriptor fd)` works like the preceding but associates the IO stream with `fd`.
- `FileDescriptor getFD()` returns the file descriptor associated with this IO stream.

26.10.2   Sequential Binary Output of Primitive Data: DataOutputStream

Class DataOutputStream provides methods for machine-independent sequential binary output of Java primitive types such as `int` and `double`. The class implements the DataOutput interface (section 26.11) and provides this constructor and method:

- `DataOutputStream(OutputStream os)` creates a DataOutputStream that writes to the IO stream `os`.
- `int size()` returns the number of bytes written to this DataOutputStream.

26.11   Binary Input-Output of Primitive Data: DataInput and DataOutput

The interfaces DataInput (implemented by DataInputStream, ObjectInputStream, and RandomAccessFile) and DataOutput (implemented by DataOutputStream, ObjectOutputStream, and RandomAccessFile) describe operations for byte-oriented input and output of values of primitive type, such as `boolean`, `int`, and `double`. Thus DataInput's method `readInt()` is suitable for reading integers written using DataOutput's method `writeInt(int)`. The data format is platform-independent.

The DataInput interface describes the following methods. The `read` and `skip` methods block until the required number of bytes have become available, and throw EOFException if end-of-stream is reached first.

- `boolean readBoolean()` reads one input byte and returns `true` if non-zero, `false` otherwise.
- `byte readByte()` reads one input byte and returns a byte in range $-128\ldots127$.
- `char readChar()` reads two bytes and returns a character in range $0\ldots65535$.
- `double readDouble()` reads eight bytes and returns a double.
- `float readFloat()` reads four bytes and returns a float.
- `void readFully(byte[] b)` reads exactly `b.length` bytes into buffer b.
- `void readFully(byte[] b, int i, int n)` reads exactly n bytes into `b[i..(i+n-1)]`.
- `int readInt()` reads four bytes and returns an integer.
- `String readLine()` reads a line of one-byte characters in the range $0\ldots255$ (not Unicode).
- `long readLong()` reads eight bytes and returns a long integer.
- `short readShort()` reads two bytes and returns a short integer $-32768\ldots32676$.
- `int readUnsignedByte()` reads one byte and returns an integer in the range $0\ldots255$.
- `int readUnsignedShort()` reads two bytes and returns an integer in the range $0\ldots65535$.
- `String readUTF()` reads a string encoded using the Java modified UTF-8 format.
- `int skipBytes(int n)` skips exactly n bytes of data and returns n.

The DataOutput interface describes the following methods. Note that `writeInt(i)` writes four bytes representing the Java integer i, whereas `write(i)` writes one byte containing the low-order eight bits of i.

- `void write(byte[] b)` writes all the bytes from array b.
- `void write(byte[] b, int i, int n)` writes n bytes from array `b[i..(i+n-1)]`.
- `void write(int v)` writes the eight low-order bits of byte v.
- `void writeBoolean(boolean v)` writes one byte: 1 if v is true, otherwise 0.
- `void writeByte(int v)` writes the low-order byte (eight low-order bits) of integer v.
- `void writeBytes(String s)` writes the low-order byte of each character in s (not Unicode).
- `void writeChar(int v)` writes two bytes (high-order, low-order) representing v.
- `void writeChars(String s)` writes the string s, two bytes per character.
- `void writeDouble(double v)` writes eight bytes representing v.
- `void writeFloat(float v)` writes four bytes representing v.
- `void writeInt(int v)` writes four bytes representing v.
- `void writeLong(long v)` writes eight bytes representing v.
- `void writeShort(int v)` writes two bytes representing v.
- `void writeUTF(String s)` writes two bytes of (byte) length information, followed by the Java modified UTF-8 representation of every character in the string s.

Example 196 Binary Input and Output of Primitive Data
Method `writedata` demonstrates all ways to write primitive data to a DataOutput stream (an IO stream of class DataInputStream or RandomAccessFile). Similarly, method `readdata` demonstrates all ways to read primitive values from a DataInput stream (an IO stream of class DataOutputStream or RandomAccessFile). The methods complement each other, so after writing an IO stream with `writedata`, one can read it using `readdata`.

```
public static void main(String[] args) throws IOException {
  DataOutputStream daos = new DataOutputStream(new FileOutputStream("tmp1.dat"));
  writedata(daos); daos.close();
  DataInputStream dais = new DataInputStream(new FileInputStream("tmp1.dat"));
  readdata(dais);
  RandomAccessFile raf = new RandomAccessFile("tmp2.dat", "rw");
  writedata(raf); raf.seek(0); readdata(raf);
}
static void writedata(DataOutput out) throws IOException {
  out.writeBoolean(true);                        // Write 1 byte
  out.writeByte(120);                            // Write 1 byte
  out.writeBytes("foo");                         // Write 3 bytes
  out.writeBytes("fo");                          // Write 2 bytes
  out.writeChar('A');                            // Write 2 bytes
  out.writeChars("foo");                         // Write 6 bytes
  out.writeDouble(300.1);                        // Write 8 bytes
  out.writeFloat(300.2F);                        // Write 4 bytes
  out.writeInt(1234);                            // Write 4 bytes
  out.writeLong(12345L);                         // Write 8 bytes
  out.writeShort(32000);                         // Write 2 bytes
  out.writeUTF("foo");                           // Write 2 + 3 bytes
  out.writeUTF("Rhône");                         // Write 2 + 6 bytes
  out.writeByte(-1);                             // Write 1 byte
  out.writeShort(-1);                            // Write 2 bytes
}
static void readdata(DataInput in) throws IOException {
  byte[] buf1 = new byte[3];
  System.out.print(       in.readBoolean());     // Read 1 byte
  System.out.print(" " + in.readByte());         // Read 1 byte
  in.readFully(buf1);                            // Read 3 bytes
  in.readFully(buf1, 0, 2);                      // Read 2 bytes
  System.out.print(" " + in.readChar());         // Read 2 bytes
  System.out.print(" " + in.readChar()+in.readChar()+in.readChar());
  System.out.print(" " + in.readDouble());       // Read 8 bytes
  System.out.print(" " + in.readFloat());        // Read 4 bytes
  System.out.print(" " + in.readInt());          // Read 4 bytes
  System.out.print(" " + in.readLong());         // Read 8 bytes
  System.out.print(" " + in.readShort());        // Read 2 bytes
  System.out.print(" " + in.readUTF());          // Read 2 + 3 bytes
  System.out.print(" " + in.readUTF());          // Read 2 + 6 bytes
  System.out.print(" " + in.readUnsignedByte()); // Read 1 byte
  System.out.print(" " + in.readUnsignedShort());// Read 2 bytes
  System.out.println();
}
```

26.12   Serialization of Objects: ObjectInput and ObjectOutput

The interfaces ObjectInput (implemented by ObjectInputStream) and ObjectOutput (implemented by ObjectOutputStream) describe operations for byte-oriented input and output of values of reference type, that is, objects and arrays. This is also called *serialization* or *marshalling*.

An object or array can be serialized (converted to a sequence of bytes) if its class and all classes on which the object or array depends have been declared to implement the interface Serializable. The Serializable interface does not declare any methods; it only serves to show that the class admits serialization.

Serialization of an object o writes the object's non-static (instance) fields, except those declared transient, to the IO stream. When the object is deserialized, a transient field gets the default value for its type (false or 0 or 0.0 or null). Class fields (static fields) are not serialized.

Serialization to an ObjectOutputStream preserves sharing among the objects written to it, and more generally, preserves the form of the object reference graph. For instance, if object o1 and o2 both refer to a common object c (so o1.c == o2.c), and o1 and o2 are serialized to ObjectOutputStream oos, then object c is serialized only once to oos. When o1 and o2 are restored again from oos, then c is restored also, exactly once, so o1.c == o2.c holds as before. If o1 and o2 are serialized to two different ObjectOutputStreams, then restoration of o1 and o2 will produce two distinct copies of c, so o1.c != o2.c. Thus sharing among objects is not preserved across multiple ObjectOutputStreams.

The interface ObjectInput (implemented by ObjectInputStream) has all the methods specified by DataInput and the following additional ones. The methods available(), close(), read(byte[]), read(byte[], int, int), and skip(int) behave like those of class InputStream (section 26.9).

- int available() returns the number of bytes that can be read or skipped without blocking.
- void close() closes the IO stream, as in InputStream.
- int read() reads one byte, as in InputStream.
- int read(byte[] b) reads bytes into b, as in InputStream.
- int read(byte[] b, int i, int n) reads into b[i..(i+n-1)], as in InputStream.
- Object readObject() reads, deserializes, and returns an object, which must have been previously serialized. Throws ClassNotFoundException if the declaration (class file) for an object that is being deserialized cannot be found. Throws ObjectStreamException or one of its subclasses if no object can be read from the IO stream, for instance, if end-of-stream is met before the object is complete.
- long skip(long n) skips n bytes, as in InputStream.

The interface ObjectOutput (implemented by ObjectOutputStream) has all the methods of interface DataOutput (section 26.11) and the following additional one.

- void writeObject(Object obj) writes the object using serialization. All classes being serialized must implement the Serializable interface; otherwise NotSerializableException is thrown.

Interface Externalizable is a subinterface of Serializable that can be implemented by classes that need full control over the serialization and deserialization of their objects.

Example 197 Serialization to the Same ObjectOutputStream Preserves Sharing

Objects o1 and o2 refer to a shared object c of class SC. We serialize o1 and o2 to the same file using a single ObjectOutputStream, so we get a single copy of the shared object. When we deserialize the objects and bind them to variables o1i and o2i, we also get a single copy of the shared SC object:

```
class SC implements Serializable { int ci; }
class SO implements Serializable {
  int i; SC c;
  SO(int i, SC c) { this.i = i; this.c = c; }
  void cprint() { System.out.print("i" + i + "c" + c.ci + " "); }
}
...
File f = new File("objects.dat");
// Create the objects and write them to file.
SC c = new SC();
SO o1 = new SO(1, c), o2 = new SO(2, c);
o1.c.ci = 3; o2.c.ci = 4;                 // Update the shared c twice
o1.cprint(); o2.cprint();                 // Prints: i1c4 i2c4
OutputStream os = new FileOutputStream(f);
ObjectOutputStream oos = new ObjectOutputStream(os);
oos.writeObject(o1); oos.writeObject(o2); oos.close();
// Read the objects from file.
InputStream is = new FileInputStream(f);
ObjectInputStream ois = new ObjectInputStream(is);
SO o1i = (SO)(ois.readObject()), o2i = (SO)(ois.readObject());
o1i.cprint(); o2i.cprint();               // Prints: i1c4 i2c4
o1i.c.ci = 5; o2i.c.ci = 6;               // Update the shared c twice
o1i.cprint(); o2i.cprint();               // Prints: i1c6 i2c6
```

Example 198 Serialization to Distinct ObjectOutputStreams Does Not Preserve Sharing

If we serialize the objects o1 and o2 from example 197 to the same file using two different ObjectOutput-Streams, each object stream will write a copy of the shared object. When we deserialize the objects, we get two copies of the previously shared SC object:

```
// Create the objects (as in above example) and write them to file.
ObjectOutputStream oos1 = new ObjectOutputStream(os);
oos1.writeObject(o1); oos1.flush();
ObjectOutputStream oos2 = new ObjectOutputStream(os);
oos2.writeObject(o2); oos2.close();
// Read the objects from file, non-shared c.
InputStream is = new FileInputStream(f);
ObjectInputStream ois1 = new ObjectInputStream(is);
SO o1i = (SO)(ois1.readObject());
ObjectInputStream ois2 = new ObjectInputStream(is);
SO o2i = (SO)(ois2.readObject());
o1i.cprint(); o2i.cprint();               // Prints: i1c4 i2c4
o1i.c.ci = 5; o2i.c.ci = 6;               // Update two different c's
o1i.cprint(); o2i.cprint();               // Prints: i1c5 i2c6
```

26.13   Buffered Input and Output

Writing one byte or character at a time to a file or network connection is very inefficient. It is better to collect the bytes or characters in a buffer, and then write the whole buffer in one operation. The same holds for reading from a file or network connection. However, buffering will not speed up input from and output to byte arrays, character arrays, strings, or string buffers.

To buffer a plain input stream `is`, create a BufferedInputStream from `is` and read from that IO stream instead; and similarly for output streams, readers, and writers.

The operation `flush()` can be used on a buffered IO stream to request that the output actually get written to the underlying IO stream. A buffered IO stream should be properly closed by a call to `close()` to ensure that all data written to the buffer are eventually written to the underlying IO stream.

Class BufferedReader has all the methods of class Reader (section 26.4) and these constructors and method:

- `BufferedReader(Reader rd)` creates a buffered reader that reads from `rd`.

- `BufferedReader(Reader rd, int sz)` creates a buffered reader with buffer of size `sz`. It throws IllegalArgumentException if `sz <= 0`.

- `Stream<String> lines()` returns a lazily generated sequential stream (chapter 24) of lines read; see example 170. An IOException thrown by the reader will cause a stream operation to throw an UncheckedIOException.

- `String readLine()` reads a line of text. A line is terminated by line feed (`"\n"`), carriage return (`"\r"`), or carriage return and line feed (`"\r\n"`). Returns the line without any line termination characters; returns `null` at end-of-stream.

Class BufferedWriter has all the methods of Writer (section 26.5) as well as these constructors and method:

- `BufferedWriter(Writer wr)` creates a buffered writer that writes to stream `wr`.

- `BufferedWriter(Writer wr, int sz)` creates a buffered writer with a buffer of size `sz`. It throws IllegalArgumentException if `sz <= 0`.

- `void newLine()` writes a line separator, such as `"\n"` or `"\r\n"`, depending on the platform.

Class BufferedInputStream is a subclass of FilterInputStream. It has the same methods as InputStream (section 26.9) and these constructors:

- `BufferedInputStream(InputStream is)` creates a BufferedInputStream that reads from stream `is`.

- `BufferedInputStream(InputStream is, int sz)` creates a BufferedInputStream with buffer size `sz`; throws IllegalArgumentException if `sz <= 0`.

Class BufferedOutputStream is a subclass of FilterOutputStream. It has the same methods as OutputStream (section 26.10) and these constructors:

- `BufferedOutputStream(OutputStream os)` creates a BufferedOutputStream that writes to stream `os`.

- `BufferedOutputStream(OutputStream os, int sz)` creates a BufferedOutputStream with a buffer of size `sz`; throws IllegalArgumentException if `sz <= 0`.

Example 199 Output Buffering
Buffering may speed up writes to a FileOutputStream by a large factor. Buffering the writes to a FileWriter has less effect, because a FileWriter is an OutputStreamWriter, which buffers the bytes converted from written characters before writing them to an underlying FileOutputStream. In one experiment, buffering made writes to a FileOutputStream fifty times faster and writes to a FileWriter only two or three times faster.

```java
public static void main(String[] args) throws IOException {
  OutputStream os1 = new FileOutputStream("tmp1.dat");
  writeints("Unbuffered: ", 1000000, os1);
  OutputStream os2 = new BufferedOutputStream(new FileOutputStream("tmp2.dat"));
  writeints("Buffered:   ", 1000000, os2);
  Writer wr1 = new FileWriter("tmp1.dat");
  writeints("Unbuffered: ", 1000000, wr1);
  Writer wr2 = new BufferedWriter(new FileWriter("tmp2.dat"));
  writeints("Buffered:   ", 1000000, wr2);
}
static void writeints(String msg, int count, OutputStream os) throws IOException {
  Timer t = new Timer();
  for (int i=0; i<count; i++)
    os.write(i & 255);
  os.close();
  System.out.println(msg + t.check());
}
static void writeints(String msg, int count, Writer os) throws IOException {
  Timer t = new Timer();
  for (int i=0; i<count; i++)
    os.write(i & 255);
  os.close();
  System.out.println(msg + t.check());
}
```

For efficiency, one should usually wrap buffered streams around file streams and socket streams as follows:

Replace	By
`new FileInputStream(e)`	`new BufferedInputStream(new FileInputStream(e))`
`new FileOutputStream(e)`	`new BufferedOutputStream(new FileOutputStream(e))`
`new FileWriter(e)`	`new BufferedWriter(new FileWriter(e))`
`new FileReader(e)`	`new BufferedReader(new FileReader(e))`

Example 200 Specifying a Particular Output Encoding
To print to a file or standard output with character encoding `enc`, create an OutputStreamWriter (from a FileOutputStream or `System.out`) with that encoding and then use it to create a PrintWriter. Some legal encodings are listed in section 26.4.1. In UTF-8, the character ' s ' is encoded in one byte, as in US-ASCII or ISO-8859-1, but the character ' ü ' (latin small letter u with diaeresis) is encoded as two bytes: 195 = (192 + 252 div 64) and 188 = (128 + 252 mod 64), because the Unicode number of ' ü ' is 252. All numbers here are in decimal.

```java
String s = "El Niño, süß, Ærøskøbing å, éclair, §2";
String enc = "UTF-8";           //  8-bit Unicode encoding
OutputStreamWriter osw = new OutputStreamWriter(System.out, enc);
PrintWriter pw = new PrintWriter(osw);
pw.println(s);
```

26.14   Random Access Files: RandomAccessFile

Class RandomAccessFile is used for input from and output to *random access files*. The data in a random access file can be accessed in any order. In contrast to IO streams, which can be read and written only sequentially from the beginning. Thus a random access file is similar to an extensible byte array stored on the file system. A random access file has an associated file pointer, which determines where the next read or write operation will begin. Setting the file pointer permits random access to all parts of the file (albeit thousands or millions of times more slowly than to a byte array stored in memory). The file pointer is an offset from the beginning of the file: the first byte in a file raf has offset 0; the last byte has offset raf.length()-1. The method call seek(pos) sets the file pointer to point at byte number pos.

Class RandomAccessFile implements the DataInput and DataOutput interfaces (section 26.11) and has the following constructors and additional methods. The methods read(), read(byte[]), and read(byte[], int, int) behave as in InputStream (section 26.9); in particular, they return -1 on end-of-file, and block until at least one byte of input is available. The methods readt(), where t is a type, behave as in DataInput (section 26.11); in particular, they throw EOFException on end-of-file.

- RandomAccessFile(String name, String mode) creates a new random access file stream and associates it with a file of the given name on the file system. Initially the file pointer is at offset 0. Throws IOException if the name indicates a directory. The mode must be "r" for read-only, or "rw" for read-write; otherwise IllegalArgumentException is thrown. If the file does not exist on the file system, and the mode is "r", then FileNotFoundException is thrown, but if the mode is "rw", then a new empty file is created if possible. If the mode is "r", any call to the write methods will throw IOException.

- RandomAccessFile(File file, String mode) works like the preceding, but associates the random access file stream with file.

- void close() closes the file stream.

- FileDescriptor getFD() returns the file descriptor associated with the stream.

- long getFilePointer() returns the current value of the file pointer.

- long length() returns the length of the file in bytes.

- int read() reads one byte, as in InputStream.

- int read(byte[] b) reads into array b, as in InputStream.

- int read(byte[] b, int i, int n) reads at most n bytes into b, as in InputStream.

- void seek(long pos) sets the file pointer to byte number pos. Throws IOException if pos<0. The file pointer may be set beyond end-of-file; a subsequent write will then extend the file's length.

- void setLength(long newlen) sets the length of the file by truncating or extending it (at the end); in the case of extension, the content of the extension is undefined.

Example 201 Organizing a String Array File for Random Access
This example shows a way to implement random access to large numbers of texts, such as millions of cached Web pages or millions of DNA sequences. We define a string array file to have three parts: (1) a sequence of Strings, each of which is in Java modified UTF-8 format; (2) a sequence of long integers, representing the start offsets of the strings; and (3) an integer, which is the number of strings in the file. (Note that Java limits the length of each UTF-8-encoded string; using a slightly more complicated representation in the file, we could lift this restriction.)

By putting the number of strings and the string offset table at the end of the file rather than at the beginning, we do not need to know the number of strings or the length of each string before writing the file. The strings can be written to the file incrementally, and the only structure we need to keep in memory is the table (ArrayList) of string lengths.

Method `writeStrings` takes as argument a file name and a string generator in the form of an Iterable<String>. The first (enhanced) `for` statement creates an Iterator<String> from the iterable, and writes the strings produced by the iterator to the file while storing the offsets in the offset table. The second (enhanced) `for` statement writes the offsets to the file subsequently.

```
static void writeStrings(String filename, Iterable<String> strGenerator)
  throws IOException {
  RandomAccessFile raf = new RandomAccessFile(filename, "rw");
  raf.setLength(0);                                 // truncate the file
  ArrayList<Long> offsettable = new ArrayList<Long>();
  for (String s : strGenerator) {
    offsettable.add(raf.getFilePointer());          // store string offset
    raf.writeUTF(s);                                 // write string
  }
  for (long offset : offsettable)
    raf.writeLong(offset);
  raf.writeInt(offsettable.size());                 // write string count
  raf.close();
}
```

Example 202 Random Access Reads from a String Array File
The method call `readOneString(f, i)` reads string number i from a string array file f (example 201) in three stages, using three calls to `seek`. First, it reads the offset table length N from the last 4 bytes of the file. Second, since an int takes 4 bytes and a long takes 8 bytes (section 5.1), the string offset table must begin at position `length()-4-8*N`, so the offset si of string number i can be read from position `length()-4-8*N+8*i`. Third, the string itself is read from offset si.

```
static String readOneString(String filename, int i) throws IOException {
  final int INTSIZE = 4, LONGSIZE = 8;
  RandomAccessFile raf = new RandomAccessFile(filename, "r");
  raf.seek(raf.length() - INTSIZE);
  int N = raf.readInt();
  raf.seek(raf.length() - INTSIZE - LONGSIZE * N + LONGSIZE * i);
  long si = raf.readLong();
  raf.seek(si);
  String s = raf.readUTF();
  raf.close();
  return s;
}
```

26.15   Files, Directories, and File Descriptors

26.15.1   Path Names in a File System: Class File

An object of class File represents a path name, that is, a directory/file path in the file system. The path name may denote a directory, a data file, or nothing at all (if there is no file or directory of that name). Even if the path name denotes a file or directory, a given program may lack the permission to read or write that file or directory. These are a few of the constructors and methods in class File:

- `File(String pname)` creates a path name corresponding to the string `pname`.
- `boolean exists()` returns `true` if a file or directory denoted by this path name exists.
- `String getName()` returns this path name as a string.
- `boolean isDirectory()` tests whether the file denoted by this path name is a directory.
- `boolean isFile()` tests whether the file denoted by this path name is a normal file.
- `long length()` returns the length of the file in bytes, or 0 if the file does not exist.
- `File[] listFiles()` returns the files and directories in the directory denoted by the path name; returns `null` on error or if the path name does not denote a directory.
- `boolean mkdir()` creates the directory named by this path name.

26.15.2   File System Objects: Class FileDescriptor

An object of class FileDescriptor is a file descriptor, an internal representation of an active file system object, such as an open file or an open socket. A file descriptor may be obtained from a FileInputStream (section 26.9) or FileOutputStream (section 26.10). The class has this method:

- `void sync()` requests that all system buffers be synchronized with the underlying physical devices; it blocks until this has been done. Throws SyncFailedException if it cannot be done.

The class has static fields `in`, `out`, and `err`, which are the file descriptors associated with the standard input (`System.in`), standard output (`System.out`), and standard error (`System.err`) streams.

26.16   Thread Communication: PipedInputStream and PipedOutputStream

Threads (chapter 20) execute concurrently and may communicate asynchronously using internal pipes. A *pipe* is a pair of a PipedInputStream and a PipedOutputStream, or a pair of a PipedReader and a PipedWriter. By contrast, communication with other processes or with remote computers uses InputStreams and OutputStreams, possibly obtained from operating system sockets, briefly described in section 26.17.

To create a pipe, create one end of it by `outpipe = new PipedOutputStream()`, then use that to create and connect the other end by `inpipe = new PipedInputStream(outpipe)`. Either end may be created first. A pipe end can be connected only once.

A producer thread writes to a PipedOutputStream (or PipedWriter), and a consumer thread reads from a PipedInputStream (or PipedReader) associated with the PipedOutputStream (or PipedWriter). If the producer thread is fast and the pipe fills up, then the next write operation blocks until there is room for data in the pipe. If the consumer thread is fast and there are no available data in the pipe, then the next read operation blocks until data become available. When either the consumer or the producer dies, and one end of the pipe is destroyed, the next `write` (or `read`) at the other end of the pipe throws an IOException.

Example 203 Reading and Printing a Directory Hierarchy

The call `showDir(0, pathname)` will print the path name, and if the path name exists and is a directory, then `showDir` recursively prints all its subdirectories and files. Because `indent` is increased for every recursive call, the layout reflects the directory structure.

```
static void showDir(int indent, File file) throws IOException {
  for (int i=0; i<indent; i++)
    System.out.print('-');
  System.out.println(file.getName());
  if (file.isDirectory()) {
    File[] files = file.listFiles();
    for (int i=0; i<files.length; i++)
      showDir(indent+4, files[i]);
  }
}
```

Example 204 Internal Pipes Between Threads

The producer thread writes the infinite sequence of prime numbers $2, 3, 5, 7, 11, 13, \ldots$ to a PipedOutputStream, while the consumer (the main thread) reads from a PipedInputStream connected to the PipedOutputStream. Actually, the producer writes to a DataInputStream built on top of the PipedOutputStream, and the consumer reads from a DataInputStream built on top of the PipedInputStream, because we want to send integers, not only bytes, through the pipe.

```
PipedOutputStream outpipe = new PipedOutputStream();
PipedInputStream inpipe = new PipedInputStream(outpipe);
final DataOutputStream outds = new DataOutputStream(outpipe);
DataInputStream inds = new DataInputStream(inpipe);
// This thread outputs primes to outds -> outpipe -> inpipe -> inds:
class Producer extends Thread {
  public void run() {
    try {
      outds.writeInt(2);
      for (int p=3; true; p+=2) {
        int q=3;
        while (q*q <= p && p%q != 0)
          q+=2;
        if (q*q > p)
          { outds.writeInt(p); System.out.print("."); }
      }
    } catch (IOException e) { System.out.println("<terminated>: " + e); }
  }
}

new Producer().start();
for (;;) {                                 // Forever
  for (int n=0; n<10; n++)                  //   output 10 primes
    System.out.print(inds.readInt() + " "); //   and
  System.in.read();                         //   wait for Enter
}
```

26.17   Socket Communication

Whereas a pair of Java threads can communicate through a local pipe (e.g., PipedInputStream), a pair of distinct processes may communicate through *sockets*. The processes may be on the same machine or on different machines connected by a network.

Sockets are often used in client/server architectures, where the server process creates a *server socket* that listens for connections from clients. When a client connects to the server socket, a fresh socket is created on the server side and is connected to the socket that the client used when connecting to the server. The socket connection is used for bidirectional communication between client and server; both ends can obtain an input stream and an output stream from the socket.

Here are a constructor and some methods from the ServerSocket class in package `java.net`:

- ServerSocket(int port) creates a server socket on the given port.

- Socket accept() listens for a connection, blocking until a connection is made. Creates and returns a new Socket when a connection is made. If a timeout is set, the call to `accept` throws InterruptedIOException when the timeout expires.

- void close() closes the server socket.

- void setSoTimeout(int tmo) sets the timeout so that a call to `accept` will time out after `tmo` milliseconds if positive. Disables timeout if `tmo` is zero; timeout is disabled by default.

Here are a constructor and some methods from the Socket class in package `java.net`:

- Socket(String host, int port) creates a client socket and connects to a given `port` on the given host. The `host` may be a name ("localhost") or an IP address ("127.0.0.1").

- void close() closes the socket.

- InetAddress getInetAddress() returns the address to which this socket is connected, as an object of class `java.net.InetAddress`; methods getHostName() and getHostAddress() can be used to convert this address to a string.

- InputStream getInputStream() returns the input stream associated with this socket.

- OutputStream getOutputStream() returns the output stream associated with this socket.

- void setSoTimeout(int tmo) sets the timeout so that a call to `read` on the input stream obtained from this socket will time out after `tmo` milliseconds if positive. If `tmo` is zero, then timeout is disabled (the default). If a timeout is set, a call to `read` throws InterruptedIOException when the timeout expires.

The Socket and ServerSocket classes are declared in the Java class library package `java.net`. The Java class library documentation [2] provides more information about sockets and server sockets.

Example 205 Socket Communication Between Processes

This example program runs as a server process or as a client process, depending on the first command line argument. The server and client may run on the same machine, or on different machines communicating via a network. Several clients may connect to the same server. The server creates a server socket that accepts connections on port 2357. When a client connects, a new client socket is created and an integer is received on that socket. If the integer is a prime, the server replies true on the same socket, otherwise false.

Each client process asks the server about the primality of the numbers 1 through 999 and prints those that are primes.

It is rather inefficient for the client to create a new socket for every request to the server, but it suffices for this example. Also, buffering the input and output streams may speed up socket communication (section 26.13).

```
import java.io.*;
import java.net.*;

class SocketTest {
  final static int PORT = 2357;

  public static void main(String[] args) throws IOException {
    boolean server = args.length == 1 && args[0].equals("server");
    boolean client = args.length == 2 && args[0].equals("client");
    if (server) {                  // Server: accept questions about primality
      ServerSocket serversock = new ServerSocket(PORT);
      for (;;) {
        Socket sock = serversock.accept();
        DataInputStream dis  = new DataInputStream(sock.getInputStream());
        DataOutputStream dos = new DataOutputStream(sock.getOutputStream());
        int query = dis.readInt();
        dos.writeBoolean(isprime(query));
        dis.close(); dos.close();
      }
    } else if (client) {           // Client: ask questions about primality
      for (int i=1; i<1000; i++) {
        Socket sock = new Socket(args[1], PORT);
        DataOutputStream dos = new DataOutputStream(sock.getOutputStream());
        DataInputStream dis = new DataInputStream(sock.getInputStream());
        dos.writeInt(i);
        if (dis.readBoolean())
          System.out.print(i + " ");
        dos.close(); dis.close();
      }
    } else { ... }                 // Neither server nor client
  }

  static boolean isprime(int p) { ... return true if p is prime ... }
}
```

27   Reflection

Reflection permits a running program to inspect and manipulate the classes, interfaces, methods, and fields of the program itself. For every non-generic type t in a running Java program, there is an object ot of class `java.lang.Class` that represents type t. From ot one can get representations of the members (fields, methods, and nested types) of type t, as well as other information. Using reflection, one can create objects and arrays, call methods, and get and set the value of fields, but one cannot directly create new types, nor add new methods to existing types. There are third-party libraries for creation of new types.

Reflection provides powerful dynamic adaptability but implies that the usual checks (of argument types in a method call, for instance) cannot be performed at compile-time. Instead they must be performed at run-time, and this takes time, so reflection is slow and may fail, possibly throwing exceptions; see section 27.4.

27.1   Reflective Use of Types: The Class<T> Class

If t is a type, then the expression `t.class` of type `Class<t>` evaluates to the unique object ot that represents type t at run-time. The type t may be a class C or an interface I or an array type such as `int[]` or an enum type or annotation type or a primitive type such as `int` or the pseudo-type `void`. It cannot be a generic type `G<T>` or a type instance such as `G<Integer>`; instead one must use the raw type G, as in `G.class`.

When o has reference type and is non-`null`, the expression `o.getClass()` has raw type Class and evaluates to the unique object that represents the run-time type of o. Class `Class<t>` has the following methods:

- `static Class Class.forName(String name)` returns the Class object representing the class called name, loading the class if not already loaded.

- `int getModifiers()` returns the modifiers of the class; see example 212.

- `t newInstance()` returns a new object of the class, created as if by a call to an argumentless constructor.

- `boolean isInstance(Object o)` returns true if o is non-`null` and could be assigned to a variable of type t, where t is the type represented by the Class object; otherwise false.

- `t cast(Object o)` of type t returns o if o could be assigned to a variable of the type t represented by the Class object; otherwise throws ClassCastException. In particular, it succeeds if o is `null`.

Thus `isInstance` and `cast` are dynamic versions of `instanceof` and type cast (sections 11.8 and 11.11).

In addition, class `Class<t>` has methods to get the fields, methods, constructors, and nested types of type t, shown below. The methods on the left return only public members, including inherited ones, whereas the methods on the right return only members declared in the class, not inherited ones:

	Public Members (Including Inherited Ones)	Declared Members (Including Non-Public Ones)
Single	`Field getField(name)`	`Field getDeclaredField(name)`
	`Method getMethod(name, parTy)`	`Method getDeclaredMethod(name, parTy)`
	`Constructor<t> getConstructor(parTy)`	`Constructor<t> getDeclaredConstructor(parTy)`
All	`Field[] getFields()`	`Field[] getDeclaredFields()`
	`Method[] getMethods()`	`Method[] getDeclaredMethods()`
	`Constructor[] getConstructors()`	`Constructor[] getDeclaredConstructors()`
	`Class[] getClasses()`	`Class[] getDeclaredClasses()`

A field is identified by its name (a String), a method is identified by its name and parameter types parTy (an array `Class[]` or a parameter array `Class...`), and a constructor is identified by its parameter types parTy. The types Field, Method, and Constructor are explained in sections 27.2 and 27.3.

Example 206 Listing Public Methods and Declared Methods
Class K1 declares two public and one private method, and its subclass K2 declares a public and a private method. The getMethods call gets K2's inherited methods m1(), m1(int), its public method m3, and those inherited from Object (equals, hashCode, …). The getDeclaredMethods call gets K2's declared methods m3 and m4.

```
import java.lang.reflect.*;
class K1 {
  public int f1;
  protected int f2;
  public K1() { }
  public K1(int f1) { this.f1 = f1; }
  public void m1()      { System.out.println("K1.m1()"); }
  public void m1(int i) { System.out.println("K1.m1(int)"); }
  private void m2()     { System.out.println("K1.m2()"); }
}
class K2 extends K1 {
  public void m3()  { System.out.println("K2.m3()"); }
  private void m4() { System.out.println("K2.m4()"); }
}
class Reflection1 {
  public static void main(String[] args) {
    Class<K2> k2o = K2.class;
    Method[] mop = k2o.getMethods();            // Gets m1() m1(int) m3() ...
    Method[] mod = k2o.getDeclaredMethods();  // Gets m3() m4()
} }
```

Example 207 The Unique Class Object of a Class and the Run-Time Class of an Object
Consider the classes K1 and K2 from example 206. The class object for a given class is unique, so the class object k2o obtained from class K2 is identical to the class object k2o2 obtained from an instance o2 of K2 using method getClass. Also, note that the getClass method returns the *run-time class* of an object, so o11 and o12 have different getClass values although they have the same compile-time type K1.

```
Class<K2> k2o = K2.class;
K2 o2 = new K2();
Class k2o2 = o2.getClass();            // k2o == k2o2
K1 o11 = new K1(), o12 = o2;           // o11.getClass() != o12.getClass()
if (o11.getClass() != o12.getClass()) ...
```

Example 208 Reflective Object Creation, Instance Tests, and Casts
Still using the classes from example 206, we can create an object o21 of class K2 from the class object k2o that represents K2, test whether the existing object o12 is an instance of K2 (it is), and test whether the existing object o11 is an instance of K2 (it is not). Also, a cast of o12 to K2 succeeds, and the expression has type K2, because k2o has compile-time type Class<K2>, but a cast of string "foo" to K2 fails by throwing a ClassCastException.

```
Class<K2> k2o = K2.class;
K2 o2 = new K2();
K1 o11 = new K1(), o12 = o2;     // o11.getClass() != o12.getClass()
K2 o21 = k2o.newInstance();      // OK: k2o has type Class<K2>, K2() exists
if (k2o.isInstance(o12)) ...     // true
if (k2o.isInstance(o11)) ...     // false
K2 k22 = k2o.cast(o12);          // succeeds at run-time: o12 can be cast to K2
K2 k23 = k2o.cast("foo");        // fails at run-time
```

27.2   Reflection: The Field Class

An object of class Field from package `java.lang.reflect` represents a static or non-static field in a class or interface. It supports the following operations:

- `Object get(Object o)` returns the value of the field (in object o if an instance field).
- `int getModifiers()` returns the modifiers of the field; see example 212.
- `String getName()` returns the name of the field.
- `Class getType()` returns the type of the field.
- `Class getDeclaringClass()` returns the class containing the field's declaration.
- `void set(Object o, Object v)` sets the value of the field to v (in object o if an instance field).

27.3   Reflection: The Method Class and the Constructor\<T\> Class

An object of class Method from package `java.lang.reflect` represents a static or non-static method and supports the following operations:

- `String getName()` returns the name of the method.
- `Class[] getParameterTypes()` returns the formal parameter types of the method.
- `Class[] getExceptionTypes()` returns the exception classes listed in the method's `throws` clause.
- `Class getDeclaringClass()` returns the class containing the method's declaration.
- `int getModifiers()` returns the modifiers of the method; see example 212.
- `Class getReturnType()` returns the method's declared return type.
- `Object invoke(Object o, Object... args)` invokes the method on object o, passing the arguments `args`, and returns the result of the method, or `null` if the return type is `void`. If the method is static, then o is ignored and may be `null`; if the method is non-static, then o must be non-`null` and becomes the current object reference `this` in the method invocation.
- `boolean isVarArgs()` returns true if the method has variable arity (section 9.9).

An object of class Constructor\<t\> from package `java.lang.reflect` represents a constructor from class t, and permits creation of objects of that class. Class Constructor\<t\> supports the same operations as class Method, except for `getReturnType`, and has this additional operation:

- `newInstance(Object... args)` returns a new object instance of the constructor's class. The expression has type t when the constructor object has type Constructor\<t\>, and it has type Object when the constructor object has (raw) type Constructor. Note that `newInstance` has variable arity.

27.4   Exceptions Thrown When Using Reflection

Operations on a Class, Field, Method or Constructor may throw IllegalAccessException (field, method, or constructor is inaccessible); or IllegalArgumentException (wrong type of object o when using an instance field or method; wrong argument type when getting or setting a field; or wrong argument type when invoking a method); or InstantiationException (the called constructor belongs to an abstract class); or InvocationTarget-Exception (an invoked method threw an exception); or NoSuchFieldException; or NoSuchMethodException; or NullPointerException (the given object reference o is `null` when using an instance field or method).

Example 209 Reflective Access to a Field
The Field object `f1o` represents the (inherited) field `f1` in class `K2` from example 206. The value of the field can be set and accessed reflectively. An attempt to get field `f2` from `k2o` will fail with NoSuchFieldException.

```
Class<K2> k2o = K2.class;
Field f1o = k2o.getField("f1");
K2 o2 = new K2();
f1o.set(o2, 117);
System.out.format("Value of o2.f1 = %d%n", f1o.get(o2)); // Gets o2.f1
Class<K1> k1o = K1.class;
Field f21 = k1o.getDeclaredField("f2");
```

Example 210 Reflective Retrieval and Invocation of a Method
Variables `m1o` and `m1io` represent methods `m1()` and `m1(int)` from class `K1` in example 206. When invoking the instance methods, a `K1` object is needed; this may be an object of a subclass such as `K2`. Note how parameter types (`int`) are specified and how arguments (`117`) are passed using parameter arrays (section 9.9).

```
Class<K1> k1o = K1.class;
Method m1o = k1o.getMethod("m1"),          // Gets K1.m1()
       m1io = k1o.getMethod("m1", int.class);   // Gets K1.m1(int)
K2 o2 = new K2();
m1o.invoke(o2);                            // Call o2.m1()
m1io.invoke(o2, 117);                      // Call o2.m1(117)
```

Example 211 Reflective Creation of an Object
The compile-time type of `ck1o` is `Constructor<K1>` so the compile-time type of `ck1o.newInstance(42)` is K1, but that of `cco.newInstance(42)` is Object. The class K1 is from example 206.

```
Class<K1> k1o = K1.class;
Constructor<K1> ck1o = k1o.getConstructor(int.class);   // Gets K1(int)
Constructor cco = ck1o;
K1 k11 = ck1o.newInstance(42);              // Compile-time type K1
Object k12 = cco.newInstance(56);           // Compile-time type Object
```

Example 212 Reflective Inspection of Modifiers: `static`, `private`, ...
The result of a `getModifiers` method can be inspected using static methods or bitwise "and" (`&`) with symbolic constants from class Modifier. This example prints the `private` methods from the Method array `mod`:

```
for (Method m : mod)
  if (Modifier.isPrivate(m.getModifiers()))
    System.out.println(m);
```

Modifier or Declaration	Test	Symbolic Constant
abstract	Modifier.isAbstract(mods)	Modifier.ABSTRACT
final	Modifier.isFinal(mods)	Modifier.FINAL
interface	Modifier.isInterface(mods)	Modifier.INTERFACE
private	Modifier.isPrivate(mods)	Modifier.PRIVATE
protected	Modifier.isProtected(mods)	Modifier.PROTECTED
public	Modifier.isPublic(mods)	Modifier.PUBLIC
static	Modifier.isStatic(mods)	Modifier.STATIC
synchronized	Modifier.isSynchronized(mods)	Modifier.SYNCHRONIZED
transient	Modifier.isTransient(mods)	Modifier.TRANSIENT

28 Metadata Annotations

Annotations are used to attach metadata to a *target*, where a target may be a constructor declaration, a field declaration, a local variable declaration, a method declaration, a package declaration, a parameter declaration, a type declaration (class, interface, enum type), or the declaration of another annotation type.

An annotation of type Anno is attached to its target by writing @Anno(f1=e1, ..., fn=en) before the target declaration. The type of an annotation argument ei can be a simple type, Object, String, Class, an enum type, an annotation type, or an array of one of these types. Each expression ei must be compile-time constant or a one-dimensional array {...} of compile-time constants. A target can have only one annotation of a given annotation type; but an annotation may contain an array of other annotations. An annotation that takes no arguments can be written @Anno instead of @Anno(). An annotation that takes a single argument called value can be used as @Anno("Ulrik") instead of @Anno(value="Ulrik").

Section 13.4 shows how to define and use custom annotation types, as well as some meta-annotations used when declaring annotation types.

The most important predefined standard annotation types are these:

Annotation Type	Target	Meaning	Section
@Deprecated	Declaration	Use is discouraged	
@FunctionalInterface	Interface	Is a functional interface	23
@Inherited	Annotation type	Annotation is inherited	13.4
@Override	Method	Must override inherited method	
@Retention	Annotation	How long annotation is kept	13.4
@Repeatable	Annotation	Allow multiple use on target	13.4
@SafeVarargs	Declaration	Parameter array T... is safe	
@SuppressWarnings	Declaration	Suppress compiler warnings	
@Target	Annotation	Legal annotation targets	13.4

The standard annotations from the java.lang package have the following meanings:

Annotation @Deprecated is used on program elements that should no longer be used. Any use of such a program element causes a compiler warning.

Annotation @FunctionalInterface is used on an interface declaration to indicate that it should be functional, that is, have exactly one abstract method (chapter 23). For instance, all the interfaces listed on page 125 have this annotation.

Annotation @Override is used on a method declaration that must override some method inherited from a superclass or an implemented interface. If it does not, a compile-time error is produced.

Annotation @SafeVarargs can be used on a static and final method declaration or a constructor declaration that has a parameter array t... xs whose type t is a generic type instance or type parameter, to indicate that the method or constructor uses that parameter safely. (Section 9.9 describes parameter arrays.) This suppresses an "unchecked" compiler warning both at the declaration site and at every call to the method or constructor. The annotation should be used only if the method or constructor body does not write to the array xs and does not leak the array reference xs.

Annotation @SuppressWarnings can be used on a declaration to indicate that the compiler should not issue specific kinds of warnings for this particular declaration. A typical use is to avoid "unchecked" warnings on generic array creation.

Example 213 Standard Annotation @Override
Standard annotation `@Override` is used here to indicate that methods `m1` and `m2` must override methods inherited from a superclass or an implemented interface. This is checked by the compiler, so applying annotation `@Override` to method `m3` would cause the compiler to produce an error.

```
static class B { public void m1() { } }
interface I { void m2(); }
static class C extends B implements I {
  @Override
  public void m1() { System.out.println("m1"); }

  @Override
  public void m2() { System.out.println("m2"); }

  // @Override // Would cause compiler error because no method m3() to override
  public void m3() { System.out.println("m3"); }
}
```

Example 214 Standard Annotation @FunctionalInterface
The `@FunctionalInterface` annotation says that CharPredicate must have exactly one abstract method (and any number of `default` and `static` methods). Otherwise a compile-time error is produced.

```
@FunctionalInterface
interface CharPredicate {
  public abstract boolean test(char c);
  public default CharPredicate and(CharPredicate p) {
    return c -> this.test(c) && p.test(c);
  }
}
```

Example 215 Standard Annotations @SuppressWarnings and @SafeVarargs
Due to limitations in Java generics, one cannot create an array whose element type involves generic type instances or type parameters; see section 21.11 and example 132. Instead, one may create an array of the raw type and cast it, but this cast is unsafe and will produce a compile-time warning. The `@SuppressWarnings` annotation suppresses this warning.

A parameter array such as `Consumer<T>... consumers` provides a way to surreptitiously create an array (at the point where the method is called) whose element type involves generic type instances or type parameters. The `@SafeVarargs` annotation suppresses the compile-time warnings that would be produced at the method declaration and at calls to the methods.

```
@SuppressWarnings("unchecked")
private static <T> Consumer<T>[] makeConsumerArray(int size) {
  return (Consumer<T>[])new Consumer[size];
}
@SafeVarargs
public static final <T> void callAll(T x, Consumer<T>... consumers) {
  for (Consumer<T> cons : consumers)
    if (cons != null)
      cons.accept(x);
}
```

29   What Is New in Java 8.0

Many new features have been added to the Java programming language in versions 7.0 and 8.0, notably:

- Support for functional programming through the concepts of functional interface (chapter 23), lambda expressions or anonymous functions (section 11.13), and method reference expressions (section 11.14).

- Further support for function-based data processing through the concept of lazy streams and pipelines (chapter 24), which also improve modularity and separation of concerns in a way reminiscent of lazy data structures in functional languages; see example 174.

- Support for data parallel programming in the form of functional parallel operations on arrays (section 8.4) and parallel stream processing (chapter 24). In many cases, a sequential data processing pipeline can be trivially turned into a parallel data processing pipeline, provided the operations are side-effect free and stateless. In many cases, this improves throughput considerably by automatically taking advantage of available parallel processor cores.

- More expressive and useful interfaces through the addition of default and static methods on interfaces (section 13.3). In particular, this is used on the Comparator interface (section 22.10), the functional interfaces (chapter 23), and the stream interfaces (chapter 24).

- The ability to indicate that an operation may not return a result, and to represent such missing results, also for primitive types via the Optional class (chapter 25).

- The `switch` statement (section 12.4.3) now works for cases of type String.

- The actual type arguments in a generic object construction may be left out as in `new ArrayList<>()` if they can be inferred from context.

- Integer constants in binary `0b1010`; underscores permitted in number constants `1_000`.

Most of these features are found also in the C# programming language, as shown by this table:

Feature	Section	Java 1.4	Java 5.0	Java 8.0	C# 1.1	C# 4.5
Looping over iterators	22.7	−	+	+	+	+
Enum types	14	−	+	+	+	+
Autoboxing simple values	5.4	−	+	+	+	+
Nullable value types/Optional	25	−	−	+	−	+
Try-with-resources	12.7	−	−	+	+	+
Generic types and methods	21	−	+	+	−	+
Run-time type parameter information		−	−	−	−	+
Generic interface co/contravariance		−	−	−	−	+
Wildcard types in generic instances	21.9	−	+	+	−	−
Annotations (metadata, attributes)	28	−	+	+	+	+
Anonymous functions, function types	11.13, 23	−	−	+	−	+
Defining streams or enumerables	24	−	−	+	−	+
Parallel array and stream processing	8.4, 24	−	−	+	−	+
Well-defined memory model	20.5	−	+	+	−	−

Example 216 New Features in Java 7.0 and 8.0

This example illustrates some of the new features. Method `getFunction` illustrates `switch` on strings, the Optional type, a functional interface (DoubleUnaryOperator), lambda expressions, and method reference expressions. It may be called as `getFunction("log2").get().applyAsDouble(32.0)`. Method `diamondExample` shows how type arguments can be replaced by `<>` and inferred from context. Method `getPageAsString` uses the try-with-resources statement to make sure the BufferedReader gets closed eagerly, uses stream operations to read a limited number of lines from a web page, and uses a collector to join the lines into a string. The useless method `getPageAsStream` illustrates the dangers of combining these features. The try-with-resources closes the BufferedReader eagerly before any part of the lazily generated stream has been consumed. Method `numberConstants` shows a variety of number constant notations; the `i1`–`i4` variables all have the same value.

```java
static Optional<DoubleUnaryOperator> getFunction(String name) {
  switch (name) {
  case "ln": case "log": return Optional.of(Math::log);
  case "log2":           return Optional.of(x -> Math.log(x)/Math.log(2));
  case "log10":          return Optional.of(Math::log10);
  default:               return Optional.empty();
  }
}
static void diamondExample() {
  List<String> alist1 = new ArrayList<String>();     // Type argument <String> given
  List<String> alist2 = new ArrayList<>();           // Type argument <String> inferred
  // List<String> alist3 = new ArrayList();          // Raw type, unchecked conversion
  List<Function<String,List<Integer>>> flist = new ArrayList<>();
}
public static String getPageAsString(String url, int maxLines) throws IOException {
  try (BufferedReader in
         = new BufferedReader(new InputStreamReader(new URL(url).openStream()))) {
    Stream<String> lines = in.lines().limit(maxLines);
    return lines.collect(Collectors.joining());
  }
}
public static Stream<String> getPageAsStream(String url) throws IOException {
  try (BufferedReader in // USELESS -- BufferedReader gets closed before the stream is consumed
         = new BufferedReader(new InputStreamReader(new URL(url).openStream()))) {
    return in.lines();
  }
}
static void numberConstants() {
  int i1 = 0b1100_1010_1111_1110;        // Binary
  int i2 = 0xCAFE;                       // Hexadecimal
  int i3 = 0b1_100_101_011_111_110;      // Binary
  int i4 = 0145376;                      // Octal
  int i6 = -2_147_483_648;               // Decimal
  int i7 = +2_147_483_647;               // Decimal
  int i8 = 0x8000_0000;                  // Hexadecimal
  int i9 = 0x7FFF_FFFF;                  // Hexadecimal
  double debt = 18_210_520_570_642.0;    // Floating-point
  char c1 = 0b00110001;                  // Character '1'
  char c2 = 0b01000001;                  // Character 'A'
}
```

References

[1] The Unicode character encoding (www.unicode.org) corresponds to part of the Universal Character Set (UCS), which is international standard ISO 10646:2014. The UTF-8 is a variable-length encoding of UCS, in which seven-bit ASCII characters are encoded as themselves.

[2] The Java class library documentation can be browsed at docs.oracle.com/javase/8/docs/api or downloaded as a zip-file from www.oracle.com/technetwork/java/javase/downloads.

[3] The authoritative reference on the Java programming language is J. Gosling, B. Joy, G. Steele, G. Bracha, A. Buckley: *Java Language Specification*, version 8, March 2014. Browse or download in HTML or PDF at docs.oracle.com/javase/specs.

[4] Floating-point arithmetic is described in the *IEEE Standard for Floating-Point Arithmetic* (IEEE Std 754-2008).

[5] The best text on concurrent programming with Java is Goetz et al: *Java Concurrency in Practice* (Addison-Wesley 2006).

[6] An excellent guide to good programming in Java is Joshua Bloch: *Effective Java*, second edition (Addison-Wesley 2008).

[7] The Java Tutorials from Oracle provide a wealth of general and specialized information on Java. See docs.oracle.com/javase/tutorial.

Index